D0013395

Anja Klabunde works regularly for the French/German cultural TV channel Canal Plus/Arte. She lives near Paris with her husband and two sons.

'An engaging and lucid account of a supposed anomaly: a cultivated woman at the heart of the Nazi regime'
Michael Arditti, *Literary Review*

'A compelling read'
Times Higher Education Supplement

'Magda Goebbel's story is fascinating'
Irish Times

Magda
GOEBBELS

Anja Klabunde

Translated by
Shaun Whiteside

timewarner
paperbacks

A *Time Warner* Paperback

First published in Great Britain in 2001
by Little, Brown

This edition published in Great Britain in 2003
by Time Warner Paperbacks

Copyright © 1999 C Bertelsmann Verlag, Munich
Translation © 2001 Shaun Whiteside

The moral right of the author has been asserted.

All rights reserved.
No part of this publication may be reproduced,
stored in a retrieval system, or transmitted, in any form
or by any means, without the prior permission in writing of the
publisher, nor be otherwise circulated in any form of binding
or cover other than that in which it is published and
without a similar condition including this condition
being imposed on the subsequent purchaser.

A CIP catalogue record for this book
is available from the British Library.

ISBN 0 7515 3448 X

Printed and bound in Great Britain by
Clays Ltd, St Ives plc

Time Warner Paperbacks
An imprint of
Time Warner Books UK
Brettenham House
Lancaster Place
London WC2E 7EN

www.TimeWarnerBooks.co.uk

In memory of Max Flesch

My thanks to Karlheinz Schädlich for his academic help and support. I am grateful to the staff of the Institute for Contemporary History in Munich for their cooperation, and to my family for their patience.

Foreword

I came upon the story of Magda Goebbels more or less by chance. When I was in Israel doing some research for a documentary, I met Dr Max Flesch, a former Berlin lawyer. Like all immigrants of his generation, he told not only his own story – he was finally able to escape to Palestine in 1939 after being arrested on Kristallnacht and spending a number of weeks as a prisoner in Dachau – but also the stories of his friends and neighbours. One of these dealt with the fate of Victor Chaim Arlosoroff, his Jewish schoolmate, who had, as a young man, been in love with a girl, a certain Magda Friedländer. Arlosoroff had developed into an unusually charismatic young politician, and become Palestine's first unofficial Foreign Minister. Max Flesch related that the young woman had later married Joseph Goebbels, and that this relationship had probably become an albatross around Arlosoroff's neck, and been responsible for his early death – an event which had, through a chain reaction, continued to exert an influence on Israel's political situation that still resonates today.

I was interested in the connections between the fate of Arlosoroff and the woman who would later become Magda Goebbels. From former girlfriend of an ardent Zionist to wife of the Nazi Minister of Propaganda – what sort of trajectory must that have been?

I decided to pursue the story, because Magda Goebbels' life seemed in a sense to reflect the tragedy and blindness of Germany in the first half of our century. At the same time I found myself asking the question: how could such an intelligent and cultivated woman fall prey to such fanaticism? That is the question that my generation has been asking time and again about a civilised, cultivated country such as Germany. How could such a state of barbarism come about, and how were we, the next generation along, supposed to relate to that era?

There is, by now, an extraordinarily rich literature dealing with the Nazi period, but there is still very little about the women who lived side by side with the major Nazi figures. It is fairly certain that they must have exerted an influence as accomplices in some form or another. And among them Magda Goebbels – particularly through her personal relationship with Hitler – occupied a special place.

We, the children born in the final years of the war or the first post-war years, have usually grown up with the silence of our parents. We have often been too shy to touch upon the past and confront our parents with the questions whose answers had weighed on our own shoulders too. As a result, our own anxieties sometimes led us to become self-pitying; we identified with the victims, or else we felt ourselves to be victims of our parents' guilt.

But we have no choice: disagreeable as it may be, we must continue to deal with the past. And the life of a woman like Magda Goebbels – with its strange discontinuities – throws up many questions that apply to an entire generation, questions of which we can only answer a very small part.

The form that I have chosen for Magda Goebbels' biography is influenced by my work on documentary films. It was important for me to allow various voices, witnesses of contemporary events, to have their say.

Every now and again I have transposed the action into dramatic scenes, in order to visualise and heighten certain impressions. These scenes can be understood as an attempt at an interpretation.

There are few reliable sources about Magda Goebbels' life. I relied to a great extent on the book by Hans-Otto Meissner. He experienced the Nazi era as a young man in Berlin; his father, Otto Meissner, was State Secretary to Hindenburg, and in this capacity he was considerably involved in the rise of Hitler. In his biography, Hans-Otto Meissner refers to conversations with Magda's best friend, her sister-in-law Ello Quandt. Although she belonged to the same Nazi-influenced milieu as Magda, Magda dared to criticise the Nazi regime in her presence.

Meissner was also granted access to the unpublished memoirs of Günther Quandt, Magda's first husband. This is no longer possible.

One further source is the notes of Magda's mother, Auguste Behrend, which were published in 1952 in the *Schwäbische Illustrierte*. In her memoirs she tries to convey the most positive possible image of her daughter.

All that remains from Magda herself are some personal letters to her father, Oskar Ritschel. The rest of her correspondence refers to areas of daily life, such as orders, bills, the search for domestic staff or begging letters.

The most important information about Magda's childhood and youth I owe to Dr Max Fleisch, who was very well acquainted with Lisa Arlosoroff-Steinberg, the friend of Magda's youth.

The story of Magda Goebbels is part of our past, a period that has changed our world and whose effects are still felt today. With the biography of Magda Goebbels I should like to help to ensure that we remember, and that we do not forget this period of our own history for the sake of the future, despite – or perhaps because of – its barbarism and terror.

Chapter 1

The rain beat hard on the windows of the train. Inside the compartment the air was damp and heavy. The passengers were crammed closely together, each compartment had as many people as it could hold, and those people who had pushed their way onto the train at the last minute had to stand in the corridor. Sweat, fear of the unknown and fatigue made the atmosphere almost intolerable. The train was slow, rolling and rattling evenly along before coming to a standstill between stations every so often. Then, with a wheeze and a groan, the locomotive would start moving again.

Magda and her mother, Auguste Friedländer[1], were among the more fortunate, who were able to push and shove their way into a seat. Exhausted, the girl pressed her face to the damp window pane. Drops of rain trickled down the outside, like tears. Her mother seemed to be sleeping, but Magda tried to catch as much as she could of the fragments of words flying back and forth among the passengers. German alternated with Belgian-accented French. Over and over she heard the words: home, war, future.

It was only a few weeks since Magda had crossed the main square in Brussels with her stepfather, Richard Friedländer[2], when, next to the cab-rank, a newspaper-seller called out the headline of a special edition: 'Murder in Sarajevo', 'The successor to the Habsburg throne, Franz Ferdinand, and his wife shot in their car!' For most of the people who greedily snatched the paper from the salesman's hand, Sarajevo seemed to lie in a wild, remote land. Nevertheless, some voices on that warm summer day expressed the worry that there might be war, because mighty Germany would stand by Austria. Over the next few weeks the terrible news came flooding in. When it came to light that Germany was declaring war first on Russia and then on France, it was clear even to Magda's parents that they would have to leave Brussels for some time. Magda bade farewell to the Flemish-style house on the Allée des Hortensias where she had only lived for a few years[3]. Later, over lunch, a business friend of Friedländer's came to call, telling them that a wave of hatred was spreading against the Germans, that the windows of German shops had been pelted with stones, and that German lives might even be in danger. Magda's mother burst into tears, a few belongings were hastily crammed into a suitcase, and a little while later the family friend drove them to the German consulate in his Belgian car. Magda was furious about this outbreak of hostility. Admittedly her fellow pupils at the convent had been rather reserved with her, but their anti-German remarks had gone no further than mild sniping, and she had responded with nothing more than scorn. But the riots that she could now observe from her friend's car frightened her, because they were the product of straightforward hatred – although no one actually said that their cause lay in the sudden invasion of the German army. When it was a question of saving one's own skin, most people preferred not to think about such things. So for Magda the fact that she was being hunted from the country at dead of night must have come as a profound humiliation. A humiliation that probably left some anger behind, all the greater for being unexpressed. This feeling may explain Magda's later indifference and coldness towards the Belgian people when Hitler invaded Flanders in the Second World War.

By now other families were seeking refuge in the German consulate.[4] Their eyes were all filled with terror, and the fear of an uncertain future. As more and more people came to find sanctuary in the protection of diplomatic immunity, they learned that they wouldn't be able to stay at the consulate. After a few hours they were led away under military guard, and given temporary refuge in a circus tent.

The next morning they returned to the Gare du Nord, from where they were to be dispatched to Germany. The soldiers were friendly, and handed out coffee, cigarettes and chocolate to the terrified, exhausted Germans. Magda asked one of them why they were being so friendly, when they didn't really want to have the Germans around any more. His answer was: 'We are staring death in the face, Mademoiselle!'[5]

Magda found herself thinking about that phrase when the train ground to a standstill once again. They had arrived at the Dutch–German border, and the direct rail link from Belgium to Germany was about to pass through what was already a battle zone. All the German passengers had to alight at the border and, as it seemed to Magda, spend an age standing on the platform in the pouring rain. The confusion seemed complete when it turned out that everyone who had been ordered to leave the train had to pay the official price for a ticket to the next German border station. But since many of the refugees had fled in a terrible hurry, they did not have the money to do this. On both sides of the border voices could be heard rising in indignation, and the atmosphere became more and more heated until a telephone call to Berlin resolved the situation: the German state bank would pay the costs. The Dutch rail officials allowed them to continue with their journey – although not in comfortable if cramped compartments, but in filthy cattle cars.[6]

For Auguste Friedländer, this involuntary return to Prussian Berlin meant a return to the past, and a past that she would have preferred to leave behind her. Judging by the prettified memoirs of her daughter as published in the *Schwäbische Illustrierte* in 1952, she had, throughout her life, said nothing of the true circumstances of Magda's birth[7], and at this point, as they set off for their true 'home', all that Magda probably knew of her true origins was that she had been born in Berlin on 11 November 1901, and baptised Johanna Maria Magdalena. At this time Auguste Behrend had been twenty years old, working as a servant to a family in Bülowstrasse, an elegant address in Berlin. Later she gave Bülowstrasse as Magda's place of birth, although the birth certificate records it as Katzler Strasse[8]. At the time of Magda's birth Auguste was single, which would have meant a severe social stigma, and which she hushed up. A short time later the probable father of the child, the engineer Oskar Ritschel, married her – although without giving the child his name. The marriage was dissolved after three years, but Ritschel maintained an interest in the child. At the time he was doing a great deal of work in Belgium, and when Magda was five years old he urged Auguste to send the child to see him there. So Magda travelled alone, with a sign around her neck and a basket full of provisions, from Berlin to Cologne[9], where Ritschel met her, travelled on with her to Brussels and put her in a convent boarding school. Here her further education was entrusted to Catholic nuns.

We don't know what had passed between Ritschel and Auguste, or why he effectively took the child away from her mother without telling her where Magda was living. It was two years before he finally yielded to her insistent requests, and told her where her daughter was. Auguste, who was still a pretty young woman, had in the meantime met the businessman Friedländer, and when she went to Belgium to see Magda again, Friedländer travelled after her and married her there.[10]

Auguste was horrified by conditions in the convent in the town of Thild. The girls slept in an enormous dormitory, draughty and freezing cold. Auguste immediately decided to transfer her daughter to another convent in Vilvoorde, which seemed less strict to her: 'Here the large dormitory was divided into cabins, which could be closed off with curtains. Each girl had a bed in her "room", a chair and a wardrobe for her clothes. At night a nun walked up and down with a prayer-book and a rosary. The days were rigidly divided: at the very break of dawn the girls had to attend early mass in the church, on an empty stomach. On one occasion Magda fainted, and for that reason was the only one allowed to eat a piece of chocolate before mass, which I brought with me on my visits.'[11]

It was difficult for Magda to make friends with her fellow pupils, but she established an intimate relationship with the Mother Superior. She was a gifted pupil, learning came easily to her, she was mature for her age, she loved music and was a talented pianist. These traits won her a special place at the school, and the Mother Superior would sometimes take her to Bruges or Ghent to visit museums or art exhibitions. Since Magda knew no other way of life, she was relatively contented, and gladly adapted to life behind convent walls.

As soon as Friedländer's business was going better, Magda's parents were able to move into a one-family house on the Allée des Hortensias in Scharbeek, one of the loveliest villa suburbs of Brussels, and Magda was able to come home to visit.[12]

When she was eleven the time arrived for her first communion. Weeks before, the tailor had come to the house bringing swatches of material and discussing patterns, and Magda had respectfully run her fingers along the edges of the lace. The cathedral was full for her big day, as she walked along the central aisle with the other girls, and Magda had a sense of having been chosen when the onlookers murmured, '*Comme une fiancée*'.[13]

A little later Magda transferred to the new Ursuline convent which had just been opened in her street, near her parents' house. Of all her fellow-pupils she was the one selected to deliver the opening address in the presence of the Cardinal. Without stumbling, she clearly declaimed her words 'before the mayor, the assembled nuns, the other pupils and their parents'.[14]

From now on Magda could go home in the afternoon. Her stepfather Friedländer was good to her, and his personal warmth was

something new for the girl, and his generosity and humour contrasted starkly with the strict rules of the convent, which was all
she had known until now. He spoke German and French equally
well, with a slightly melancholy undertone in his voice.
Friedländer was a Jew, probably from an haute-bourgeois family.
He was assimilated, but he respected the solemn holidays such as
Peshach and Yom Kippur. In many mixed marriages it was customary to give the children an insight into the religious practices
of both partners, so Magda grew up having a degree of familiarity
with Judaism, particularly since she had, as we know, assumed
Friedländer's name.[15]

Magda remained an outsider in her new convent as well. After
school she escaped to her books. She locked herself in her room
for hours, sitting in her rocking chair and reading. To the dismay
of her mother she read great literature, devouring the classics and
books about art[16] as though the questions arising out of her adolescence might find answers there.

But Magda also closed herself away because she wanted to be
undisturbed. Like all young girls, she was aware of the changes in
her body. During her life in the convent the girls had even had to
wear long shirts in the bath so that they wouldn't see their own
nakedness, and one repeated question in confession was whether
they had had immodest thoughts or deeds. It had been hard for
Magda to imagine anything beyond childish curiosity. Now she
was able to observe the changes in her body. She also noticed
that she was more fully developed than her classmates, but she
remained alone with her indefinable longings and emotional fluc-
tuations. Magda's need to lock herself away shows that on the
one hand she wanted to dissociate herself from the outside world –
perhaps from her mother – while at the same time she was willing
to limit her own freedom, just as a caterpillar wraps itself up in a
cocoon to re-emerge at some point as a butterfly. This gradual
entry into the world of adulthood was now severely disturbed by
the outbreak of war and flight.

By now they had been travelling for several days, and the rattling of the cattle truck, which pitilessly shook everyone's limbs, the constant noise and dirt were taking their toll on the general mood. At each station where they were given drinking water and something to eat, they asked the station staff the same question: when would they finally get there? But no one could give them a precise answer, the trains taking the young soldiers towards the border in the opposite direction had right of way, because the Kaiser had sent them to war against France. Magda saw the laughing faces of the young men, filled with a spirit of euphoria. 'Paris by breakfast-time', it said on the side of the wagons. And Magda found herself remembering the words of the Belgian soldier: these young men, singing their way to war, clearly aren't staring death in the face. But on this endless, uncomfortable journey she herself must have become aware that she had lost her only home, that her childhood was over and that her sheltered life would now make way for another, harsher reality.

On the sixth day they finally reached Berlin.[17]

The expulsion of the Germans from Brussels at the start of the First World War, which made enemies of friends and neighbours and which the young Magda had experienced at first hand, and especially that degrading journey in the cattle cars, calls forth images which recall the deportations and expulsions that would occur in Germany and throughout Europe three decades later.

Chapter 2

'Victory to the Kaiser!' came the confident call as young soldiers, drunk with victory, marched along the platform while Magda and her parents, hungry, tired and dirty, alighted from the train. 'We'll meet again, back in our homeland,' sang the men who had clambered into their compartments and, beaming, waved their handkerchiefs, to the wives or girlfriends they were leaving behind. They had stuck flowers into the barrels of their rifles, and the euphoria of departure left little room for the grief of farewell. Even the mothers of fresh-faced, boyish volunteers had to remain surreptitious as they dabbed the tears from their eyes.

'The spirit of the nation' had gripped the Germans: Germany must and will be victorious, 'simply because that is a necessity for human and divine history of the spirit on this globe.'[1] These were the words intoned from church pulpits across the country.

In the USA and France a national sense of self-understanding had come into being as a result of events expressing those countries' will to political freedom and self-determination, as in the American War of Independence, or, in France, the Tennis Court Oath and the storming of the Bastille. Nothing comparable had happened in Germany.[2] Instead, the decision in 1871 to bring about the unity of the German Reich through warfare had been made over the heads of the population itself, and did not lead to the political emancipation of the country's citizens – although large sections of the population greeted that unity with cries of victory. Even now, with the outbreak of war, we cannot necessarily speak of political self-determination. It would be more accurate to say that war was given a sacred, religious significance which politics elevated into an apotheosis: the 'Kaiser should apply the laws of global justice to Germany's enemies'.[3] The fanaticism of these views, with their apocalyptic tendencies, finds expression in a frequently-occurring image: Germany is compared with a phoenix that will arise, renewed, from the ashes. The nation of 'poets and philosophers' also crafted verses in its warlike enthusiasm. In August 1914 alone, more than a million German war poems were written,[4] some by such well-respected names as Richard Dehmel, Rudolf Alexander Schröder, Ina Seidel, Gerhart and Carl Hauptmann, but most by unknown authors, by 'suddenly blessed dilettantes of the cultivated bourgeoisie,'[5] expressing the supposed superiority of the Germans. 'The religiously-minded set to work with similar industry. During the first two years of the war more than a thousand sermons and other tracts were published about the war, and individual publications ran to editions of several hundred thousand.'[6] People had not been 'German' for very long, and the philosopher Johann Gottlieb Fichte's 'Addresses to the German nation' were quoted both by Protestant vicars in their sermons and by university professors in their war-lectures.[7] Fichte and his colleague Arndt were the first to have spoken (with reference to the wars of liberation) of the special 'mission of the German nation' and its supposed intellectual superiority, and a contemporary of theirs, Max von Schenkendorf, had summarised Fichte's ideas about the spirit of the nation and the Germans in particular, in the following lines, which suddenly seemed to have a contemporary relevance once again.

In Germany shall blossom
Salvation for all the world[8]

But behind this warlike cry, this 'furor teutonicus', lay hidden the anxiety and uncertainty of German society at that time, because the gulf between the working class and the class constituted by the nobility and the bourgeoisie was growing ever deeper. As industrialisation had progressed, the workers had grown in political importance. At the same time a new sector of society, the rising petty bourgeoisie, had come into being in the form of the technical professions. Along with these there were the many bank and office workers, who streamed each morning to their work places wearing collars and ties, no longer devoted to the humanistic cultural ideal of the bourgeoisie, which was based primarily on idealistic philosophy and classical theatre. The old academic intellectual values of the elite had started to show cracks, and were being rendered irrelevant by the mass Social Democratic party, with its emphasis on the material interests of trade and technology.[9] The threatened cultivated bourgeoisie saw the war as an integrating means of forging a kind of unity. As one war sermon had it: 'In this army of ours we have an embodiment of our national spirit!'[10] and the jubilation at the start of the war, over the 'rise of the German national soul', which was seen as a 'magnificent miracle'[11], promised to grip the nation as a whole, as a 'spiritual movement', and drove thousands of young men into recruitment offices throughout the Reich, determined to go to war as volunteers.

In the recruitment office of the Berlin district of Schöneberg, a young man had joined the queue of volunteers. He was of medium build, wearing dark horn-rimmed glasses, behind whose lenses alert and resolute eyes flashed. He had thick, black curly hair, and although his German was unusually eloquent, he spoke with a slight Russian accent. When his turn came, and the doctor in charge of examination asked him how old he was, he confidently replied that he would be sixteen next year. The doctor benignly shook his head. 'Too young,' he announced. 'You should go back to school!' The boy tried to argue that he was physically and intellectually on a par with many eighteen-year-olds, and that the Kaiser needed everyone he could get for his war against Russia, but the doctor waved him aside. 'Next!' Disappointed, Victor Arlosoroff stepped out of the queue. Outside in the street his mother and younger sister Lisa were waiting for him. When his mother saw his downcast face, she was relieved, and clutched Lisa's hand in a secret gesture of agreement.

The family originally came from the Ukraine, where Victor's grandfather was a famous rabbi.[12] In 1905, when the Russian pogroms against the Jews broke out, the Arlosoroffs, like many other Jewish families, had fled to Königsberg. There the three children, Dora, Victor and Lisa grew up with two cultures, but events made them feel more German than Russian, although as a Russian family they were obliged to renew their residence permit every year. This they were able to do without difficulty. In her memoirs of her youth, Victor's sister Lisa describes the situation of the family a few days before the outbreak of war: 'In July 1914 Victor had an operation on his nose. Our parents watched as the boy, without twitching an eyelid, made his way to the operating table, knowing that the operation would not be an easy one. In the clinic, where he was supposed to spend only a few days, he fell ill with a threatening disease. Victor was still lying there when war broke out. He didn't know that in the first days after the declaration of war a rifleman had appeared in our house and taken us, on the basis of an expulsion order issued twenty-four hours previously, out of the fortress city of Königsberg. Only the fact that Victor happened to be laid low by a serious illness concealed from us the fate of the first emigrants who had been dispatched to Russia, their cases unexamined. Victor knew only that war had broken out and his fatherland was in danger, and he, a boy of fifteen years, implored his parents to allow him to join the army as a volunteer. His parents refused their permission, but he declared that he would only agree to take his doctor's advice if they allowed him to join up. Eight days later we boarded the train to Leipzig. The rumour was circulating that foreigners were not allowed to enter Berlin, and only once we had reached Berlin, where that rumour turned out to be a lie, did our parents decide to leave the train after a thirty-six-hour journey.'[13]

Arriving in the capital, once Victor had been turned down as a volunteer on the grounds of his youth and instructed to continue his school career instead, his father tried to find his feet in Berlin and feed his family. But as no foreigner who had recently arrived in the capital could find work of any kind, he was forced to resume his old business contacts with St Petersburg and travel to Russia. In the meantime Arlosoroff's mother was to stay in Berlin on her own and try to eke out their small savings so that they could all live on them. Lisa Arlosoroff writes: 'We didn't know that we would be separated for ever. Our father died of cholera on 9 August 1918 in Petersburg, just as he was about to come back to us.'[14]

The Arlosoroffs and the Friedländers were not the only ones who had come to the capital as refugees. In the summer of 1914 there had been massive shifts of population. Not only were trains full of volunteers and conscripts leaving the stations for the eastern and western boundaries of the Reich, but at the same time refugees were flooding in, waiting until further notice to be housed and looked after. Among them, Magda and her family were at first sent to the Hohenzollernstrasse, on the corner with Tiergartenstrasse. They lived with other homeless refugees in a beautiful old villa, which had known better days and affluent inhabitants. Every family was assigned a room, bachelors and single women had to divide up rooms between them, and each family had to feed itself, although without any cooking facilities.[15]

At noon each day Magda went with her mother to Lützowplatz, where a Red Cross kitchen distributed hot meals. This temporary arrangement made her very unhappy. In the queue Magda came into contact with people from all walks of life, most of them either deracinated or destitute. They included immigrant day-labourers who thought they would be able to make more money in the city, impoverished Russians who had had to abandon their luxurious life in St Petersburg after the first Revolution, old proletarian women who could no longer work and young women whose terrible experiences of life, standing there with their little children, would have melted the heart, while their husbands were off fighting somewhere at some unimaginable front.

Magda had problems understanding these people. Her German was not as good as her French, and the brash directness of Berlin slang was utterly alien to her. In the home for refugees, on the other hand, where the women sat peacefully together knitting and chatting about their lives then and now, noble words were heard about heroism and sacrificing oneself for the Fatherland. Magda, who had so enjoyed having her own room at home after her time in the convent, found it difficult to get used to the constant presence of so many strange people. No secret, no indiscretion could remain hidden for long. But one of the women occupied the imaginations of the rest more than any other: Frau Kowalsky, an elderly East Prussian with wide, high cheekbones, a wan face and crazed eyes, who had fled with her daughter for fear of the Russians, was believed to keep herself busy with astrology, fortune-telling and palmistry, and was often happy to lay out the cards when her daughter, who did not have a high opinion of this passion of her mother's, was not nearby.

When the women were sitting together as usual in the afternoon, the other women would pester their room-mate to lay out the cards for them. Even Magda, who normally seemed quite rational, was interested in fortune-telling, and begged and pleaded until the cards were laid out for her. Her mother later recalled: 'The fortune-teller put Magda's left hand to her heart, carefully laid out the cards in four rows and quickly shuffled them all together again. "I don't want to see that," she said, "a single person cannot have so much good fortune!" Then she took Magda's hand and studied the lines long and hard. After a while she said, "One day you will be a queen of life, but the end, when it comes, will be terrible . . ."'[16]

That autumn Magda – by now almost thirteen – attended the Kollmorgen Lyzeum in Keithstrasse, to keep up to date with her schooling. It was not hard for her to follow the lessons, since she had been well prepared in the convent school in Brussels, but she still had some difficulties with the German language. At first, if she tried to begin a sentence in German, she would inevitably have to finish it in French. On the other hand, it meant that she shone in French lessons.[17] Once again Magda was playing the part of the outsider, but her fellow pupils were kind, and curious about this unusual girl, in many respects more advanced than they were.

Soon afterwards the headmistress brought a new girl to the class. Reticent but self-confident, the girl of about thirteen with the thick dark plaits and the brown eyes introduced herself: Lisa Arlosoroff.

Chapter 3

From now on Magda's life changed: all of a sudden she had a friend.[1] After only a few days Lisa had gone up to Magda at breaktime. She had heard Magda's accent, and concluded that Magda, too, had been brought to Berlin by the war. The two girls quickly discovered that they had both lost a home, and that they both had to find their feet in their new surroundings.

By now Magda's mother, Auguste, was running from one office to another trying to find a new place for the family to live. But times were hard, because Friedländer's money was locked up in a bank in Brussels, and he himself was temporarily without work in Berlin, before being employed by the elegant Eden Hotel. By the autumn of 1915 the Friedländers were finally able to move to their own flat,[2] not far from the Arlosoroffs, and the two girls visited one another every day after school.

One fine September day – the war was entering its second year – Magda and Lisa were strolling home from school. The gentle warmth of summer was still in the air, but over everything there shimmered a gauze of silvery light, anticipating the melancholy of the coming autumn. The lovely weather had enticed many people out of doors, and while Magda and Lisa carelessly swung their satchels, other walkers, young women with perambulators and older schoolchildren, walked towards them, glancing at the two girls. They had become used to walking one another home: first Lisa went to Magda's, then Magda accompanied Lisa and so on, until they had exhausted all the topics of the afternoon. This time they had an unusual amount to discuss, because it was the beginning of the high Jewish holidays, and Lisa would not be coming to school for the next few days. By the time they stood before Lisa's front door they were so immersed in their conversation that they almost bumped into the telegram boy, who turned to them in annoyance and asked if they could at least tell him where a family called Silberstein lived. He had a telegram from the front for Eisenacher Strasse, but it was hard to make out the house number. Lisa was happy to oblige. While the telegram boy was leaving, the girls stood together for a moment. All of a sudden they heard a terrible cry that sounded almost inhuman, as though of a fatally wounded animal. 'He's dead! They've killed him!' they heard a voice shrieking, and shortly afterwards they heard that same cry, which soon turned into a wild sobbing, gradually subsided and finally fell silent. Magda stood as though rooted to the spot. Only in whispers did they dare to remember the young Hans Silberstein, who had just a few weeks previously interrupted his studies to go off to battle.

Hans Silberstein was one of the many Jewish and other volunteers who had given their lives for the Kaiser at such an early point in the war. For the war was not going as everyone had anticipated: those soldiers who had hoped to spend the Christmas of the first war year with their families were instead lying in trenches in the midst of pitched battles on the Eastern and Western fronts. At home, on the back pages of the newspapers, the lists of the fallen were growing ever longer. Society decreed that the wives and mothers left behind should practise 'self-discipline'. They were to take the heroic deaths of their husbands or sons with equivalent heroism, and they were expected to devote themselves to the less seriously wounded casualties who were home to recuperate before they were once again dispatched to battle.

The seriously wounded, who could not be treated at home but who filled the military hospitals, presented a pitiful picture. As battles at the front were often fought hand to hand – and with bayonets – the injuries were terrible. The men were missing arms and legs, their heads were swathed in blood-drenched bandages. Then, too, there were the shocking reports of these sad figures on their crutches, considerably dampening the enthusiasm of the civilian population. The ones who were told whispered tales of gas attacks – the first of these launched by the Germans on 22 April 1915 at Ypres, a little town in Belgium – were seized by fear. Something crucial had changed in this war. Now battles were being decided by the development of military technology either at home or in enemy territory, and victory and defeat no longer had much to do with individual courage.

Along with the fear of war that was felt by many, almost everyone suffered from daily hunger. Germany was in the middle of a serious food crisis. Because of the Allied blockade, supplies were used up by the second year of the war, and anyone without special privileges was obliged to go hungry. After a damp summer, all food was rationed. Black bread, the only kind that one could normally find – and only then for a considerable sum – was mixed with sawdust, and the only available spread had for a long time been artificial honey.

Magda and her mother generally suffered less from rationing than the rest of the population, because his work in the Eden Hotel meant that Friedländer now and then managed to set aside something for his family, and if they had any leftovers, Magda would sometimes bring them to her friends, the Arlosoroffs, on Shabbath.

On 11 November 1916 Magda turned fifteen: she was an unusually pretty girl, of medium height and slim, with thick dark-blonde hair, blue eyes and a confident bearing that made her look older than she was. For her birthday Friedländer had managed to get hold of a cake – a great surprise to everyone – which Magda and her friends Lisa and Dora enjoyed at a little party.[3]

A few days later, when Magda took the remains of the birthday cake to the Arlosoroffs, through the November dusk on the badly lit street, a disagreeable, damp cold crept through her limbs. Actual winter had not yet come, and even now it had become impossible to heat apartments so that they became really warm and dry. Coke left fine black soot in the air, to clog up the airways. Many people suffered from chronic bronchitis. Friedländer, too, was ill more often than he had been before, and Magda noticed that the atmosphere between her parents was more often irritable, that her mother used a harsh tone when talking to him, and that after arguments the doors fell silently shut.

Magda's steps echoed in the empty street, she was almost alone, because people only left the house if they absolutely had to. The trees had shed their leaves, and stood black and gleaming by the side of the street. In the distance Magda could see the gaslights being lit, and their milky light cast cold, long shadows. The Arlosoroffs' staircase in Eisenacher Strasse was badly lit as well, and cold and wet. Music could be heard coming from the apartment, Dora and Lisa were playing piano duets, and it was a while before Victor opened the door. Magda had not seen him for some time. He attended the Werner Siements Realgymnasium, a very progressive school with its own student parliament, high entrance requirements and an open-minded body of teachers, who readily discussed anything with their pupils. Magda knew from Lisa, who had a very high opinion of her brother, that Victor was a brilliant pupil, and that outside of school he led a very independent life, was a committed Zionist and even led a Zionist youth group. Now he stood before her, took her clammy hands in his own as if it was the most natural thing in the world, and greeted her with an audibly Russian accent. Magda had a sense of well-being as she walked in to join Lisa and Dora in the music room, a feeling that she did not know from her own household. In the Arlosoroff home the children set the tone, their mother was a cheerful, intelligent woman and gave her children a great deal of space, so the apartment was often full of young people enthusiastically discussing the events of the day. Naturally, the progression of the war and all the deprivations that it entailed was often at the centre of these discussions. Victor's youthful, combative patriotism had long since vanished, and he had instead become a convinced pacifist, with his attentions focused on the coming collapse of bourgeois structures in Germany, the 'monopoly-capitalist form of the economy', as he called it. He spoke with passion about the misery of the workers and the terrible poverty of the Russian–Jewish refugees. Victor was a fiery and persuasive orator, very sure of his arguments, but it was above all his voice, his alert and intelligent eyes, the vitality and energy in his gestures that fascinated Magda so much that she could not take her eyes off him. The evening echoed with music: Dora and Lisa played piano, together with Victor they sang songs by Schubert and Beethoven and, finished up with some old Russian ballads that directly addressed the young people's emotions. When Magda had to leave, Victor showed her to the door. As they said goodbye he said only that he would like to see her again.

Over the next few weeks Magda and Victor saw each other more often, first of all when Magda came to visit Lisa, and then when Magda asked Victor – just as Lisa did – to allow them to attend the Zionist youth meetings he organised. In her memoirs Lisa wrote how Victor's passion came into being:

Even in December 1914, when our father had already left us, our mother had gone to the Palestine Office in Berlin to find a good Hebrew teacher for Victor. That same month Jisrael Reichert began teaching Victor Hebrew. Reichert was the first Palestinian who had come to our house, the first who could tell us anything about life in Palestine and talk to Victor about it. Victor's interest in Palestine grew and grew . . . He feverishly learned Hebrew, Jewish history and the history of Zionism, and had only one thought in his head: the idea of Zionism.[4]

Zionism came into being as a political movement in the late nineteenth century. The founder of the movement, Theodor Herzl, an Austrian journalist and author, still influenced by the notorious Dreyfus trial of 1894, anticipated a further wave of anti-Semitism. His vision for resistance to that anti-Semitism consisted in revitalising the Jewish nation by founding a Jewish state. The name of the movement, 'Zionism', referred to the unique bond between the Jewish people and its biblical home-land, Zion, because since the laying-waste of Zion almost two thousand years ago, and the Roman destruction of the temple in Jerusalem, the Jewish people had been living through the pain of exile. In 1896 Herzl published his thoughts in the essay 'The Jewish State'. Here he writes: 'I consider the Jewish question neither a social nor a religious one, even though it sometimes takes these and other forms. It is a national question, and to solve it we must first of all establish it as an international polit-ical problem to be discussed and settled by the civilised nations of the world in council.

'We are a people — one people.'[5]

At the first Zionist Congress in Basle, which was called by Herzl in 1897, it was decided to create a 'publicly and legally secured homeland in Palestine'[6] for the Jewish people. In the face of great difficulties, the immigration of the Jews was increasing, and the first Jewish city, Tel Aviv, was founded in 1909; in 1911 the first Kibbutzim (collective settlements) were established, and by 1914, twelve thousand Jews were living in fifty-nine agricul-tural colonies. But very soon – contrary to Herzl's original intention – various different strands of Zionism developed: a reli-gious tendency and a modern, socialist wing.

Victor identified so strongly with the ideas of socialist Zionism that he tried to create such a circle at school among his Jewish fellow-pupils. One of his followers, Robert Sternau, relates the great influence that Victor, or Chaim, as he began to call himself, exerted upon them:

He showed us the sources of Jewishness, and Zionism as the
only goal . . . At first we resisted his influence: initially we
could see nothing in his Jewish nationalism but an
additional national separation from the world at large. But
it was not long before he conquered our hearts. His entire
personality, his profound humility, the sympathy with
which he responded to every honest opinion influenced us
more and more. Everything that later made him the overall
leader of Zionism made its appearance during this time.[7]

Some twenty pupils under his leadership formed a close circle
that they called 'Tikvat Zion' (Hope of Zion). The young people
met almost every day in the Arlosoroff household, and Victor's
authority had such a convincing effect on them that he even
handed out homework and organised a real training seminar.
Sternau remembers that they did not only discuss Jewish subjects:
'With what feeling he would sometimes read to us and explained
works from German literature, which he loved with his whole
heart. He was able to make Hölderlin, Liliencron and even Goethe
more vivid to us than our schoolteachers could. The Jewish and
the human elements formed an organic unit in him, and his great
influence upon us was based on that many-sidedness.'[8]

Magda regularly took part in these meetings. Friedländer's influence meant that Jewish life was not alien to her, and although she
had not yet paid it a great deal of attention, she suddenly found
herself fascinated by Victor's passion for the Zionist cause. She
sensed instinctively that he had the strength and the will to realise
his ideas of a new life in a Jewish Palestine. And like all his
friends, Magda too was convinced that because of his natural
authority Victor would assume a leading role in the coming Jewish
state. Victor paid her a great deal of attention in any case, and
within the little circle the brilliance of his charisma worked its
charms on her. The stimuli that she absorbed in those discussions
promised to give her life structure and direction. For his part,
Victor very quickly became used to the young member of the

group, and soon she was not only his little sister's friend, but a young girl whom he found very attractive, and with whom he was able to discuss his ideas.[8]

Again and again the subject of war appeared in these discussions. Among the young scholars at the Werner Siemens Realgymnasium the mood had changed just as much as it had among the majority of the population. When it first broke out, and for its first year, the war actually did create the desired social integration between the different social classes, it cut through the monotony of the bourgeois world, and the world of the working class which had itself practically become bourgeois. The internal tensions of German society were concentrated on an external enemy. Now those trends were changing. A polarisation was taking place: the broad centre of the population, which had supported the war, was shaken by a left wing that no longer acted as a support to national solidarity but pressed for an end to the war, a peace settlement. On the right, on the other hand, extreme forces were assembling, who were not only ready to accommodate a further drastic deterioration in quality of life in order to achieve a final victory, but who wanted to achieve that victory by means of a militarised society. Within these circles the concept of 'total war' made its first appearance, a war whose weight the civilian population would have to bear, both through their willingness to endure deprivation, and through their psychological support.

Off at the front another feeling was coming to the fore with the increasing brutality of war. It was based on isolation from all civilian life, daily confrontation with death and the experience of soldiers who had spent months living in the trenches and depending solely on each other. At the same time Ernst Jünger's diary *Storms of Steel* began to mythologise the notion of the heroic death, a phenomenon that went hand in hand with an unheard-of aestheticisation of cruelty and violence.

At home, the underprivileged classes suffered most terribly from the increased hardships of the front, and felt the most vulnerable to 'the ones at the top'. One of the government measures which was perceived to be unjust was the general mobilisation of the population, introduced in December 1916; according to the law of Support for the Fatherland, the government could force any worker to work where it thought necessary. Consequently the armaments industry was given free rein. At the same time living conditions were deteriorating continuously, a black market for food had come into being, and people were beginning to sell off their valuables to buy meat, fat and pulses at extortionate prices. In February 1917 the news of the Russian workers' uprising reached Germany, and in April the country saw its first major wave of strikes, above all among the well-organised armaments workers in Berlin. The government tried to keep the population in line with hortatory slogans, and at the same time it developed a war propaganda based on chauvinism, hatred and concepts of the enemy, and which spread the conviction of the superiority of the German nation.

Chapter 4

In summer 1917 Victor sat his *Abitur*, his school-leaving certificate. Magda was sitting with Lisa, Dora and Victor's mother in the big school hall when the headmaster delivered his end-of-year address, once again talking of the duty of perseverance, of German culture, of those tendencies towards fragmentation that must be held in check and of the duty of each individual towards his humanist inheritance. Then silence fell in the hall, as the headmaster read out the names of former school-leavers who had died in the war over the past few years.

Victor began studying Economics at the Humboldt University. He escaped the difficulties a young man of his origins might have had in entering the university thanks to his successful school career and the sympathetic headmaster who attested to his excellent German convictions:

Victor Arlosoroff, b. 23.2.1899, attended our institution for two and a half years until Easter 1917. I can in all good conscience attest that he felt himself to be a German in every respect. His fellow-students proved that they shared this opinion by electing him to the head of the pupils' committee . . . Thus, despite the fact that he is nominally still a Russian subject, I can thus only approve the matriculation of Victor Arlosoroff.

Prof. W. Wetekamp[1]

Even during his studies, Victor remained a passionate advocate of Zionism. Magda stood by him in all his enterprises, as though this was the most natural thing in the world, and accompanied him to his meetings and lectures, even when he was, for example, distributing food supplies that he had organised to the poor Russian and Polish Jews. These Eastern Jews were the poorest of the poor. After the most terrible experiences, the pogroms in Russia and Poland, they had fled to Berlin, where they now led pitiful lives around Alexanderplatz. Victor felt the need to help these people in any way he could. Their outward appearance, their sidelocks, long caftans and hats, looked exotic, and they were treated as undesirable aliens by assimilated Jews. Victor tried to recruit these lost souls for Palestine, and to explain to them that they had no future in Germany, and described Eretz Israel[2] as their only possible perspective.

Victor's persuasive powers were so great that everyone who belonged to his circle shared his views. Conversations and lectures always revolved around the question of how it would be when they lived in that country which would once again flow with milk and honey when the Jews had returned.

These idealistic ideas of a better life contrasted starkly with the general mood. Magda's parents, Auguste and Max Friedländer, were not only downcast by the lengthy duration of the war, but also in a state of profound insecurity. The outbreak of the October Revolution in 1917, with its terrible side-effects, prompted strong and subliminal anxieties throughout the entire population.

Because of these insecure, oppressive times it seemed important to Auguste to provide as best she could for the pretty and intelligent Magda. So when, in the last year of the war, her father

Ritschel wrote from Bad Godesberg to invite his daughter to visit, after a brief hesitation Auguste and Friedländer agreed.[3]

The journey brought Magda further support from Ritschel: he was still paying the fees for her school, the Kollmorgen Lyzeum, in addition to three hundred marks a month, a sum with which Auguste presumably supplemented her housekeeping.

Magda's relationship with her biological father was reinvigorated by this trip. It may not have been warm and tender – they simply did not know each other well enough for that – but her father, who had, as an engineer, been responsible for several inventions, and whose family owned a factory in the Rhineland, introduced her to a haute-bourgeois world in which she would have liked to live, but in which she was not quite accepted. We do not know how aware she herself was of the 'stain' of her illegitimate birth at this time, but she must have sensed the customary rejection on the part of bourgeois society – although not on the part of Ritschel himself. Her biological father was not only wealthy, but a cultivated man. He took a particular interest in the ideas of Buddhism, which he explained to Magda during her visit, and which would fascinate her for the rest of her life.

This inclination towards Buddhism reappears throughout Magda's biography, but no contemporary gives us any reason to suggest that she ever spoke of it or outwardly engaged with it. Perhaps she was more concerned with establishing a shared interest and a connection with her biological father through something that might have seemed mystical and alien to others, and which belonged only to the two of them. Much later, when Magda was married to Goebbels, books about Buddhism still lay on her bedside table. The journalist Bella Fromm, however, was officially forbidden to mention this fact in an article about Frau Goebbels. Clearly the ideas of the peace-loving Buddha were no more reconcilable with the philosophy of National Socialism than the game of chess, which Magda played from time to time, but which had the reputation of being a Jewish, intellectual hobby.[4]

After Magda's return from Bad Godesberg, the final winter of the war was just beginning. As in the previous year the schools were still unheated. Pupils were expected to make sacrifices for the Fatherland, collecting – for example – gifts for the army at the front. Magda refused to have anything to do with this, instead continuing to spend as much time as she could with Victor.

Victor's circle had enlarged since he had begun his university studies. He was not only valued for his political views, however, but soon received the nickname 'the poet' because of his tendency, in the middle of a polemic, to quote a poem by Heine or Rilke. This made him universally popular, so receptive were young people at that time to poetry.

This was the age of the youth movement, in opposition to the false emotionalism of the older generation. The young Zionists around Victor differed from other young people only in their political goals. Emotionally they were all gripped by a striving for inner authenticity and self-defined responsibility, although for some of them these emotions led to a new kind of romanticism and estrangement from the world. For Victor it was quite natural to live outside bourgeois conventions even in his personal relationships, and Magda, who had left the prohibitions of her Catholic upbringing far behind her, agreed with his precocious ideas about morality. In this way – perhaps more out of curiosity and the desire to seem like an adult than out of great love – she became his girlfriend.

While in these pacifist circles the end of the war was something devoutly yearned for, government declarations were filled with hollow slogans about perseverance, supported by news of the desperate victories of the German army on the Western Front, a last attempt to halt the advances of the Allies. Newspapers were no longer permitted to print the long lists of the dead, but there was barely a family that could not lay claim to someone wounded, fallen or missing in action. 'At the end of September 1918 Germany faced military collapse. The block of the central powers was beginning to fall to pieces. Bulgaria had already laid down its arms, and on 29 September signed the cease-fire. Since mid-September,

Austria–Hungary had been attempting to introduce peace negotiations, when a new major entente offensive in the west brought
the entire German front into extreme danger.'[5]

In these circumstances the 1st General Quartermaster, Erich
Ludendorff, was obliged to admit total military defeat. But since it
was nonetheless his goal to save the army – its existence and its
honour – he concealed the true military reasons for this, instead
passing the blame to the Social Democrats, who had been urging
peace for some time. As a result of constitutional change 'from
above', which turned Germany into a parliamentary democracy
overnight, they now saw themselves in the role of the government, and compelled to put a request for a cease-fire to President
Wilson. Thus, as Sebastian Haffner describes, the 'stab-in-the-
back legend' was born. The political left stabbed the 'victorious'
army in the back, they were ready to capitulate.

> At that point constitutional changes were relatively
> uninteresting to the German masses, and they took place
> over most people's heads. What counted was the end of the
> war, defeat, capitulation, the end of terror and the terror of
> the end: and that immediately divided the entire country
> into two camps. Some heard it with despair, others with
> relief. The war-weary, starving masses gave a sigh of relief;
> the belligerent bourgeoisie, hungry for victory, were
> reduced to sobs of grief. Some of them groaned: 'Finally!'
> The others cried, 'Betrayal!' and the two camps were
> already starting to look at each other with hatred.[6]

But for the time being the request for a cease-fire had not yet
been accepted, and President Wilson of the United States was
not sure how to respond to Germany's attempt to democratise
itself. 'The question of the Kaiser had not yet been solved,
because for a democracy wishing to follow the western model
it did not seem possible that the King of Prussia should, with
his army, have effectively forced a "revolution from above" on his

people'[7] and when Wilson didn't move, the Social Democrats under Friedrich Ebert began to raise fears that if the cease-fire were to collapse over the issue of the Kaiser, the country would be threatened with revolution.

On 5 November 1918 Magda and Lisa were let out of school early. One pupil's father had telephoned the headmistress and spoken of mutinous sailors in the city. The streets were still peaceful, but he wondered how long they would remain so. Arms linked, in groups of five or six they were colonising the pavements, their uniform jackets open at the neck, their cap bands missing, red armbands on their sleeves.

That was the start of a revolution that had been started by war-weary sailors in Kiel, and which had continued among sections of the army and the general population, demanding a final end to hostilities and involvement of the people in government in the form of workers' and soldiers' councils.

On 9 November 1918 Berlin was in uproar. Sebastian Haffner describes the day: 'Processions bearing Red Flags stormed the Reichstag. There was an eternal coming and going. That afternoon, the streets of central Berlin resembled a surging ocean of people.'[8] It was dangerous in the streets, there were shoot-outs between the regular army and revolutionary workers and soldiers. In the evening the Kaiser abdicated, fled to Holland and vanished from history once and for all.

Two days later, on 11 November 1918, the day of Magda's seventeenth birthday, the cease-fire was signed in the forest of Compiègne in Northern France. The Kaiser's empire had ceased to exist, and an era was at an end.

But the war had had terrible effects, particularly among young men: half of the fallen were between the ages of nineteen and twenty-five. Defeat had been conceded, but those in charge had refused to shoulder the blame. Many had had to endure the loss of their loved ones, and when humiliation was heaped upon grief, they felt a sense of injustice that made them even more resolute in their resistance to political reality. [9]

Chapter 5

Victor hurried to get home from university. That afternoon the Humboldt University, as they put it, had been temporarily closed 'by military decree'.

Berlin was in the midst of a civil war. After the 'bloodless revolution' in November of the previous year, in January 1919 the Berlin workers' movement had made a further attempt to win back the rights that they had fought for and lost once again. This attempt was condemned to failure. The workers might well have drummed together a massive march, militant forces had even occupied the newspaper district – later the building of the Social Democrat paper *Vorwärts* would be completely destroyed by government forces armed with cannon – but the Ebert government reacted with violent measures. In doing so it was relying on a strange and – as it would later turn out – unfortunate alliance, with Berlin government forces. These were troops from the former Reichswehr, the imperial army, who felt politically lost in the new situation and neither supported the soldiers' councils nor really agreed with a Social Democrat government. But while this – largely Social Democrat – government was admitting the possibility of reacting with force to the Spartacists, those forces were able to vent their frustrations. Within this sector of the military, which also included the notorious Freikorps, brutality and a hatred of dissidents were already clearly apparent; even now we can see the emergence of the attitudes of the future SA and SS, whose members were drawn from this faction.[1]

Arlosoroff tried to buy bread somewhere on the way home, but all the shops were closed, their blinds were down and their doors barricaded. People everywhere feared the aggression of the rising masses, because hunger was worse than it had been during the past year. It must have seemed as though everything had got worse since the end of the war.

From Wilhelmstrasse and the Brandenburg Gate the sounds of explosions reached Arlosoroff. A fellow-student had warned him, but by now even Dönhoffplatz was echoing with gunfire. Since both gas and electricity were in short supply, he had to find his way in the quickly falling darkness. Spectral groups of people were standing around everywhere, and it was hard to tell friend from foe. Suddenly he heard the familiar cry: 'Achtung, achtung! Clear the street at the double! Sniper fire!' He darted into a house door-way, and could already hear the bullets striking the suddenly empty streets. Events such as this had become a part of everyday life – as had the anti-Jewish propaganda. The older Jews who had already lived through such things in Russia or Poland feared the outbreak of a deliberate pogrom, and Arlosoroff could not quite ignore his mother's fears. It was important always to be careful, one could never predict how the dullards of the former Reichswehr and the Freikorps might suddenly wish to work off their aggression. Talk of the 'stab in the back' was universal, and leaflets were being distributed blaming the Jews for everything. A few confident Jewish associations protested against this and declared their position, making it clear that they hadn't been the ones who had instigated or prolonged the war. They, in contrast, had stood side by side with their comrades in the trenches, and this rabble-rousing propaganda was merely the expression of a hopeless search for scapegoats. They did not achieve a great deal.[1]

The same rabble-rousing mood had led a few days previously to
the deaths of Rosa Luxemburg and Karl Liebknecht, co-founders
of the German Communist Party.[3] The news of their brutal
murder had shocked Arlosoroff, even if he didn't agree with all
their political views. It was clear to him that the blind hatred
with which they had been persecuted had to do both with their
political aims and with Luxemburg's Jewish origins. This was a visiting card from the 'Guard Cavalry Riflemen's Division', which
had set up its headquarters at the feudal Eden Hotel, and which
had unofficially been called in for assistance by President Ebert
and his Armed Forces Minister Noske.[4]

As Arlosoroff was approaching Eisenacher Strasse, things
became quieter. The closer he got to his mother's apartment, the
more he comforted himself with the thought of Palestine. He
reflected that now of all times he should concentrate his forces not
on German politics, but on Eretz Israel. He was convinced that
there was no secure long-term future for the Jews in Germany,
only in their own country. His family, his mother and sisters,
would come with him, that much had been decided, but whether
Magda would come remained uncertain. She seemed to have too
great a longing for a certain bourgeois quality of life.

Victor was genuinely fond of her, but something about her
remained strange to him. She wore the Star of David[5] that he had
given her, but he was never sure whether the symbol really meant
anything to her. She was probably unable to understand how
important it was for him to commit himself to that ideal, to create
a situation whereby Jews might really belong somewhere rather
than being at best benevolently tolerated guests.

At home his mother was preparing dinner, and Lisa and Magda
were studying for their *Abitur*. Victor helped them a little and
later walked Magda home.

As he was walking back home alone, the sky opened up above
him. All day it had been grey and damp, the air had smelt of
snow, but now it had grown colder and clearer, and he could
smell frost. The glittering stars reminded him of Königsberg,

where he had often seen that clear winter sky, and he felt a little calmer.

Over the next few months, until May 1919, a bloody civil war continued to dominate Germany, one that demanded thousands of victims and left great bitterness in its wake. What Victor had already sensed in Berlin now continued in other regions of the country. In the midst of this chaos the new government also lost its support, even among its original sympathisers. It was simply unacceptable that it should be making common cause with the volunteer troops from the old imperial army, and attempting to re-establish order with a bloody 'Counter-Revolution'. With this alliance it was defending its proclaimed democratic values in an undemocratic way, and had thus quickly lost credibility. Always tottering on the brink of the abyss, the government could never really convince anyone, least of all those who yearned for the strict, glorious days of the Kaiserreich. These people saw their need for the re-establishment of order – of whatever kind – satisfied by the forces of the Freikorps and the former imperial army. These were the people who greeted the troops with gratitude and jubilation, in some areas even with beer, chocolate and black, white and red flags.[6]

Magda did not take much interest in contemporary politics, but the effects of the riots, the hunger and the endless strikes were apparent to everyone, and of course she had no great desire to have constraints imposed on her life. The Spartacists, the Communist groups, too eagerly called into question the right of her bourgeois world to exist, and Magda, along with her mother, tended to side with those who greeted the counter-revolution and perceived it as a liberation, rather than those who criticised the behaviour of the government.

In autumn 1919 Magda sat her *Abitur*,[7] but she had not yet made any decisions about the future. Although she was very ambitious, her ambition did not focus on any particular area. Her friend Lisa was studying music with a view to teaching in Palestine one day. Ritschel had suggested a course of studies to Magda, which he would finance himself, but she could not find any enthusiasm for anything, and her stepfather Friedländer, who was devoted to her, became concerned about her future. Magda's sole wish – perhaps in order to avoid making a real decision – was to go to a finishing school. Auguste had failed to deal with this issue in time, and accordingly Magda was annoyed with her mother[8] and made her dissatisfaction felt. If she went to a finishing school, she would be assured of access to bourgeois society, and, given their domestic circumstances – Friedländer was by now, it seems, working as a waiter at the Mitropa – that was not something they could rely on.

Mother and daughter agreed, however, that Magda would soon marry. As her mother knew from her own experience, she had a chance of making a good match. But for the time being Magda's first concern was to leave home.

Her friendship with Lisa and her relationship with Victor were losing some of their sparkle for her. It could not have escaped her that the Jews had lost some of their social status in Germany for the first few years after the Versailles Treaty. Society was making life difficult for them with unjust accusations, and even Victor's charisma could not conceal his helplessness in the face of these slanders. In addition to that, he had less and less time for her. Not only were his obligations within the Zionist community making increasing demands on him, which further estranged Magda and Victor from one another, but he was also putting more of his energies into his economics studies, always with a view to developing economic and agrarian reforms in Palestine. Magda, on the other hand, was hungry for life, and the other distractions, hikes in the open-air, sleeping in bales of straw, which Victor loved and on which she had often accompanied him with the Zionist youth group in the summer, had come to bore her. So she waited impatiently for something to happen.

When the finishing school in Holzhausen near Goslar surprisingly agreed to take her, she was delighted.[9] Arriving in a new outfit supplied with the help of Ritschel's generous support and equipped with everything she needed, she soon discovered that the institute, which prepared young ladies for their roles as wives and mothers, was a remnant of another age, terribly boring and an infringement of her liberty. But she had to endure this fact for a few months, and used that time to make herself popular with the head of school and her fellow-pupils. Finally, in February, she was suddenly presented with the opportunity to ask officially for a holiday, since her stepfather was celebrating his birthday.[10] One further excuse for her was Victor's twenty-first birthday, which fell in the same week.

'Le Chaim!' Magda raised her glass and drank to Victor's health – to his original name, Vitaly, Victor in German, he had now officially added the Hebrew Chaim, meaning life. Everything in the Arlosoroff household was as it had been: the many friends who thronged around Victor, the lively discussions about Zionism and the related issue of nationalism, the scraps of Russian and Yiddish, the diverse opinions, violently asserted, about how secular a Jewish state would have to be, to which Victor stated his resolute opinion that the state could not do without assimilated Jews. On the table, for the celebration of the day, stood the home-made chicken-liver vol-au-vents, decorated with little onion rings and halved hard-boiled eggs, and dark bread: delicacies of which Victor had sometimes dreamt during the war. While his friends were still admiring the hors-d'oeuvres, Victor's mother came to the table with the big soup-bowl, and as soon as she removed the lid, the scent of hot borscht wafted through the dining-room. Clutching her glass, Magda stood somewhat apart, by the window, and turned her gaze from the lively dining-table to the world outside. The window was covered with condensation. When she rubbed at the pane with her handkerchief she saw the half-melted slush lying on the black road. Inside, everything was as familiar as ever, and yet all of a sudden she no longer felt part of it. This world, with its liveliness and warmth, was not really her own. She was not a Jew. However kind everyone was to her, she still remained an outsider, a blonde 'schicksa', as the young Jewish men called the Christian girls, half with contempt, half with desire. She was only accepted in this circle because she was Victor's girlfriend. Sometimes, particularly with young religious Zionists who wore the kippa, she had noticed the questioning glances, and then moved more demonstratively to Victor's side. Victor had been delighted about her surprise appearance at his birthday, but for a while now he had not paid her any attention. Magda saw that he was deep in conversation with a girl with light blonde hair. When Lisa approached her friend to bring her back into the circle with the others, Magda asked in passing who the girl was, and learned that she was also Jewish, from a very good if impoverished Königsberg family. Here in Berlin she lived entirely alone, studied medicine and earned a little money by giving piano lessons.[11] Magda felt a pang, not so much a feeling of jealousy as more a kind of envy that the other girl really belonged to this community – like everyone else gathered here – and that she did not. With the finely honed senses of the rival she could also tell that something had developed between Victor and the girl, and that she could do nothing to stop it. Slightly annoyed, her vanity injured, she made up her mind to leave early, although Lisa, who was pleased to see her friend again, would have liked to hear more about life in an elegant finishing school

Magda was still in a bad mood the following morning when her mother brought her to the train to Goslar. Since the war trains in the country had been less frequent, because along with its high war reparations Germany had had to supply a certain number of railway trains. Many trains had been destroyed during the war, and the few that remained were constantly filled to capacity. Magda and her mother had pushed their way through the full corridors – in vain. Now Magda was standing outside a reserved compartment while Auguste went off to try and find a seat for her daughter. By the time she came back, Magda sat beaming in the reserved compartment. The two gentlemen for whom it was reserved had invited the pretty young woman to join them.[12]

Chapter 6

Magda forgot the previous evening's dark mood and sank into the soft, plush-covered upholstery. The gentleman who had been the first to speak to her introduced himself with a bow: 'My name is Günther Quandt'.[1] Magda enjoyed the obvious interest that the two men took in her, and reacted with charm and confidence. Noticing the gentlemen's astonishment that she was travelling back to her finishing school, and becoming aware that they thought she was older than she looked, she was flattered. She in turn took Dr Quandt to be in his mid-forties, as his hair sparsely covered the beginnings of a bald patch, and he also seemed very stout. But his well-turned-out appearance, the pleasant smell of after-shave, the good tweed of his suit, the freshly starched collar and the white sleeves with the smart gold cufflinks all made a very attractive impression on Magda, particularly since at this time, so shortly after the war, very few people were able to take such care of themselves and dress so well, and also because Quandt's appearance reminded her of Ritschel.

While the winter landscape of snowy mountains and forests glided by them, this otherwise rather reserved man felt the need to open his heart to the young woman – as sometimes happens in trains when travellers, feeling removed from time and space, reveal things to strangers that they would otherwise never dream of. Günther Quandt was a widower, his wife had died a good year previously during the terrible flu epidemic, leaving him alone with two boys of eleven and thirteen. Magda, with her freshness and youth, enchanted the mature man, and later, in his memoirs, he described his first meeting with her:[2]

> . . . By now I had discovered that I had an unusually beautiful creature before me: pale blue eyes, beautiful, thick blonde hair, a well-formed, regular face, a slim figure. We talked about the theatre in Berlin, travel and the things that interest a young girl like that. Time flew by.
>
> When she left the train in Goslar at about one o'clock in the morning, I helped her, and while fetching her luggage I was able inconspicuously to find out her address in Goslar. Upon my arrival in Kassel my first letter was dispatched to Goslar the same night. I would take the liberty of interrupting the journey in Goslar on my return journey at three o'clock in the afternoon, to visit her headmistress and introduce myself as a friend of her father – I was thirty-eight years old at the time! I said I would be delighted if she could reply to me with a letter or telegram in time to tell me whether my visit was desirable.
>
> The postal connection – I must say, looking back – was surprisingly good. By the morning of my departure I was already holding her reply in my hand, including, along with a delighted acceptance on the part of the head of school, some advice upon my correct behaviour. Arriving in Goslar I found a room in the Achtermann district, bought a bouquet of lovely Maréchal Nil roses – not for the young lady, but for her headmistress– and so armed I made my visit. I was very sweetly welcomed as a friend of the father, whom, of course, I knew not at all. After about half an hour's conversation the question came: 'Now you must

be wanting to see Magda?' 'But of course, my dear lady,' and she already had the telephone in her hand and was saying, 'Magda, please come down. A friend of your father's is here, passing through.' And Magda came, and our greeting was accompanied by mixed emotions. Stiff, like people who barely knew one another, friendly, like people who were happy to see one another again, cordial, like a friend of her father: that was how we faced one another.[3]

Quandt won the trust of the headmistress with his generosity and good manners. On his next visit he invited Magda and the whole school to the most elegant pastry-shop in the town,[4] and over the weeks that followed he was even allowed to take Magda out without a chaperone. In this way he was able to get to know her better and assure her, with his first kiss, of the seriousness of his feelings. He portrayed an economically glittering situation, and on a car journey through the Harz Mountains he asked her to be his wife.[5] Magda, who enjoyed these excursions, still needed some time to reflect. She felt flattered to be courted by such a man, she knew how much the other girls envied her when Quandt's limousine turned up and, at each visit, he brought flowers and chocolates, not just for her, but for all the others as well.[6] This attentiveness was something quite special in the hard times after the war, and conveyed an impression of luxury and wealth. Compared to Quandt's lifestyle, life in the finishing school seemed monotonous and oppressive, but Magda still did not say yes.

A few weeks later, when Magda was to stand in for her mother as godmother to her great-niece in Magdeburg – Auguste had to stay in Berlin to look after Friedländer, who was seriously ill – she took the opportunity not to travel back to Goslar but, much to her mother's astonishment, to arrive in Berlin early the next morning: 'You can do what you like, I'm not going back to Goslar,' she declared resolutely, when her mother expressed her reservations. 'What do you think I've seen of the Harz all the time I've been there? The shoes of the girls in front.'[7] In the face of her mother's objections, Magda refused to stay at the finishing school. She stayed in Berlin, from where, as promised, she telephoned Dr Quandt. The next day the industrialist arranged a meeting with the girl and her mother. He invited them to his villa on the Griebnitzsee in Babelsberg for the coming Sunday. He was amused that Magda had refused to return to Goslar, and he was sympathetic, since this also concurred with his own plans.

Mother and daughter were both impressed by the villa and the big park in Babelsberg: 'The view from the drawing room across the well-tended park-land to the Griebnitzsee presented such a fairy-tale scene that without thinking I exclaimed, "My dears, how lovely!" Magda was standing behind me at the big window that reached from the floor to the ceiling, and said furiously, "Mama, be under no illusions, if I don't love him I won't marry him!" [8]

Magda was certainly not in love with Quandt in any romantic sense, yet after a brief period of reflection she decided to marry him, since he emanated a dependability and certainty that she had never experienced in her own life. Despite good marks at school and a knowledge of foreign languages Magda could not imagine any professional prospects for herself. Her social position was not unambiguous. She was entirely aware of her mother's simple origins, and reacted to them in her own way by feeling dependent on her mother while at the same time refusing to take her advice or follow her recommendations. Friedländer's health had by now deteriorated even further, as had the relationship between Friedländer and Auguste. So the situation at home gave Magda no security. Ritschel, her biological father, offered her only external, financial support. Magda found his haute-bourgeois way of life very attractive, but in the circumstances she could hardly feel accepted by the family in Bad Godesberg, since she did not even bear Ritschel's name. Her acquaintance with Quandt, on the other hand, outweighed all these insecurities, and it was an enticing notion to marry into such a family, into a social stratum that would otherwise have remained out of her reach, but of which she dreamed nonetheless. If Arlosoroff's attraction to her lay in the passion with which he put forward his ideas, with which he inhabited them, in Quandt's case it was the tangible power of the successful industrialist. Magda found the notion of sharing in this power as Frau Quandt seductive, and was undaunted by their twenty-year age-gap. She was probably unaware that in order to meet him on his own level she would have to skip certain stages in her emotional development. She probably believed that the generous lifestyle that he had promised might compensate for any difficulties.

On 31 July of the same year, on Quandt's thirty-ninth birthday, they celebrated their engagement. Her mother's later recollection reveals how childlike and immature Magda's response to her relationship with Günther Quandt was at this point, how concerned she was with outward appearances and how little she valued Günther Quandt as a lifelong partner with an independent personality. Instead, she acted out her role as one with feminine power and youth:

The day before the engagement Dr Quandt had gone rowing with Magda. I should mention that even then my first son-in-law had a bald patch, which he tried to cover up as best he could. He had allowed the hair on his crown, which surrounded his baldness in a horseshoe-shape, to grow long, and then combed it from left to right over the exposed area. We called these long hairs 'anchovies'. As luck would have it, a gust of wind seized hold of these 'anchovies', ruffled them and thus revealed his dome. Magda, who was sitting opposite her betrothed and watching Dr Quandt pumping industriously away with the oars to keep the boat in motion, used this favourable moment to express her opinion about the anchovies: 'I'm not going to marry you until you cut off your anchovies!' Dr Quandt rowed silently back to the boat-house. The next morning, the day of their betrothal, he came to

breakfast without his beloved anchovies. He had cut them
off himself with a pair of nail scissors before his morning
shave.[9]

But Quandt, for his part, also set certain conditions. Coming as
he did from an old Protestant family, he requested that his future
wife should also convert to Protestantism.[10] In the six months
between the engagement and the date set for the wedding, Magda
received confirmation instruction from old vicar Kritzinger, who
had taught at the Kollmorgen Lyzeum. It was before him that she
was baptised into evangelical rites in the Kaiser Wilhelm
Memorial Church in Berlin.[11]

In addition, she had to lose her given name of Friedländer.[12] In
the little village from which Quandt came, Pritzwalk in the
Prignitz region of North-Eastern Germany, where the rest of his
family still lived, it seemed impossible to introduce his fiancée as
a Fräulein Friedländer. Quandt's parents were still completely
stuck in the world of the previous century, and had taken note of
the bride's age with some consternation. There was something
not quite respectable about such a young woman, not to mention
one from the city of Berlin.

One generally remained within one's own social circles, and did
not marry just any young girl about whose family history one knew
nothing. A Magda Friedländer, not herself of Jewish origin, but
with a typically Jewish surname, would give rise to endless speculations which would, in this case, be better avoided. The first Frau
Quandt, who came from the same part of the world, had only
died about a year ago, and was still vivid in everyone's memory. To
make Magda reasonably acceptable in the eyes of the provincial
relations, Ritschel had to become involved. He too had been originally opposed to the marriage because of the great age difference,
but he had been won over by Quandt's excellent circumstances
and his solid and dependable demeanour. So, out of social necessity, after all these years he officially acknowledged Magda as his
daughter, gave her his name, and in her capacity as Günther

Quandt's fiancée, Fräulein Magda Friedländer briefly became Fräulein Magda Ritschel.[13]

Victor received the news of her engagement with equanimity. Sometimes Magda heard of him from mutual friends, and sometimes she saw him in the street in the distance. He would be walking side by side with Gerda, the blonde girl from Königsberg. Victor had his arm around her shoulder and carried her bag. They laughed together, looking very happy and very much in love.

Content as she was with her new and promising situation, Magda could not close her eyes to the fact that Günther Quandt – in love though he was – would not be an easy-going partner. He was authoritarian and accustomed to enforcing his decisions with a certain degree of harshness where necessary. As an eighteen-year-old he had had to reorganise his father's textile factories.[14] His fortune had grown over the next few years, and his influence and reputation had increased along with it. He worked extraordinarily hard, and expected the same strong-minded commitment from those around him.

On more than one occasion there was a difference of opinion between the girl and her future husband, since Magda could not get used to the idea of behaving according to his conventional ideas. One day before the wedding their different views collided so violently that Quandt wanted to dissolve the engagement.

Two days before the wedding, Magda arrived in Bad Godesberg, where Ritschel, who lived there with his family, generously wanted to organise the wedding. Magda and her mother were staying with his parents, Magda's grandparents, and a few friends and relations were staying at the Godesberger Hof. The afternoon before the wedding, when Magda visited her grandmother – without telling Quandt anything about it, lest he worry – he was so outraged to discover that his fiancée was visiting people without her husband-to-be, that he wanted to call off the wedding.[15]

Ritschel managed to calm him down, because it would have been a social scandal in the little town of Bad Godesberg to break off the relationship a day before the marriage. The next day, 4

January 1921, everything had been forgotten, and the wedding took place as planned. Magda wore a wedding dress of Brussels lace, and the elegant dinner held in the Godesberger Hof Hotel united the ill-matched couple with family and friends. The guests from the family circle included Quandt's brother Werner with his wife Ello,[16] who was just as young as Magda and felt just as much of an outsider in the rigidly Protestant family clan of the Quandts, along with their two sons, Hellmuth and Herbert, and business associates of Quandt and Ritschel. We do not know why Quandt's parents did not attend the festivities. There is no mystery, however, about why Friedländer was not invited.

A stage of Magda's life came to an end with this wedding. What she thought of the conditions of her marriage, for example, the fact that she had to drop the name Friedländer before she could be married, is not known. After living with her Jewish stepfather and her friendship with Victor and Lisa, Quandt's demand, revealing his anti-Semitism, must have come as a shock – particularly since Friedländer had really been a devoted father to her. It would have been the loveliest present to him for his stepdaughter to bear his name.[17] But the name-change does not seem to have been an emotional matter for either Magda or for her mother, and Auguste divorced her husband the same year. Friedländer disappeared from both their lives, and from that moment onwards he might as well never have existed.[18]

In her memoirs Auguste mentions that Magda, who was brought up a Catholic, did not find the conversion to Protestantism difficult. When asked why this might be, she replied only, 'Religion doesn't matter to me, I have my God in my heart.'[19]

Chapter 7

Everything was perfectly still. Magda looked out of the window. Deep snow covered the lawn that stretched far down to the lake, engulfing any sound there might have been. On the surface of the water the water-lilies blossomed in summer, white and pink, but now the lake was covered with a thin layer of ice punctuated with occasional patches of black water. Life seemed muffled in the house, too, as the staff went silently about their business. Quandt had bought the villa after his wife's death but before his meeting with Magda, and what had seemed a little paradise to Magda on her first visit in the summer now seemed to have vanished, leaving her with a terrible feeling of loneliness. The villa was not excessively large or luxurious – that would not have been in line with Quandt's intentions – and yet Magda lost herself in it. She tried to familiarise herself with Quandt's former life, the life that had gone on here before her arrival, and whose traces lingered on the furniture that he had brought from his family home. Everything was still alien to her, as indeed was Quandt himself.

After the wedding Magda and Quandt spent some days travelling together, before Quandt was called back to Berlin on business.[1] Magda went with him, planning to continue the honeymoon in Italy once his work was completed. But during this journey their differences came to the fore. Magda was disappointed: by love, by marriage, for Quandt was not the tender and experienced lover which, despite his apparent coolness, she had longed for him to be.

Magda had entered into marriage with different ideas of a shared life, shaped by her upbringing and her experiences in her own family and among the Arlosoroffs; while we can only assume that she had an intimate relationship with Victor, she had previously been surrounded by people who had responded to her emotions with warmth and cordiality. Victor did everything with great intensity and passion, whether it was a matter of his own self-imposed social and political tasks or his engagement with literature and music. Art was as important to him as politics or his daily bread. Quandt, on the other hand, was a pragmatist, sober and hidebound in his daily habits, a man who devoted all his energies to social matters. Although he was in love with his young wife, he did not seem able to express these feelings. After the honeymoon Magda hoped at least to run a socially great house in Berlin, but here too the reality was to be different. First of all she had to learn to impose her will on the staff. The housekeeper, who had been in Quandt's service for a long time, thought she would be able to run rings around the inexperienced young woman. But Magda complained to Quandt, and the housekeeper was fired.[2] After this she got on well with the other servants, the cook, the maid, the gardener and the chauffeur, for Magda was friendly, and where possible she didn't involve herself in the running of the household. From Quandt she learned to consider the running of the household in much the same way as the running of a business. There was a very precise budget set aside for the purpose, and Magda kept a book, accurate to the last ten pfennigs. At the end of the first month, like a child hoping for its father's praise, she presented the accounts to her husband. He gladly set aside his stock market reports, silently checked page after page, wrote something in red ink with his silver pen and, still silently, handed it back. When Magda, who had been hoping against hope for a positive reaction, read the remark: 'Read and authorised, Günther Quandt', she forgot her posture of self-control, ripped up the book, threw it at his feet, and yelled at him: what did he mean by treating her like his firm's lowliest accountant? Then, furious and tearful, she ran upstairs.[3]

From the first, Magda developed a warm relationship with her stepsons, Hellmuth and Herbert. She had a great deal of sympathy for the two adolescents. The everyday life of the boys, with its major and minor concerns and its scholarly duties was so familiar to her that she was able to share in it without further ado. Particularly with Hellmuth, the older boy, she formed something like friendship.[4] He had become very lonely after the sudden death of his mother, and matured early. His way of seeing the world, his artistic interests, his quick responsiveness and youthful spontaneity and vitality were very attractive to other people, including Magda. As well as his personal aura, he had the sensitivity and vulnerability of his age. Magda felt naturally closer to him than she did to the businessman Günther Quandt, when he came home after a long day in the office needing peace and quiet. Herbert, the younger of the two sons, was very shy and introverted. He was extremely short-sighted, and because of this he had still not attended a public school.[5]

There had been major changes in the Arlosoroff household. Victor's friendship with Gerda, the young medical student, had not been without its consequences, and she was expecting a child. They both refused to terminate the pregnancy, and since Gerda was entirely self-reliant Victor's mother welcomed the young woman into her household. As always, she asked no questions, but simply offered her help.[6] Victor did not give the matter too much thought. As a revolutionary of sorts, and taking free love for granted, ideas of marriage were still remote from him for the time being. Gerda's parents, who still lived in Königsberg, and, in the end, Victor's mother still wanted to see the relationship legalised, so one day they went together to the register office in Berlin, although they personally could not show 'the correct understanding of the social meaning of the founding of a family'.[7] After the birth of Shulamit, at the end of the high festivals, everything at first remained exactly as it had been. Victor thought it quite natural that she should go on living in his mother's house, since this was only a temporary arrangement before their emigration to Palestine. He went on studying until late in the night, or talking to Palestinian workers' leaders who had come to Berlin.[8] By this time he had already joined the socialist wing of the workers' party Hapoel Hazair, and spent much of his time at meetings examining the issues of Zionism and Marxism.

After the birth of her child, Gerda initially continued her studies and was about to begin her clinical training when Victor and the Palestinian workers' leaders, who often came to visit, convinced her that Palestine would be better served by practical people than by academics. As she was in any case preoccupied with exam worries, she was relieved to abandon medicine and, like Victor, switched to economics, pleased to be useful to the movement in this way.[9]

In the course of the winter Victor had finally moved from theory to practice. He was preparing for his first journey to Palestine, moderately satisfied that his little family was adequately catered for.

After a few months of marriage, Magda also knew that she was expecting a child. After a trouble-free pregnancy, on 1 November 1921 her son Harald was born, and Quandt happily rushed to the hospital with a bunch of carnations. But he had to consult his mother-in-law about another present for his young wife, since he couldn't think of anything himself. Astonished by this lack of imagination, Auguste advised a toiletry set, and when Magda came home from the hospital she found a silver comb, mirror and brush waiting for her in her bedroom.[10]

Quandt was very proud of his third son, but did not spend any more time at home than he had before. The social possibilities of the post-war period were numerous, and represented a great challenge to his ambition, particularly in a city like Berlin, which had undergone a fundamental change. In the past the city had been shaped above all by the Prussian monarchy, the nobility, militarism and the mentality of the landowning Junkers, a society in which officers were the 'masters' and ordinary soldiers the 'lads'. But with the war and its consequences the whole of Germany was shaken to its foundations and found it difficult to consolidate itself under the new government. Social structures had been hollowed out from within, and everything seemed built on a shaky foundation. In the capital, Berlin, the uncertainties and adversities of the whole country – the loss of moral values, poverty and misery, speculation, the pursuit of quick money – seemed to be rising to a shrill crescendo. The carpet-baggers from the provinces made their way to Berlin along with political discontents who wanted a new world order, the conmen and market criers, and the city's magical powers of attraction did not seem to be waning. Each day a stream of new arrivals poured into the anonymity of the lively streets, where by now automobiles had replaced horse-drawn cabs. Many new arrivals managed to do small deals, they distributed themselves among the back courtyards and lived from hand to mouth, others used the heaving city as a temporary staging post. Everything was in flux, everything was pushing towards change, nothing was constant. But this openness, this fragility provided plenty of opportunity for anyone determined enough to exploit the situation.

As a boy during the Kaiser's time, Günther Quandt had come from the provinces of Brandenburg, where his father, Emil Quandt, owned a textile factory in Pritzwalk, to Berlin, where he attended secondary school. It was there that he sat his *Abitur*, and after a few years of professional training he was earning a substantial income as co-proprietor of another textile factory.[11] When war broke out he stayed on the home front, and at the age of thirty-four became director of Reichswoll AG. His textile factory provided the material for the army uniforms, an inexhaustible source of commissions, and the basis of his millions. From 1915 until 1919 he was also appointed consultant in the Reich Ministry of Economics, a position which gave him useful insights into the economic structures of the state.[12] After the end of the war, when the beginnings of inflation destroyed so many small and medium-sized companies, Quandt was able to profit from his knowledge and contacts – like a skilled chess-player who is always one move ahead of his opponent – and from the bankruptcies and mergers of other companies. Even during the war his fortune had grown to ten million, and by the end of the twenties it was estimated at seventy to one hundred million.[13]

Inflation began only very gradually, and seemed to be controllable, but suddenly money was losing more and more of its value. The workers' families, war widows with their children and old people lived on the edge of the poverty line or below it, and soon the middle class, the comfortably-off bourgeoisie, found itself slipping into crisis. In this way the gulf between rich and poor became ever greater. Quandt did not bring these political events home, of course, they were not something with which he wished to burden his young wife, and in any case Quandt was too tense for such discussions after a long day at work; his proverbial fatigue was attested to in anecdotes about his falling asleep, time and again, at some social occasion or other, or in the dark warmth of the theatre, probably dreaming about numbers. Magda, who was not interested in the darker side of the city, would have preferred to go out and participate in the brilliance of its cultural and social life, which continued to develop with all its intensity despite economic problems, but she had to content herself with a small number of business-related invitations, and keep an eye on her husband lest he nod off in the middle of important discussions.[14]

Her daily routine consisted entirely in bringing up her three children and supervising the staff. Her occasional distractions included visits from her mother, who would bring some gossip with her. This remote life in the villa with the fairy-tale park, in the middle of a small circle of people, was in many respects like life in the convent, where Magda had been equally cut off from the world by a pane of glass.

The few friends that Günther Quandt saw as guests in his own home, apart from his social connections, included a family by the name of Schulze. Magda, too, had made friends with the rather older wife of the family, and liked to talk to her about children, since Frau Schulze was herself such a contented mother. The shock was all the greater when she suddenly died after a brief and serious illness. Her husband, still devastated by the sudden death of his wife, was seriously injured shortly after this, when he inattentively walked in front of a moving train. He never regained consciousness, and died in hospital. All of a sudden the three half-grown children were orphans, and Quandt saw to it that they were educated in various boarding schools. But Magda had other ideas. She wanted to look after the three children herself, and jokingly told Quandt that this meant that her desire for twelve children would be at least partially satisfied. The idea that these three, having grown up in a warm and loving family, should have to endure the impersonal coldness of a boarding school on top of the loss of their parents struck Magda as so terrible that, when Quandt did not immediately accede to her joking request, she tearfully begged him, something that does not seem to accord with her otherwise proud and controlled manner. After lengthy consideration Quandt agreed, and from now on the house was full of children.[15]

This emotional request to take in the orphaned children is the first hint we have of an intense emotional reaction on Magda's part. We cannot know precisely whether it was her own memories, her feelings of having been abandoned as a little girl separated from her mother for five years. Or did she hope to find in the half-grown children the solidarity and friendship that she had probably never had with her husband? Even later on she stayed in contact with her foster-children, and visited her foster-son Heino in Leipzig, where he was training as a book-dealer. From him she ordered a ten-volume work on Buddhism.[16]

Chapter 8

Arlosoroff had been en route for Palestine for several weeks now. From Berlin he had taken the train via Vienna to Trieste, where he had boarded a ship to Haifa. For the whole group of Zionist emigrants travelling with him, and who were seeing the sea for the first time – many had never left the confinement of the East European *shtetls* and the narrow alleys of the cities – there was something overwhelming about the sight of the Mediterranean. The reddish glow of the winter sun, turning a darker violet along the coast as the hours of evening drew on, made them think of the Promised Land. But very soon after embarkation the Mediterranean showed its unpredictable side, and when they had left the coast behind a typical winter storm broke out, tossing the unstable ship around in the waves like a ball.

Arlosoroff was standing with the captain on the bridge when he thought he could finally make out the restful pink patch of the coming twilight between the outstretched wind-clouds, promising an improvement in the weather. His frightened protégés in the belly of the ship wished the voyage would come to an end. Up on the top deck he could hear the melancholy Russian and Jewish songs of the orthodox Hassidim, because along with the active, free-spirited pioneers were those who sought refuge in Palestine with their families, a part of the Aliyah.[1] They were trying to banish their fear of the unknown with the familiar sounds of the past.

Victor had prepared well for his journey, and when he finally reached dry land at Haifa, he was met by other Zionists who were to bring him to Tel Aviv, where his friend Lufban, a Palestinian workers' leader, would receive him. Years later he recalled their meeting:

> It was a winter day in Tel Aviv. It had just stopped raining. A train stopped at the sand-dune – the only sign that this was a 'railway station', an inhabited place, was a little wooden shack open on all sides, and out jumped a young bespectacled man who moved rapidly. He was pale and haggard, wearing sports trousers of greyish-green corduroy, and a grey jacket of some military material like the ones worn after the war by certain civilians who didn't think clothes were especially important. On his back was a fully-stuffed rucksack, and in his hand he carried a large, worn, shapeless case, heavy and fully packed. Through his glasses gleamed two piercing and astonished eyes.
>
> Tel Aviv did not immediately reveal itself to the newcomer's eyes. In those days it was still hidden behind sand-dunes and the remains of foul-smelling vineyards. I felt the need to explain this curious fact to the guest that I was supposed to be welcoming, lest he suspect that we had cheated him – and to reassure him that Tel Aviv, however small, really did exist behind this piece of barren land. He replied with a quiet smile, the smile that played around the left-hand corner of his mouth and never disappeared from his face – a sign of his intelligence and reason. With an energetic gesture he turned to go – [2]

By this point Arlosoroff had already made a name for himself by publishing several major articles and essays on the subject of Zionism. But here he did not appear 'in the cold, serious figure of

the academic, but with the smiling face and warm soul of the
poet, living in the age of romanticism, more inclined towards
bohemianism than towards an orderly lifestyle. His heart was open
to friendships beyond the party-political, full of magnanimity and
wisdom, youthful cheerfulness and radiant humour. Light and
warmth poured from him, even if this was only apparent to his
closest friends.'[3]

For Arlosoroff the next few months were a period of learning.
The intellectual had initially been treated with a certain suspicion, and he himself did not immediately strive to adopt public
postures, but tried to absorb as much as he possibly could. In the
eyes of the other speakers and the workers he was seen as the type
of the 'matmid', the eternal scholar.

Once in Palestine, Arlosoroff encountered the daily problems
arising out of coexistence with Arabs. Although the proportion of
Jews in the population had barely risen above ten per cent until
the First World War, the immigrations were already spreading
unrest among the Arab population. Admiration and envy mingled
at the sight of these light-skinned Jews who were starting to buy
up land and till the desert soil.

Shortly after Arlosoroff's arrival in January, in April 1920 the San
Remo Conference took place. It was here that the Allies reached an
agreement about the division of the Arab provinces of Turkey, the
former Ottoman Empire: France was to have the mandate for Syria,
including the Lebanon, and Great Britain would be responsible for
Mesopotamia (Iraq). Palestine was declared the mandate of the
League of Nations, which was to transfer it to Great Britain.

This transfer was preceded in 1917 by the Balfour Declaration,
called after the British Foreign Minister Arthur Balfour, in which
it was declared that the British government would support a
national homeland for the Jewish people in Palestine, while the
rights of existing non-Jewish communities would remain unaf-
fected. In December 1919, representatives of the Zionist
organisation negotiated an outline for a Palestinian mandate
which to a large extent corresponded to Zionist ideas.

The outbreaks of violence which Arlosoroff could now immediately feel were based in part on the still ambivalent attitude of the British Mandate authorities both towards the Jews and towards the vague concept of the national homeland for the Jewish people, which was so unclear that it unsettled the Arabs, particularly since after the end of the First World War in Europe living conditions there were becoming ever more desperate.

It was the period between the pogrom in Jerusalem in 1920 and the pogrom in Jaffa in 1921. Floods of immigrants were pouring into the land. The third Aliyah was emerging from all parts of the Jewish world in Eastern Europe, from Poland, Lithuania, the smoking ruins of the Ukrainian shtetls and from Russia. And in the country – hastily erected white tents in the wide desert, Jewish boys and girls were building roads, breaking stones, doing work that neither they nor their parents had ever done before, work which in Jewish eyes was contemptible, the occupation of inferior and miserable types.'[4]

Relations with the Arab population became increasingly tense, and serious disturbances broke out in May.

For the first time the theory and practice of Zionism blew apart before Arlosoroff's eyes, and he had to engage very concretely with the fact that Zionism had a potential for violence among all involved, as this letter to his mother in Berlin reveals:

Tel Aviv, 11 May 1921

Dear mother,

I hope you received the telegram I sent you during the first few days of the disturbances in Jaffa to put your mind at rest. Jewish Palestine is going through difficult times the like of which the Yishuv, which knows desperate times, has not, in my opinion, seen before. As far as I am concerned, fate spared me this time, too, without giving me a second glance. It was only by chance that on the first of May, the day of the worst of the riots, I was not in Jaffa. During the first holy days I was sitting in Tel Aviv taking part in a writers' meeting that was taking place at the time. That was why I could not travel to Jerusalem.

When I returned the next day, unaware that anything had happened, twenty people were already lying dead in the school building. As I was among the few bearing firearms, after an hour I was sent to a militia group based in the Neveh–Shalom post. I stood guard there the whole time, and was therefore unable to write to you in greater detail.

Apart from that the situation has not yet been resolved, and nerves are so tense that it is almost impossible for me to write to you clearly. . .

After all this, you can imagine the oppressive atmosphere in which we are all living.[5]

After nine rich months in Palestine, Arlosoroff wanted to return briefly to Berlin to finish his doctorate with Werner Sombart. He also felt responsible for Gerda, his wife, and their little daughter Shulamit, as well as for his mother and sisters. His purpose in returning was not solely to resolve fresh financial problems, but also to deal with the estrangement that had arisen between himself and Gerda.

His return was also rendered difficult by the general economic situation in the capital, which had by now become so bad that the German inability to keep up with payments had begun to look dangerous, and no change in Allied reparations policy was on the horizon. The population was still looking for Jewish scapegoats in the government, as the anti-Semitic bacillus spread, going beyond the boundaries of public institutions such as the university.

Each day Victor passed by the Werner Siemens Realgymnasium to ensure that the Zionist group did not fall apart. They could only feel quite free in their own faith community, Sternau had told him, and in Victor's eyes it was important that the group should learn intensive Hebrew, to have a solid foundation if they decided to emigrate to Palestine at any point in the future.

On 24 June 1922, a domestic political bombshell exploded in the midst of the general dissatisfaction, insoluble financial problems, the anti-Semitic and revanchiste sloganeering: on 24 June 1922 the Reich Foreign Minister Rathenau was murdered in broad daylight on his way to the Foreign Office.[6] Rathenau had repeatedly been victim to hate-filled attacks by the conservatives, because, as the son and successor of the founder of the largest electrical company in Germany, AEG, he radiated an upper middle-class, liberal intellectual aura – long before the war he had published essays of cultural criticism under a pseudonym. In addition to this, Rathenau made no secret of his Jewishness, and although throughout his lifetime he felt like an alien in Germany, both as a Jew and as an intellectual, he loved his country. He paid for that love with his life.[7] The murder of Rathenau was not an individual incident, but the climax of a series of attacks and assassinations that had begun with the murder of Rosa Luxemburg and Karl Liebknecht. The murders of Kurt Eisner and Matthias Erzberger had followed, and the series had continued through to the assassination of Rathenau. Many people were possessed with hatred of the leaders of the Weimar Republic, and popular drinking songs echoed those horrendous prejudices ('Shoot down Walther Rathenau/ the God-accursed Jewish sow.') As Hagen Schulze puts it, quoting these lines: 'Given this much sympathy and public support, the act itself can hardly have been a problem for the murderers.'[8]

At the other end of the political spectrum the news of

Rathenau's death unleashed a violent wave of sympathy, peaking in an ardent speech by Chancellor Wirth to the Reichstag, which closed with the words: 'There stands the foe [turning to the right], dripping its poison into the wounds of a nation. – There stands the foe – and there can be no doubt: the foe stands on the right.'[9]

Chapter 9

The foe was indeed on the right, and not only in Berlin. At this time Munich was the capital of nationalist movements and conspiracies. It was here that countless German nationalist splinter groups were setting up their headquarters, the Freikorps was holding its meetings, leagues of young soldiers and officers were paraded and exercised with secret funding from the Reichswehr, organisations formed with a view to abolishing the Republic.[1]

But Munich was also a popular university city, a city of fine art with baroque architectural monuments, little cafés and pubs, particularly in Schwabing, where artists and writers met.

But the young Joseph Goebbels, who had already spent a term studying in Munich, and who returned there in 1922, came not for the city's stimulating cultural atmosphere, but to be among the conspirators who were crude and uncivilised – unlike Goebbels himself – free of inhibitions and determined to give full vent to their hatred of the Republic. They were close friends of Rathenau's assassins, and spoke of the crime as of a heroic patriotic deed.

Shortly after his arrival in the city, Joseph Goebbels attended a meeting called by one of the many nationalist parties. Huge posters around the Bavarian capital had attracted his attention. He was astonished that Munich's biggest meeting-hall, Zirkus Krone, was filled to capacity: eight thousand people – a large number for a city with not much more than half a million inhabitants.[2]

Goebbels had heard of the speaker whose name was announced, Adolf Hitler, and his rhetorical gifts, and now he was curious to listen to his speech-making. After he entered the circus building, he first had to allow his eyes to become accustomed to the semi-darkness. Even then, Hitler liked to give his performances a mystical aura, so the lighting was arranged in such a way that his face was half in shadow and could not fully be seen. After a few minutes of his oratory, Goebbels was swept away:

> I barely notice that there's someone up there, and that he's starting to speak. Halting and shy at first, as though looking for the words for things that are too large to fit into a small form. Then, all of a sudden, the flow of oratory is unleashed. I am caught up in it, I listen carefully . . . People begin to glow . . . Rays of hope gleam on their grey, ragged faces. Then one man gets to his feet and raises his clenched fist. The man next to him is finding his grey collar too tight. Sweat stands out on his brow. He wipes it away with the sleeve of his coat. In the second seat to my left sits an old officer, weeping like a child. I feel hot and cold. I don't know what's happening with me. All of a sudden it is as though I could hear cannon roaring. . .
> 'I no longer know what I'm doing. I feel almost demented. I cry 'Hurrah!', and no one is surprised. The man up there looks at me for a moment. Those blue starry eyes strike me like rays of fire. It is an order. From that moment onwards I am reborn . . . I know where my path will take me . . .'[3]

At the end of the meeting Goebbels stepped up to the table by the exit, bearing a sign with the inscription: 'Applications for membership of the National Socialist German Workers' Party are accepted here.' He filled in a form, paid a few marks and received membership number 8762.[4]

Who was this Joseph Goebbels, who up until that point had not found his true path, and despite his intelligence and his recent doctorate, had just been waiting to follow a fanatical orator and obscure politician?

Paul Joseph Goebbels was born on 29 October 1897 in the industrial city of Rheydt on the left bank of the Rhine. Joseph's father, Friedrich Goebbels, worked in the candle factory W.H. Lennartz, working his way up from runner to company secretary.

His father was described by the family as a hard-working, serious man, although he did have a sense of humour. His children benefited from his industry and thrift, and he hoped his sons would be able to rise from the petty-bourgeoisie to solid middle class society.

Joseph's mother, Maria Katharina, was the daughter of a blacksmith, a woman from a working-class family. Her children loved her, Joseph most of all. She was a plain-minded, modest woman. Joseph had two older brothers and a sister twelve years younger, Maria.

Despite their simple, constricted circumstances, life in the Goebbels family was harmonious. The parents loved their children and did everything they could to ensure that they were better off than their parents. Joseph was particularly close to his mother, and they supported one another even when, after the end of this higher education, he changed in a way that worried and alarmed her.[5]

Joseph was an ugly child, weedy and pallid, with an over-large head on narrow shoulders. When he was seven, he fell prey to an illness that was to influence the whole of his later life. He developed an inflammation of the bone-marrow in his left thigh, and had to have an operation. The consequence of this was that his left leg was some eight centimetres shorter than his right, and remained thin and weak. The doctors told his parents that their child would have a limp for the rest of his life, and that he would have to wear splints and orthopaedic shoes.[6]

It was later said that Goebbels was born with a clubfoot. This theory assumed an almost official status, and, when it was not too dangerous to mock him, his limp was compared with the hoof of Mephistopheles, which tells us something about the aura that surrounded him.

Joseph was a lonely child. He kept himself aloof from his brothers, and was unable to keep up with the games of the neighbours' children and his schoolmates, being slower and weaker than they were. This exclusion made him envious of the others, of the natural way they were able to run, scrap and play sports, and the roots of his later cynicism and the misanthropy that he felt for those around him should probably be sought here. But if he was physically disadvantaged, he was intellectually quicker than the rest, and a verbal match for any of them. He loved mocking others with spiteful remarks, which made him unpopular and won him the reputation of being argumentative and arrogant. He fled into books and read everything that came his way. In his parents' house, though, all he found was Meyer's two-volume *Lexikon*, Mommsen's *Roman History* and a few volumes of poetry. His mother watched his development with concern, taking him to church and praying for him in the hope that he would find his way to faith. She was firmly convinced that God had given him a great intellectual gift to compensate for his physical deformity. She hoped he would study theology, and Joseph himself was open to this idea, no doubt influenced by the Rhineland's sumptuous form of Catholicism. He was already attending Gymnasium when his mother managed, with the help of some acquaintances, to arrange an interview with an old priest about the encouragement of her talented son. Goebbels tried to make a good impression, but the experienced cleric quickly saw through him: "'My young friend,' he said, 'you don't believe in God.'"[7]

When war broke out on 1 August 1914, and the sixth-formers at Joseph's Gymnasium began, in the generally belligerent mood of the time, to volunteer to fight at the front, he wanted to do the same. When he failed his medical, his reaction was an outbreak of despair. To imagine that he might have passed was surely the triumph of hope over experience.[8]

At Easter 1917 he sat his *Abitur*, winning very good marks. After this he spent five years studying at eight different universities. This constant change of location suggests that the student of philosophy, history and literature might have been trying to escape from himself and his own insecurity and dissatisfaction. 'What am I actually studying?' asks his novelistic protagonist, Michael, who shares biographical traits with his author. 'Everything and nothing. I am too lethargic, and I think I'm too stupid for academic work. I want to be a man! To have proper outlines! A personality!'[9]

During these first few years as a student his first love affair ended in a fiasco. Anka, a tall and pretty fellow-student, came from a good family whose members were not enthusiastic about her connection with the overwrought, impoverished student. The relationship lasted four months, and then Anka chose someone else, leaving Goebbels to surprise them in each others' arms.[10]

For Goebbels this break-up became a wound which refused to heal, and which only reinforced his complexes, his feelings of hatred and revenge towards the whole world. This unhappy affair led to a lifelong suspicion of women, and behind his cynicism there may have lurked a doubt about whether he would ever be loved for his own sake. Time and again he would hurl himself into new relationships, as though compelled, to prove to himself that, small, frail and handicapped though he was, he still had something that would set women's hearts fluttering. And his many amours do suggest that he could be very attractive to women.

After his disappointment with Anka, philosophical and political conversations with one of his friends became increasingly important. This friend, Richard Flisges, was one of those disappointed soldiers who occupied the auditoriums after the loss of the war, who felt their heroism had been betrayed and looked upon 'cowardly bourgeois' life with a sneer of contempt. Most of them were on the far right, and united in their rejection of the Weimar Republic, which they associated with a rotten compromise. A small minority stood on the left and looked towards Russia. Richard Flisges was one of the latter. He had pacifist, anarchist and, above all, Marxist leanings. He introduced his friend to the works of Marx and Engels, Lenin and Dostoyevsky, unleashing further religious doubts in Goebbels, as well as calling forth the longing for a strong, new leader figure who promised salvation.

But Flisges' influence on Goebbels did not last long. Although Flisges seemed outwardly to have everything that Goebbels could have wanted, like Goebbels he risked being drawn into the nihilistic maelstrom of the time. He was bitter and demoralised; he despised everything to do with Germany, and his Communism seemed to Goebbels to be the expression of his terrible hatred for all things German.[11]

In the autumn of 1920 Goebbels went to Heidelberg to attend lectures by one of the most prominent minds of his time, Friedrich Gundolf. Gundolf, whose Jewish name was Gundelfinger, had written books about Shakespeare and Goethe, and was the most important and brilliant personality in the 'George-Kreis', the elite circle of young literati and aesthetes around the poet Stefan George. Goebbels wanted to become a member of the circle, but although Gundolf acknowledged Goebbels' intelligence, something about the young man repelled him. Goebbels was turned away, which he took as a terrible insult. Nonetheless he continued to attend Gundolf's seminars, and in 1921, after studying with a colleague of Gundolf's, he was awarded his doctorate for a dissertation on the Romantics.[12]

But the fresh-faced doctor of philosophy, who from now on never signed a document without mentioning his qualification, and who spent a considerable amount of time working out how to incorporate the word 'doctor' most elegantly into his signature, remained unemployed for the time being. He tried his hand at journalism, writing articles and reviews, which he sent to Theodor

Wolff, the editor-in-chief of the *Berliner Tageblatt*. His pieces were sent back. He applied for a post as an editor. Theodor Wolff, whom he greatly admired, once more turned him down. He kept on writing applications: for a post as an editor in publishing, as a theatrical script-editor – and was rejected once again. There was nothing more to it but to return to his father's house in Rheydt. There his brothers looked upon the 'Herr Doktor' with displeasure. He became a burden on the others, and suffered from depression, because he knew very well, even if his parents didn't say so, how disappointed they were that their most talented son, for whom they had made every possible sacrifice, had clearly not managed to rise into bourgeois society. He was also a source of torment to himself. 'I live in a constant state of nervous disorder,' he laments in his diary. 'This miserable skiving. I rack my brain about how I can bring this undignified condition to an end. Nothing – nothing is going to work. One must first discard everything that one might call one's own opinions, courage, personality and character, in order to become a number in this world of protection and career. I'm still not a number. Just a big zero.'[13] Anti-capitalist and anti-Semitic prejudices, latent in the Catholic petty-bourgeoisie, arose out of envy for the 'world of patronage'. It was in the sphere of 'international Jewish finance' that he discovered the appropriate scapegoat for the economic misery of the time, as well as for his own personal failure.

But he went on undauntedly writing, he spent night after night writing poems, plays and articles. Finally he wrote the novel *Michael*, in which he merged his own character with that of Flisges in diary form. In this autobiographical novel he allowed Michael to shake his fist at God, who is to blame for his failure. He hates the others for not being like him, and scorns his mother for being able to like a cripple like himself. At the same time 'Michael' – as an early response to international Marxism – has typical German nationalist traits. Curt Riess writes of the feelings of inferiority that arose out of Goebbels' nationalism: 'This nationalism did not arise out of a knowledge of Germany's real interests; Goebbels knew nothing of those. It was not based on real love of the German people; Goebbels had no feeling for the people, close physical contact with the masses always made him feel ill. What he sought was something with which he could identify. What he needed was a great and reputable Germany.

> Neither did that nationalism have anything to do with love of home, family or friends: it was not an affection for the great family of the entire nation. On the contrary: it was the result of a flight from his previous surroundings. Flight from the bosom of the family, from the town of his birth, which would not allow him to forget that he was a cripple. Flight from left-wing intellectuals; from Professor Gundolf, from the editors of the *Berliner Tageblatt* who had turned him away, from Flisges, who had tried to convert him to Communism; from the aesthetic view of the world, from romanticism, from the wisdom of the philosophers, from Goethe, whom he revered (and later scorned).[14]

This is how Curt Riess sees the man who Magda declared to have been her God, and who would later 'become her devil', a phrase recorded by her first biographer, Hans-Otto Meissner, who heard the remark from Magda's sister-in-law, Ello Quandt.

This characterisation might prompt us to a comparison with Arlosoroff, who was a classmate of Riess.

As we already know, from childhood onwards Arlosoroff was swept from one great love to another: his love of his own people, his love of the Germans, their literature and music. He did not exclude the 'other', the 'alien', he was open to everything, and he was always able to call his own authority into question.

How different Goebbels appears! Even as a boy he felt contempt for his fellow man, a contempt which he really felt, deep down, for himself, and which intensified into a passionate hatred as he sat in his attic after being awarded his doctorate, unable to find his niche anywhere. 'I have learned renunciation,' he wrote in his diary, 'and a boundless contempt for the rabble that is mankind!' His intelligence spurred his ambition onwards, but it had no real goal, circling instead around his own ego, until he found something that could win his allegiance. For this reason it should not come as a surprise if Curt Riess writes that Goebbels, in becoming a nationalist, in a sense betrayed everything for which he had hitherto been striving.

For the time being all his writings were rejected. But it never occurred to him to doubt his gifts, and perhaps he traced this rejection to the fact that the two most important publishing houses to which he applied, Ullstein and Mosse, were in Jewish hands. The *Berliner Tageblatt*, too, was run by a Jew, Theodor Wolff, and they had turned down about fifty of his articles. And had Professor Gundolf not turned him away, too, for no good reason? He chose to ignore the fact that non-Jewish editors showed no interest in his work either, preferring instead to turn himself into a victim. Rejection by the capital cohered precisely with his view of the world: the owners and the most successful journalists of these publishing houses were, after all, of Jewish origin. The world that refused him access and income had been infected with the spirit of Jewry.[15]

He was ripe for a party of discontents, of losers who could not find their place in society, and who needed recourse to a myth to rebuild their injured confidence. He was ripe for a mass party that longed for a saviour, and which was to find him in Adolf Hitler, a failed artist.

After his experience in Munich, listening to Hitler's speech, Goebbels knew what route he would have to take. In mid-August 1924 a friend, Fritz Prang, who had joined the (still forbidden) Nazi Party in 1922, took Goebbels with him to a Party rally in Weimar, which saw the consolidation of the already-existing electoral association of the National Socialist Freedom Movement, formed from the Deutschvölkische Freiheitspartei and a section of the forbidden NSDAP[16]. Here a role was found for the unemployed weakling from Rheydt. He was to assume the editorship of the Saturday newspaper *Völkische Freiheit*, a campaigning paper for a *völkisch*, nationalist Germany,[17] which was prepared to print the polemical essays of 'Dr G.' – although unpaid at first. Soon almost the entire content of the newspaper came from Goebbels' pen, and shortly afterwards he took over the editorship – 'with thankless idealism' as a salaried employee, with great satisfaction. 'I am a tiny little bit happy. The first visible success of my striving,' he remarked in his diary, 'Now I am back on top.'

With our character-study of Joseph Goebbels we have raced ahead in Magda's story, which we left with the Reichskanzler's speech to the Reichstag on the occasion of the Rathenau's assassination.

Chapter 10

The attack on Rathenau was so monstrous that it led in the short term to a reinforcement of the existing system. But the burdens of war and the costs of reparation continued to lead towards a lasting financial crisis, which the government attempted to solve by means of a trick that Hagen Schulze describes in the following terms:

> The massive and widening gulf between the income and expenditure of the state was filled with a loan from the Reichsbank, which was in turn financed by the steady production of new bank notes. The government deliberately accepted the increasing chaos in the balance of payments, the unstoppable slide towards a predictable breakdown of the entire currency system. The final result of this inflation was the same as it would have been if the state had gone bankrupt, but the political consequences were far less dramatic, and the government was able to pass the blame to its opponents, those who believed in reparation, and whose demands were the prime cause of the German currency's fall in value. And so the bank note

presses rattled away night and day, by the end of 1923 no
fewer than 1783 presses in 133 printworks, and the state
found itself in terrible straits each time the print workers
went on strike. For the state, this inflation resolved the
problem of internal war debts as at a stroke: on 15
November 1923 the entire internal war debts of the
German Reich, 154 billion marks, had the value of 15.4
pfennigs in 1914. But another social class was paying the
price, and becoming completely impoverished in the
process: small businessmen, craftsmen, shopkeepers,
freelance professionals, office workers, civil servants – in
short, a significant proportion of the middle class. All the
money they had saved became worthless, and consequently
this class was financially ruined.[1]

People on small and moderate incomes could only live hand to
mouth, and after their daily wages had been paid they immediately
had to buy bread for the next day, because value would have
plummeted once again.

Big businessmen, on the other hand, were able to increase their
fortunes. Quandt also managed to win credits for himself through
favourable bank connections, and quickly invested them in material assets such as buildings, while his debts were resolved very
quickly. In this way, amongst other things, in 1923 he bought a
pharmacy in Berlin for Magda's mother, who was consequently
well catered for after her divorce.[2]

Auguste was now able to take charge of her own life, she was
busy, and visited her daughter more rarely at the Babelsberg villa.
For Magda this meant even more loneliness. By now, she and
Quandt had hardly anything to talk to one another about. At
seven o'clock in the morning, while she was still asleep, he left the
house, lunching in the city – often with business colleagues – and
did not come home until late in the evening. Magda was not the
kind of woman to complain or seek her husband's attention with
caresses and sweet nothings, she was too proud for that, and

instead closed herself off from him. Her only option was to concentrate on the children, who were not much of a claim on her time since, apart from Herbert and Harald, they were all at public schools. For Herbert, because of his bad eyesight, a private teacher came to the house, and a nursery nurse looked after little Harald. At midday she had lunch with the teacher, but the meal was prepared by the servants, so that despite the fact that she had a large household to run, consisting of fourteen people including the employees, she still had a great deal of time to fill. But her position in the house had improved in the meantime, she was able to budget for herself and have work done by the best tailor in Berlin. But that was not enough. Magda missed people, company, acknowledgement, having some kind of outward effect. Her social ambitions, her desire to shine by the side of a successful man, all the hopes that she had entertained upon entering her marriage, remained unfulfilled. At home she practised the piano, did a bit of singing, checked her children's homework – and got bored. During this time her sister-in-law Ello, who, as we have already mentioned, was also unhappily married, became her best friend and confidante, and she was able to talk to her about the lack of fulfilment in her marriage,[3] because Magda felt thoroughly neglected. Quandt, she believed, no longer valued her properly or admired her as the lovely young woman that she was. She found his conservative ideas oppressive, and he had his reservations about her, objecting, for example when she appeared for breakfast in full make-up but still in her dressing gown, and on more than one occasion he criticised her clothes, which he found too risqué.[4] Little remained of his quiet charm when he had been in love, which had won her over at the time. Instead affection grew between Magda and Hellmuth, her adolescent stepson. The young man was enchanted by his beautiful stepmother, and his admiration and his imaginative sympathy did something to assuage her feelings of loneliness. He made Magda feel that she too was still young, making no secret of his devotion, and his romantic infatuation gave her fresh inner life. In the meantime outsiders all

believed her marriage to Quandt was still perfect, because Magda
kept her emotions fully under control, and even her mother, who
repeatedly stresses in her memoirs how warm-hearted, albeit
clumsy, she had felt her son-in-law to be, had no idea how
estranged her daughter and Quandt had become.[5]

The monotony of this 'doll's house' was lifted slightly on those
days when Quandt did not need his car and chauffeur. Then
Magda cautiously enjoyed her freedom, but since she had completely severed contact with her former friends, all she could do
with the car was visit Ello or her mother, who, being unaware of
her daughter's problems, was often too busy to chat to Magda.

One dull winter's day, when Auguste, as usual, had no time to
talk to Magda about the many trivial matters of daily life, Magda
decided to visit her old neighbourhood. Otherwise untouched by
the political situation and the general economic crisis, she now
noticed the changes in the place where she had grown up. The
atmosphere was generally depressed; the streets were full of people,
but most of them were badly dressed, some were begging, and the
children looking for rubbish at the side of the road looked in
astonishment as the elegant car passed by. Darkness was slowly
falling when Magda recognised Victor's mother in the queue outside the kosher butcher's in her old street. The old woman looked
tired, and her worn-out coat looked too big for her frail figure. She
was holding a little girl by the hand. Magda asked the chauffeur to
stop on the next corner and got out of the car. The old woman was
surprised to see Magda in her elegant fur-collared coat, but straight
away she proudly told her about Victor, who had almost completed his dissertation and, as a member of the Yishuv,[6] was
travelling to various conferences and, despite his youth, had
already assumed important diplomatic missions in England and
Switzerland. The little girl she was holding by the hand, and who
was by now impatiently shifting from foot to foot, was Victor's
daughter. Magda quickly jotted her address on a piece of paper for
Lisa. Then she made her way back to the waiting car, which was
out of sight around the corner. She had not dared ask about

Victor's relationship with Gerda, and in any case his mother would probably not have been able to say anything very precise about it, because Victor was now head over heels in love with someone else.

As Victor's mother had proudly related, he was being sent as a young delegate to various Zionist conferences to deliver lectures about the movement. At one of these conferences, in Lithuania in 1923, he met a pretty young student. Sima came from Riga, and after Arlosoroff had delivered a lecture there with his group, Sima's father invited him to dinner. After this Victor and Sima took a long walk along the Baltic shore. They were soon walking hand in hand beneath the clear night sky, and Victor opened up the romantic side of his personality to the young woman, once more becoming the young man whose friends had called him the 'poet'. Now he talked not about politics, about Zionism or social-ism, but about his suddenly awakened feelings for Sima, as well as about his situation with Gerda, his young marriage which really existed only on paper, but which obliged him to behave responsi-bly towards his wife and child. He spoke of his longing to move to Palestine once and for all, and perhaps to take Sima there as well. The young woman listened to him, enraptured by his charm and persuasiveness, and shortly after he left they wrote one another love letters[7] in which Arlosoroff seems the more urgent and demanding partner in the relationship. He wrote that he would like her to share in his life, at least in her thoughts, while bearing in mind the Zionist movement would always remain centre stage.

But Arlosoroff, repeatedly described by his comrades as some-one who united the coldness of the visionary with the fire of the prophet, was sometimes plagued by doubts. While the British were greatly admired for their statesmanship, the 1923 publication of their first White Book, in the clash between the Palestinians and the Jews, showed that they sided unambiguously with the Arabs, and for that reason imposed severe restrictions on immigration policy. For Arlosoroff this was particularly hard to bear.

In the winter of 1924, while Arlosoroff was being tormented by weighty concerns such as these, the whole Quandt family holi-dayed comfortably in the snow with the children and Quandt's company secretary. Then Magda and Quandt travelled on alone from Cortina d'Ampezzo into the spring-like weather of upper Italy. Magda sent her mother photographs and postcards from Bordighera,[8] the elegant resort on the Ligurian coast, but the *froideur* that prevailed between the couple could not be warmed back to life by the luxury of the hotels and the beauty of Italy. If anything, without the protective routine of daily life with the children, Magda's loneliness became even greater here.

She could not shake off her memory of the meeting with Victor's mother, and found herself thinking over and over again about her former life, but even about this her feelings were ambivalent. Her life then had, admittedly, provided stimuli more appropriate to her age, but at the same time it had been socially and materially impoverished, and her status had been far less priv-ileged than it was now.

Once they had both returned home, Magda decided after lengthy ruminations to return once more to the old district to visit the Arlosoroffs in their apartment in Eisenacher Strasse – perhaps to see Victor again. She knew that she could cover over any feelings of insecurity she might have had about Victor, who had clearly achieved so much, with her present elegance and her social status. They had not seen each other for some years, and Magda knew very well that she now possessed even more of an aura than she had before.

Everything in Eisenacher Strasse was as it had been: the slightly stale smell in the stairwell, the worn-out, creaking wooden steps that Magda climbed to the first floor. When she rang the bell she heard tired, hesitant steps approaching the door from inside. Old Frau Arlosoroff could hardly conceal her astonishment when she saw Magda standing in front of her. Hearing her cry of surprise, Lisa came to join her. Touched and delighted, she embraced the friend she hadn't seen for so long, and asked her in. Victor was not at home, he had too much to do at the moment, since they had unexpectedly discovered that they were all to emigrate to Palestine in a few days. Magda was thunderstruck: she had nearly missed seeing her friends. Now she asked a hundred questions, and when Lisa had patiently answered them all she too talked about her own life, about her loneliness, her disappointment with her marriage and the uncertainty about her own future. Lisa invited her to stay longer, but Magda could and would not wait for Victor. To see him again right now would be too much to bear. Instead she promised to come and see them all off at the station.

On the day of their departure, the platform was full of people. Apart from the young Zionists, some of whose faces were familiar to Magda, groups of Eastern Jews were also assembled in the station: old men with beards and long caftans gesticulated to their wives, young orthodox mothers, their hair hidden under head-scarves, tried to calm down their excited children. They had all brought a very few belongings with them, and were accompanied by friends and relations who repeatedly embraced them telling them how much they hoped to see them again soon.

Arlosoroff was standing further towards the back, and Magda impatiently pushed her way through the crowd. By now Victor wore a beard, he had become a man rather than a boy, and in the circle of friends and relations surrounding him he looked much more domineering than Magda had remembered. She finally reached him. Standing next to him were his mother and Lisa, and nearby Magda also recognised Gerda, clutching a collapsible child's bed under one arm and holding her little daughter under the other.[9] Magda cautiously approached her friends, and with some embarrassment she greeted Victor, who overcame her hesitancy with his familiar heartiness. One final embrace for Victor, and another for Lisa, whose eyes were filling with tears – and the train was slowly moving off. Handkerchiefs fluttered, and the people left behind briefly ran alongside it. Magda ran with them, her throat tight with grief and tears running down her face as, with a sob, she called out to Lisa, who was waving from the open window: 'Maybe I'll come after you!'[10]

In fact, the Arlosoroffs had left with unnecessary haste. Shortly before Easter 1924 the Histadrut, the directorate of the Zionist workers' organisation, started up a council in Palestine at which Chaim's presence was urgently requested, so he had decided that this would be the ideal moment to move. Somehow the family managed to find themselves an immigration permit. Even then this was not easy, since the English, after the first Arab uprising in protest against the claim to a 'Jewish homeland', had produced the White Book mentioned above. Nonetheless Arlosoroff managed to get hold of a passport, stating that he was born in Rechovot, in Palestine.[11]

They had neither time nor money to prepare or buy anything for Gerda and the child, so, armed only with a large trunk and Shulamit's iron bed, they boarded an Italian steamer in Trieste. As 'pioneers' it seemed quite natural to them that they should not travel in a cabin but between decks, despite the fact that none of them was quite clear what it would mean to travel without comfort with a little child. They were hardly on board before Gerda and Shulamit became severely seasick. With the help of a generous tip Arlosoroff managed to persuade a sailor to find a cabin for mother and child. But when, after six days' crossing, they reached land, this time in Alexandria, they were still so weak that they could barely walk. They were immediately overwhelmed by the Orient, with its strangeness, its heat, the strange noises of people and animals, the intense and varied smells, the incomprehensible cries and wild gestures. They travelled on by train, amongst proud Bedouins and poor fellaheen, to Tel Aviv, where they were put up by Dora, who had emigrated there with her husband a year before the rest.[12]

Immediately upon his arrival Arlosoroff found himself completely preoccupied with discussions and meetings in the directorship of the Hapoel Hazair and the various institutions of the workers' body. In theory he should have been receiving an income from the day of his arrival, but in fact finances remained a problem. Since his first trip to Palestine, Arlosoroff had been famous for trying to reach an accommodation with Arabs, which meant that the British and the Arabs held him in equally high esteem. He was invited to the Moslem festival of Nebi Mussa,[13] for example, at which the then first British High Commissioner, Herbert Samuel, received him on the Mount of Olives in Jerusalem. Herbert Samuel was himself a Jew, although the Arabs also acknowledged him. The fact that he, a handsome, imposing man, was present with his son and his little grandson, was a clear demonstration of the continuing patriarchal domination of the British Empire, which still seemed to be at the height of its powers.[14]

After the first few weeks Arlosoroff and Gerda parted company, partly because of the external circumstances, partly for personal reasons, for it was clear to both of them that they had had enough of each other for some time.

Arlosoroff had rented a little house near the beach of Tel Aviv, which was then a suburb of the much older Arab city of Jaffo, a suburb in which European immigrants tried to recreate something of the atmosphere of their former way of life. Unlike Jaffo, Tel Aviv was not dominated by the claustrophobia and noisy business dealing of oriental alleyways and souks hidden from the sea. Instead the settlers made a point of building houses with gardens and balconies, incorporating light and shade, wind and views of the Mediterranean.

Arlosoroff's little house was set somewhat apart, and he was for this reason accused of aristocratic tendencies, but he loved and needed the loneliness. Here the beach was still wild, and the view of the sea was blocked by dunes. Only once one had climbed over them did one see the horizon stretching away into infinity. Every day when he was at home Arlosoroff took this ever-changing walk through the dunes, and every day, once again, he felt that sense of freedom, when all that could be heard was the rushing of the wind and the rolling waves. Once he had reached the beach he would swim far out,[15] unafraid of the currents that had cost several people their lives on this patch of coast.

Europe was far away, another world. And yet he felt bound to it, not only for the sake of Zionism, but also because his thoughts repeatedly returned to Sima. By now Sima was having a child by another man with whom she had had a relationship before she had known Arlosoroff. This did not change matters much for Arlosoroff, who promised to acknowledge the child as his own after his planned divorce from Gerda.[16]

Daily life was extraordinarily difficult for the pioneers: along with all the other problems there was terrible unemployment. The groups waiting for dwellings were forever being put off because there was neither the land nor the money for new building projects. The Jewish workers in the colonies engaged in bitter competition with the Arab workers, who had a low standard of living and were satisfied with lower wages than the Jews, although the Jewish workers in Palestine also endured the severest of deprivations.

But they did not starve, since they were all living to some extent on credit on the assumption that they would at some point be able to pay their debts. On the other hand all the European Jews suffered from the sun and the heat; with their light skin they were unused to planting tobacco under the burning heat, or breaking stones to surface the roads. If these difficulties could be overcome with such cheerful solidarity it was only due to the fact that everyone believed in the construction of a new world that had nothing to do with traditional forms of society and economy, but which depended solely on the desire to create something. There was something intoxicating about this hubris.

While Arlosoroff was tirelessly travelling around the country in the most primitive conditions, Gerda had met another workers' leader, and moved in with him.

When she accompanied him on his tour of Europe, Arlosoroff was in Berlin at the same time, and they decided to be divorced by a rabbi.

'After the very brief – or abbreviated – divorce ceremony, we went to drink coffee together, and Arlosoroff quoted a saying from the Talmud: When two people divorce, God weeps.'[17]

Despite his youth, which he sometimes saw as an obstacle, Arlosoroff had already been elected on to the Zionist Action Committee and the Commission for Economy and Finance. The better the public got to know him, the more popular he became. But his character prompted some to hostile polemics. Even within the party he was not always a man of peace; he courageously and stubbornly advocated his own positions, and spared no one in his struggles, least of all himself.

His relationship with Sima was a constant stream of conflict and reconciliation. She was capricious, and still had some problems with settling down, and yet Arlosoroff married her in 1927. But immediately afterwards he had to leave for America once more, this time for a longer period.

The economic situation in Germany was slowly stabilising. By virtue of the fact that inflation had reduced the cost of reparations to the Allies to a laughably small sum, the state bank was to some extent able to recover. But as a result of this coup, not only had the savings of the lower and middle classes been unscrupulously destroyed, but many previously large and successful businessmen faced bankruptcy. Günther Quandt, on the other hand, had so skilfully distributed his fortune among different enterprises that it had continued to grow. On one occasion he profited from the unfortunate situation of another businessman, who, to avert bankruptcy, needed a certain sum of money in a short space of time – in cash, of course. Quandt was flush, and helped him out – in return for the man's perfectly appointed, elegant villa. In one move Quandt – at a knock-down price – was the owner of a representative town-house in the Frankenallee in the smart area of Charlottenburg in Berlin. Everything in the house was in place: paintings, carpets, antiques and table-silver had been selected and matched with impeccable taste.

But when he came home glowing with delight at the news, Magda did not share his enthusiasm for the new villa. As far as she was concerned the 'perfect' house was a terrible disappointment, since she was unable to contribute anything to its decoration. There was no space for her own personal needs, and she would always feel a stranger there.[18] She now had two houses at her disposal, and in both she was more a guest than the lady of the manor.

Up until this point Magda had not really taken charge of her own life, and remained strangely uninvolved. But it is curious that the two men who had played an important role in her life so far represented two of the most important trends to have influenced the twentieth century. Arlosoroff's contemporaries saw him as the most brilliant mind and the most charismatic personality in Zionism, and Quandt was a major player in large-scale capitalism, who would manage to save his fortune even beyond the end of the Second World War and the subsequent economic collapse.

What these two men, otherwise so different, had in common, and what made them so attractive to Magda was surely the passion with which they devoted themselves to their tasks, and the unerring way they pursued their paths. While Magda shared in Victor's ideas, she thought she was partaking in his charisma, his power and his energy. Standing by his side, she had wanted to play an important part in the construction of the Promised Land. But that was not to be, because Victor would have demanded that she bring her own commitment to the project, and as far as we can tell, that was something that she, unlike Gerda, had been unable to do. Then Quandt happened to cross her path, and she very quickly changed direction. This man, twenty years older than she was, represented a powerful father-figure, more powerful than the two fathers she had had so far. Perhaps it was the longing for such a father that led her to settle down with Quandt. At the same time, because of his powerful position, she expected to play a social role that would enhance the value of her vague social origins. But that hope, too, was to be shattered.

Chapter 11

The leaden summer sky hung over Paris like a pall of smog, grey as the stones of the pavement and the endless rows of buildings, where the day's warm air lurked until well into the night. The streets were still cluttered with the remains of the big Bastille Day celebrations. The people had danced, sung and drunk wine in streets and squares and on the Seine bridges, celebrating their '*liberté* and *égalité*' in such a way that rigid social divisions seemed to have been broken down.

Magda barely noticed the relaxed atmosphere of the holiday, any more than she was really aware of the stale smell that lingered in the air, or all the cats looking for scraps among the rubbish and rubbing against her legs. She distractedly walked along the broad boulevards, which mutely witnessed her grief. From an open window came the tune of the old chanson *Les temps des cérises*. She was very familiar with the words, which said that love was as brief as cherry-picking time, and that anyone fearing its pains should give love a wide berth . . .

Quandt had stayed back at the hotel. Magda wanted to be on her own. It was as though she was paralysed, her pain was too terrible for tears, and she could not share it with her husband.

Only much later, once she had returned to Berlin, was she able to spend hours immersed in conversation with her mother, and to reconstruct the events that had led to the unhappiness that had opened up like a deluge over her life. Even after her daughter's death, Auguste would remember that summer in all its details.[1]

The year had begun so promisingly: Hellmuth, who was sitting his *Abitur*, was to spend a few months with business friends in London and Paris to improve his linguistic skills, because Quandt thought it was very important that his children should gather experience abroad before they began their university studies. He had probably also noticed that his son was in love, and hoped that his new impressions would be enough of a distraction to make his beloved stepmother retreat into the background. Hellmuth began his foreign stay in London.

In early summer Quandt went to London on business. He travelled, as he almost always did, in his own car, a red Maybach, which attracted a great deal of attention in the capital. Magda went with him. When they met Hellmuth, they could tell immediately that he had settled in well in the city. He was as familiar with the sights, the Tower and Westminster Abbey, as he was with the little corner tea-shops. But for some time he had been suffering from severe physical pains, for which the English doctors he consulted could find no satisfactory explanation. They prescribed him some medication, recommended a hot water bottle before bedtime and advised him against spicy foods.[2]

When Quandt had finished his negotiations in London, he had to travel on to France for business reasons, and therefore suggested that Hellmuth and Magda should accompany him.

So they left behind the London of King George V, where, as in Germany, there were frequent political tensions between right and left. Even before their departure they witnessed clashes between English Fascists and Communists in Hyde Park.

They were all thrilled by their journey through the summery hills of Southern England. On either side of the country roads nestled little cottages, wild roses blossoming in their gardens and raspberries ripening on their canes. The mild, pale blue summer sky welcomed them on the other side of the Channel as they drove through Normandy to Paris. Magda enjoyed hearing and speaking the language of her childhood, and looked forward to visiting museums and galleries in the French capital.

They had set aside only a few days for Paris, but for Magda and Hellmuth those days were filled with enchantment.[3] The cafés along the great boulevards were filled with the intellectuals of the day, the artists, authors and musicians. Some days before their arrival Paris had seen the première of Stravinsky's oratorio *Oedipus Rex*, with its libretto by Jean Cocteau, and Magda and Hellmuth could even, had they known them, have lunched with James Joyce and Nora in La Coupole while Quandt occupied himself with his business deals. They enjoyed a performance by Mistinguette and heard Maurice Chevalier, who seemed to be singing, with his melting voice, *Parlez-moi d'amour* specially for them. No one would have taken them for mother and son as they strolled hand in hand through the Tuileries, visited the Louvre and climbed the tower of Notre Dame before settling down to a *café crème* on the Champs-Elysées to admire the elegance of the Parisian women. But time flew by, and after Magda and Quandt had left, Hellmuth, who knew only a little French, found himself very much alone in the strange city. He was staying in a little hotel between the Madeleine and the Opéra, and spent most of his time walking along the Seine. While he had been in Magda's company, taking in the sights, he had paid no attention to the pains in his body, but now he felt them once again, more strongly than before. The attacks became more frequent, and one afternoon it was all he could do to drag himself to his hotel. Hoarse with pain, he begged the concierge to find him a German-speaking doctor. When the doctor came and examined Hellmuth, he recommended an immediate operation, diagnosing the final stages of appendicitis.[4]

Hellmuth had his operation in a Paris clinic, but there were complications. Quandt and Magda were informed by telegram, and travelled back to Paris, forty-eight hours after their arrival in Berlin.

Magda was horrified when she entered the clinic where Hellmuth lay. The whole hospital struck her as neglected and dilapidated. She immediately set all the machinery in motion to ensure better hygienic conditions for Hellmuth, and organised a private nurse to attend to him. All her efforts were made more difficult by the fact that on 14 July, the national day of celebration, there was a shortage of staff.

Hellmuth was happy to see Magda, but he did not recover. The sepsis advanced. He suffered terrible pains, and even the morphine injections that he was given did little to alleviate them. On the third day after Magda's arrival Hellmuth died, fully conscious to the end, in his mother's arms.[5]

Quandt was terribly shaken, and Magda was inconsolable, but they were too deeply estranged to comfort one another, and with Hellmuth's death a further bond between them was broken. Hellmuth's body was taken to Pritzwalk, where he was buried.

The notes of her mother and her biographer Hans-Otto Meissner indirectly suggest that Magda had reciprocated Hellmuth's affection for her. But the resulting conflict was unspoken, and only Magda could have resolved it. To do that she would have had to have the strength to break away from social conventions. But as she did not have that freedom, her love for Hellmuth was never to become a reality.[6]

But Magda seems to have been unable to act – in all likelihood she was unaware of her feelings, because otherwise the conventions of the day would have led her to keep them secret. So she was unable to take the chance of listening to her feelings.

While the private tragedy of the Quandt family was being played out in Paris, on 15 July 1927 the Palace of Justice in Vienna was being consumed by flames. As in Germany, the loss of the war, the harsh conditions imposed by the Allies' peace terms in 1918 and the end of the monarchy had led to unsolved problems. In Vienna, too, the socialists had clashed with the right-wingers, the 'old warriors'. The original cause for this was the acquittal of three old warriors of the anti-socialist front, who were believed to have killed two Communists. The left-wing press was horrified by this acquittal, and called for violent protests. The workers took to the streets, set fire to buildings and smashed windows, and finally thousands of people furiously stormed the Palace of Justice. The police fired brutally into the crowd and the Chancellor called in the armed forces. The workers and trades unionists then declared a general strike and called for the resignation of the Chancellor, who instead brought even more troops from the provinces into the capital. The Viennese press held Moscow responsible for the riots, and the German press wrote that the situation in Austria could only be improved by the country becoming part of the Reich.

Chapter 12

Hellmuth's death made the gulf between Magda and Quandt in their new Charlottenburg villa even more palpable. When their foster-daughter Carola married and little Harald was sent to school, Magda hardly had any domestic duties left, and she accepted Quandt's suggestion that she accompany him on a major trip around the United States.[1]

So Magda, who was presented to the world as an entirely loveable and exemplary mother, decided to leave her six-year-old son on his own for six months, when the boy had just undergone a considerable change in his life, having lost his brother a short time previously. For Quandt's son Herbert, too, the loss of his elder brother must still have been very fresh in his mind, but in spite of all this Magda saw no need to stay with the children, preferring to go travelling with the husband she no longer loved.

A family by the name of Köhler came to the house to look after the boy, and in mid-October Magda and Quandt, in the company of some friends, another married couple, boarded the British Cunard liner, the *Berengeria*, a former German vessel, the *Imperator*, requisitioned and renamed after the war.[2] Magda had a poor crossing and suffered severely from sea-sickness, probably still so shaken by the events of that summer that she was unable to put up much resistance to the ship's rocking and swaying. While Quandt enjoyed 'captain's night' with their mutual friends, dressed in dinner jacket and full evening regalia, Magda's evening dresses remained in the cupboard. As well as sea-sickness she had flu and a high fever, so that when they arrived in New York she was unable to go up on deck to see the view of the Statue of Liberty under the mild autumn sky, or the skyline of Manhattan growing from toy-size to a massive silhouette. Instead she was immediately brought by ambulance to the nearest private hospital. Here she very quickly recovered under careful medical attention. As soon as she was better, she and Quandt went to look at the sights of New York. Quandt was fascinated by Wall Street for the Stock Exchange was booming, and Quandt was not blind to the business opportunities that might be exploited here in relation to Europe, particularly since holders of foreign passports had only recently been allowed to trade here. Meanwhile Magda enjoyed the social life. Prohibition was still officially in place, but cocktail parties and dinner parties in the town houses or the great country houses of Long Island and Connecticut displayed a degree of luxury – even in Protestant and Anglo-Saxon families – unknown in Germany. The atmosphere was like that of Fitzgerald's *Gatsby*: wealth, excess and always enough staff to spoil the guests with every imaginable comfort. In this society Magda was the centre of attention, not only because she was pretty and radiated an old-world charm, but also because she held a promise that could no longer be taken for granted in the New World: the sense that American women had gone too far with their striving for emancipation, and that a woman should, in her opinion, still be subordinate to her husband.[3] With this attitude she conquered the hearts of the American men, including the industrialist nephew of the future president, Herbert Hoover.

Quandt had had his red Maybach shipped over, and they now continued their journey with the other couple by car: along the East Coast, to Boston, Buffalo, Niagara Falls, Philadelphia and

Chicago. Along the route, of course, they visited industrial plants and car factories, and the ladies were expected to join in. Quandt writes in his memoirs: 'When we took our ladies to two dry-cell battery factories, and in Chicago led them through the huge slaughter-houses of Armour, the ladies went on strike and declared that they had had enough of their factory visits.'[4] So they left the ladies behind until the journey continued to Florida and Mexico, from where Magda wrote to Auguste at New Year: 'The romance and beauty here are hardly to be surpassed. Günther is ever cheerful, and I am – as he always likes to have me – up for anything. As might have been predicted, I am an attraction here. A blonde, blue-eyed white woman – they've never seen such a thing here. I'm forever being gawked at and stared at. It won't be long before some enthusiast hurls himself at my feet. Everyone else in our party is dark and old! So I often have the dubious pleasure of being the sole recipient of admiring stares. . .'[5]

Later Magda wrote to her mother that she was suffering as a result of the primitive travelling conditions and accommodation. She also had problems with the differences in climate and altitude. But her visit to the pyramids of the sun and moon in Mexico City and an authentic Mexican bullfight, about which she reports with a slight shudder, compensated for so many deprivations – and also for the fact that she was once again so ill that the worst was feared. Once more she was taken to the hospital, although this time with Quandt, who had also acquired an intestinal infection. After they had both recovered, Havana was the final stop on their trip. From there Magda wrote, as Auguste remembered, 'only in a tone of drunken enthusiasm'.[6]

The hardships of the long journey had weakened Magda. Even later in Berlin she did not feel particularly well. She suffered a miscarriage, had a heart complaint and, on the orders of her doctor, went for a cure to Bad Nauheim and later, for a post-cure, to Graubünden in Switzerland.

To take his wife's mind off these matters, Quandt, clearly having discovered a taste for travel, suggested a trip to Palestine and Egypt the following spring, but Magda refused. Quandt could not understand her refusal, but then how could she explain to him that Palestine was wrapped up in the dreams of her youth, with Arlosoroff and her former wish to start a new life there? After their emotional farewell at the station she had, after some reflection, severed contact with Lisa, but the memories of this past time had left her with a wound that would not heal. Even Quandt's proposed trip to the French Riviera did not appeal, and he had to go there on his own.[7]

Magda's sole desire was a separation from Quandt. She had had enough of her unfulfilled marriage. Her difficulties with her health, her 'heart-pains', were like an echo of the emotional problems from which she had been suffering for ages, her lack of joy in life. She wanted to live as she felt she had never lived before. But there was no legal reason to separate, and Quandt did not want to take their mutual estrangement to its conclusion. On the contrary, he tried to save what could still be saved, by granting her greater outward freedoms than ever before. She was able to dress with the most exquisite elegance, she attended operas and concerts, and Quandt was even prepared to take her to important dances – although he would also invite along a young cousin to spare himself the tiresome duties of dancing – and yet Magda was still dissatisfied. She was accused – even among her friends – of moodiness, and those around her were believed to fear her temper.

On one occasion she was invited with Quandt to a benefit dance. Her dancing partner had walked on to the balcony with a cigarette and Quandt had immersed himself in the financial pages, and Magda's eyes wandered across the crowded ballroom. At the other end she saw a little group of young men apparently engaged in an intense discussion. She was struck by their shabby clothes, particularly in this society, where most people came from the moneyed aristocracy, people who had come into money either

during or after the war, along with some old bankers or successful
businessmen like the owners of the large department stores.
Nonetheless, they aroused Magda's interest, and a vague curiosity
prompted her to stand up and approach the group. Quandt barely
glanced up from his stock market report when she said she wanted
to go and freshen up. While she was walking slowly through the
hall, she recognised her old friend Victor, despite the change in his
appearance. A number of years had passed since their last meeting,
and Victor was now more mature, more gaunt, his face more chis-
elled and tanned brown, but his full, dark hair looked as tousled as
ever. The same moment he too recognised her, apologised to the
other men, walked over to her and took her spontaneously in his
arms. Once again it was his warmth, his cordiality, his genuine joy
at seeing her that immediately took possession of Magda. Of
course she noticed how badly cut his suit was, that the material
was not of the quality to which she had by now grown accustomed, but she was not bothered by such things. After their initial
greeting, and after he had explained to her that he had only come
to the ball to request donations from industrialists, he told her he
could tell that she was unhappy. Magda did not reply to this, but
allowed him to ask her to dance. When he asked to see her again –
they had a lot to say to each other, and this was clearly not the
right place – she agreed.

Once again Magda was fascinated by Arlosoroff. When they
met, the years of their youth came flooding back. She heard of his
divorce from Gerda and his difficult marriage with Sima, who
didn't write to him often enough, who made scenes and who was
said, behind his back, to have countless lovers. Magda poured her
heart out to him, too, telling about Quandt, her unhappy marriage, all their travels and the emptiness that still filled her life, of
her longing to be loved and desired. Arlosoroff listened. We do
not know what level of reawakened intimacy was reached between
them. They were both going through difficult times, but Arlosoroff
could not fill the void in Magda's life. His warmth, his friendship,
perhaps his tenderness never allowed her to doubt that he felt

bound both to the Zionist movement, in which all his energies were wrapped up, and to Sima, whom he continued to love in spite of all their problems. He was not in a position to free Magda from her unsatisfactory situation with Quandt, and in turn Magda knew very well that she would not be the right woman to go with him to Palestine. In addition, Arlosoroff did not have much time, he had to travel within Europe, and when disturbances broke out in Palestine again he was called back more quickly than he had anticipated.

The position in Palestine had fundamentally changed. Between 1925 and 1928 the situation had been relatively stable for Jewish immigrants, and Arlosoroff in particular had been on a good footing both with the Arabs and the British. The following anecdote dates from this period: one day when Arlosoroff was sitting chatting on the terrace of the British Officers' Club, a Bedouin prince demanded to speak to him. As a surprise, and a gift of friendship, he had brought him a thoroughbred Arab stallion. To the great astonishment of the British officers, Arlosoroff mounted the horse without a moment's hesitation, and rode the temperamental creature elegantly around in front of everyone.

After the appointment of Sir John Chancellor as High Commissioner, such an episode would have been unthinkable. The new man was unable to reconcile the tensions between the Arabs and the Jews, and the Arab population was increasingly reacting with violence. Never before had the Jews been refused the right to pray at the Wailing Wall in Jerusalem, but in August 1929 they were brutally hounded from it, their holy books were burned and an unprecedented blood-bath ensued. The violence in Jerusalem spread to other parts of Palestine. The mounted police, largely Arab, refused to intervene against its own population to protect the Jews, and British troops were forced to put an end to the bloodshed. This they did reluctantly, seeming rather helpless. After these events the battle lines were drawn up. The British formed an investigative commission and came to the dubious conclusion that the Jews bore full responsibility for what had happened, and that immigration must be restricted for that reason. The consequence of this change in mood was that the Socialist Workers' Party, Arlosoroff's party, lost members, and the revisionists, the conservative right-wing as well as the Misrahi, the ultra-religious groups, gained in influence and power.

In the midst of this conflict Arlosoroff intensified his political work in Palestine by the side of Chaim Weizman and David Ben Gurion. All three were convinced of the extraordinary importance of not allowing the negotiations with the British to break down. But this attitude struck some other Jews as meaning that the Socialists were co-operating with the British.

After Arlosoroff's departure Magda felt even lonelier than before. During this time, yearning for a loving relationship, she met a young student – and from this point onwards her biographers contradict one another: Hans-Otto Meissner calls the young man 'Ernst', but points out that this is a pseudonym. Meissner met him after the Second World War, a father of three, living in the Rhineland and wishing to protect his anonymity. Meissner describes the young man as a perfect romantic lover, of good family, with excellent manners and a generous allowance, which enabled him to neglect his studies and instead spend a great deal of time with Magda. Perhaps his greatest charm for Magda lay in the fact that he had time, time to go to exhibitions with her, to accompany her to the theatre, to enjoy the cultural diversity of Berlin life with her – and that he had time for love. Because 'Ernst' took a great deal of time for the woman he was in love with. Magda was just a few years older than he was, but she emanated a great deal more maturity. 'Ernst' admired her elegance and gave her a sense of being desirable, a sense that he saw it as a great good fortune to be her lover. In her memoirs Auguste mentions the young man with his – supposedly – correct name: Fritz Gerber.[8]

But some people also suspect that the pseudonym of the young student 'Ernst' conceals Victor Arlosoroff. Ello Quandt in particular speaks of his mysterious persona and his passionate temperament, which feeds into this supposition.[9] I consider it unlikely that Arlosoroff would have wanted to get involved in this kind of relationship with Magda, since his obligations were pushing him in another direction. And the development of the affair suggests the behaviour of an impetuous young man, and this, given what we know of him, would not have applied to Arlosoroff.

Magda clearly abandoned herself to her romantic infatuation. She appeared openly in public with 'Ernst', made no attempt to conceal their relationship and even stayed in elegant hotels with her young friend. Despite all these 'demonstrations', however, it remains open whether she was really in love with him or only enjoyed him being in love with her, or whether she was primarily using him as a means to an end, the end of provoking Quandt with her careless behaviour. The demonstration of this affair demanded a reaction from Quandt. The impression arose that Magda could only break away by force from Quandt's all-powerful father-figure. It was as though all that remained was the possibility of a complete break, as though to free herself from Quandt she had to make it impossible for herself to go back, even at the risk of ruining herself financially and socially. The choice of her young chaperone, who was charming, cultivated and good-looking, but who was unable to give her any security, meant that she was unable to seek the safe haven of those around her.

As predicted, Quandt was not someone to tangle with. He was profoundly hurt when he learned of Magda's trip with 'Ernst' to Bad Godesberg, where they stayed in the Hotel Dreesen, the same hotel where Ritschel had put up some of their wedding guests. On her return Quandt interrogated her. Magda admitted everything. All she would say in her defence was that she had pleaded for her freedom before, and that in having this affair she had only been taking the estrangement in her marriage to its logical conclusion.[10]

Quandt was beside himself. He barely gave her time to pack a few suitcases, before she was standing in the street. She took a taxi to her mother's. She gradually realised that she alone was responsible for the collapse of her marriage. In those days no divorce court would have taken the slightest interest in the emotional reasons for her situation. What remained was the fact of adultery, quite unambiguous and confirmed by Magda herself.

This meant that she was unable to claim maintenance, and would also lose custody of her son Harald. So after eight years of marriage she stood on the brink. She had no access to Quandt's bank account, and she herself had no savings, she had no expensive jewellery that might help her through a difficult time, and she had no professional qualifications.

She hired one of the best lawyers in Berlin. In conversation with her he tried to detect any shortcomings on Quandt's part – in vain. As things stood, no lawyer was able to help her. But in this cul-de-sac Magda suddenly had an idea, and since what was at stake was her future life, the end justified the means. She suppressed any possible scruples she might have had. And in making her claim for maintenance and custody of her son she felt fully in the right.[11]

One lovely spring day she took a taxi to her old villa in the Frankenallee. She was forbidden to enter the building, and the staff were not allowed to let her in, but she was willing to take a risk. She remembered that Quandt was waiting for visitors from England that week, and was sure not to be at home. By now Herbert was attending a public Gymnasium, and little Harald was at school, too. Magda asked the taxi to wait outside the villa. Everything was unchanged, the well-tended garden, the tulips and narcissi heralding the spring. She received a shy greeting from the gardener, who was raking the last winter leaves away from the lawn. The maid opened the door. She was almost a child, and was unable to counter Magda's authority. In any case, she had not understood why the lady was no longer living in the house. Magda explained that she had forgotten something very important, and the maid shyly curtseyed and left her on her own. Magda went into her old bedroom. It was untouched, as though she had never been away. The curtains were half opened, and the smell of her perfume still seemed to float through the room. Magda remembered that in the top drawer of her chest of drawers, amongst all kinds of bits and pieces, were the keys to the villa in Babelsberg. These keys were the purpose of her visit. She looked around. She had closed the door behind her. She looked out of the window, and the gardener was nowhere to be seen. While she stood by her chest of drawers, rummaging through the drawer for the keys, she kept an eye on the door in the mirror. Everything was still. Her hand immediately found the keys, and she quickly slipped them into her pocket. Then she cast one last glance into the silver-framed mirror; this time she considered only her external appearance, and she was pleased by what she saw: an elegant young woman, every hair in place. Without yielding to sentimental feelings and looking around the house or Harald's room, she left the villa, climbed into the waiting taxi and set off for Babelsberg.

Although the coming spring could be sensed in the park here too, and the buds on the trees were cautiously opening, the house itself was still deep in its winter sleep. The heavy door opened easily. It was cold in the unheated house, and the wooden shutters were closed, allowing the bright morning sun to fall on the parquet floor only in delicate narrow strips. The air in the house was heavy, damp and stale, and mixed with the smell of naphthalene from the mothballs with which the curtains and carpets had been carefully treated. The chairs and sofas were draped with sheets.

Magda walked into Quandt's study. Her steps rang out in the empty house. His desk was also covered with a sheet. Magda's hands had grown cold, and with clammy fingers she now opened one drawer after another.

Somewhere in this desk, years before, one winter evening when Quandt had stayed late in the office again, she had decided to have a rummage, and found a bundle of well-hidden letters. They were letters from women to Quandt – clearly not from ladies of his own social class – with whom he had at some point had a

relationship, and who were now asking him for financial
help. Magda had been shocked, although these relationships had
dated from a time before their marriage, but of course she had said
nothing.[12]

She remembered those letters, and now she was determined to
get her hands on them. Quandt had changed nothing in his desk,
and the documents were still in the same place. Magda hastily
took them and, like a thief, crept from the house where she had
lived for many years.

When she handed the bundle of letters to her lawyer, she knew
that she had won the game. Because although Quandt was legally
in the right, he was too much the gentleman not to find the revelation of this private matter extremely embarrassing. And by
now he had achieved a certain amount of detachment, and was
able to acknowledge certain mistakes he had made in his relationship with Magda.

In his later memoirs, too, Quandt remained the gentleman,
regretting 'that he had, because of his many obligations, not been
able to devote himself as fully to Magda as he should have done,
and as much as she deserved.' He concluded with the words: 'But
how often do we shoulder blame when we are not really at fault?'
When, in a later passage of his memoirs, he speaks of his broken
marriage, he writes: 'In the summer of 1929 I separated from
Magda Ritschel. We divorced on good terms, and had drawn up a
contract some time before, to the effect that our son Harald would
stay with his mother until the age of fourteen, and afterwards, or
in the event of his mother marrying again, he would return to his
father's house. Since then we had been on amicable terms, and I
was often a guest in her house on the Reichskanzlerplatz'.[13]

The divorce was not without its difficulties. Quandt, otherwise
so thrifty, proved extraordinarily generous. Magda received, for
herself and Harald, a monthly allowance of almost four thousand
marks, as well as the sum of fifty thousand marks, to set up a new
apartment for themselves. In case of illness Quandt left twenty
thousand marks. In addition she continued to have free use of

Quandt's farm at Severin in Mecklenburg, which consisted of about a thousand acres and which was administrated by Quandt's brother-in-law, Granzow. Quandt had previously invested a large amount of money in the farm to ensure a livelihood for his partially-sighted son, Herbert (although this later proved unnecessary). The farmhouse itself was carefully renovated and enlarged, and furnished with lovely old furniture from Quandt's inheritance. The permission to use this farm as she saw fit was another generous gesture towards Magda, who loved to go there. The divorce was by now only a matter of form, a 'gentleman's agreement', and afterwards Quandt sent flowers and took Magda to Horcher, Berlin's smartest restaurant.[14]

Now Magda was free. Her relationship with Quandt was friendlier than it had ever been before, and Harald was now in stable contact with his father.

From one day to the next Magda had won every opportunity to shape her life as independently as it was possible for a woman to do at this time: she was young, healthy and pretty, she spoke several languages, she was intelligent, well-travelled and open-minded. Her life with Quandt had brought her into contact with the upper middle-class, and she had mixed with people from all over the world. But although she had her son with her, she still felt a great void within her. Clearly, she had no pronounced interests or passions to which she could devote herself.

Chapter 13

On 24 October 1929, a few months after Magda's divorce, the stock market crashed on Wall Street. The economic earthquake, whose tremors reached the old continent, shook Europe to its foundations. Germany had made a relatively confident economic recovery, but now the collapse of the stock exchange led to mass unemployment, and intensified discontent among right-wing and left-wing political parties, which had never been able to reach an accommodation with the western-style democratic government of the Weimar Republic.

So the twenties in Germany came to an end in a mood of deep dissatisfaction, with arguments, anxiety and a profound loss of orientation. Only in retrospect would they become the 'golden twenties', and the myth of Weimar culture only came into being once most of the intellectuals who gave the twenties their glitter and brilliance had been driven into exile, carted off to prison or simply killed.

If we talk about the myth of that time, and its unprecedented intellectual richness, we must understand that it was born out of the neurotic sense of insecurity and rootlessness that permeated post-war intellectual and political life after the war. The constant quest for something radically new was based on a deep suspicion of the past, and found expression in an explosion of new ideas and experiments, although these never really captured the public imagination in their own time. The culture of the period remained the preserve of an intellectual elite, and was played out chiefly in a small layer of writers, painters, musicians, thinkers, philosophers and researchers – somewhere between the cultured bourgeoisie and bohemianism.[1] The representatives of this elite were not popular, because they also took issue with the deceitfulness of past ages, and saw through the hollowness and megalomania of rising nationalism. They tried, with new aesthetic and scientific theories – Arnold Schönberg in music, Walter Gropius in architecture, Wittgenstein in philosophy, Kafka, Musil and Broch in literature, Sigmund Freud in psychoanalysis and Albert Einstein in physics – to establish new standards and values. These names stand like milestones in the culture and science of this century. They were not popular in their own time, because the ideas associated with them shattered the final certainties of a society that was already destabilised and insecure.

The intellectual and cultural posture of this elite, which called the old values into question, was formed by the experiences of the First World War. Kurt Tucholsky wrote 'militantly' pacifist texts for cabaret, Brecht and Weill's *Threepenny Opera* hacked away at the relationships of a corrupt contemporary society, and Erwin Piscator produced political theatre by updating the classics. Most representatives of the critical, 'left-wing' cultural scene were city dwellers. The culture was largely Berlin-based, and many of its chief participants were Jewish intellectuals. In the wider population, on the other hand, the gap which had opened up between the artistic avant garde and the aesthetics of the nineteenth century grew ever deeper. The First World War, with its intellectual disruptions, had reopened this gap, and it now seemed barely bridgeable.[2]

On the other side of the divide, in the right-wing camp, the experience of the war was the focus of the present – although in the opposite sense. Here, war was not seen as a site of horror and inhumanity, but as a *Stahlgewitter*, a 'storm of steel', in which the new man was to be forged from blood and iron. Ernst Jünger was the head of this movement, writing: 'Nowhere will we stand where the tongue of flame has not broken a path for us, where the flamethrower has not wrought its great cleansing through the void . . . We are sons of warriors and soldiers, and only once all this, this dumbshow of circles revolving in the void, has been swept away, only then will we see unfolding that part of nature that still dwells within us, that which is elemental, true wildness, the capacity for authentic procreation with blood and semen. Only then will the possibility of new forms be created.'[3]

What was appearing was the concept of an archaic, violent life which, in these anti-democratic pamphlets, was placed in opposition to the subversive, dissecting intellect. There is something intoxicating, Dionysian about life, it is secure against any form of criticism because rational analysis would only weaken life. Ernst Jünger's younger brother, Friedrich Georg Jünger, wrote: 'Life is not unrestricted mind-play. It is rigidly bound . . . it is above all a matter of the blood, a component of a community of blood, in whose life-core it participates . . .'

If one understands the connection between 'blood and life' in the sense meant by the brothers Jünger, the next logical step is National Socialism. Friedrich Jünger continues: 'National Socialism has something intoxicating, a wild, blood-kin pride, a heroic and powerful feeling of life. It has no critical, analytical tendencies. It does not want tolerance, because life does not know tolerance. It is fanatical, because everything related to the blood is fanatical and unjust.'[4]

With this attitude a return to old Teutonic values is undertaken, it is as though the Enlightenment never happened. There are echoes of Wotan and the Nibelungs, and in the work of F.G. Jünger the rather nebulous-sounding betrayal of the blood as life's most sacred fluid becomes a betrayal of life *per se*.[5]

In this charged atmosphere, nourished by language that is filled with references to blood and soil, using unambiguous images to manipulate a torn society whose confidence had been badly shaken, the complex structure of the Weimar Republic meant that it could only keep hold of those people who were consciously and sophisticatedly engaged with it. Where the rest were concerned, everything cried out for revenge, for reparation, the re-establishment of the wounded feeling of self-worth through a new, dynamic nationalism. So literary outpourings like those of the brothers Jünger prepared the soil for Hitler and his rising National Socialist Party. And Hitler knew very well how to make use of that.

By now Goebbels had not only achieved journalistic success in the party newspaper of the right-wing *Völkische Freiheit* splinter party, but also excelled himself as a speech-maker. If he at first struck his audience as comical, almost ridiculous, with his small stature and large head, he soon learned to cast a spell, as Guido Knopp describes:

The strangely fascinating sound of his voice, which could cut through the noisiest hubbub, the formulations, keen and precise, which could be understood by every last party member, the untrammelled aggression and the biting wit made the auditorium fall silent in devotion. He himself remained completely cold, paying careful attention to every reaction. With unerring instinct he found the turns of phrase that caught his listeners' nerves at exactly the right moment. Flattering, searing, radiant, melancholy by turns, he drew from his repertoire the tones that best matched the mood in the hall. He won his greatest accolades when he drenched his opponents in cutting sarcasm. Every speech was an enormous task for him, he would finally totter from the podium, hoarse, exhausted and drenched in sweat, with the applause of the masses behind him.[6]

In 1924, when Hitler was in prison and the Nazi Party was in temporary stagnation, Goebbels put his talent as an orator at the disposal of the competition, the equally right-wing and national-istic '*Völkische Freiheitspartei*'. For this he drew a feeble monthly income of one hundred marks.

Hitler's right-hand man and party representative, Georg Strasser, was present at one of these speeches, listening to the attacks on Hitler. He recalled that a few months previously this same Goebbels, with his rhetorical talents, had founded various Nazi cells in the Rhineland. After the rally Strasser approached Goebbels and suggested that he would be better off working with the NSDAP, and promised to raise his meagre income. Without much hesitation, Goebbels switched sides. At Christmas 1924, when Hitler was pardoned and released from prison, he temporar-ily offered his services to the party once again – replacing Strasser's private secretary, Heinrich Himmler – and soon became business leader of the North-Rhineland Gau. Strasser had bought him, it was thanks to Strasser that he could now let loose on the podium, and so he was Strasser's man when conflicts arose between Strasser and the senior members of the Munich party. Strasser and Goebbels represented the party's socialist wing in this conflict, while Hitler drew his support, amongst other things, from the dis-affected former monarchists. Goebbels wrote in his diary on 22 November 1926: 'I no longer fully believe in Hitler', and at a party rally he bellowed into the auditorium: 'I petition that the petty-bourgeois Adolf Hitler be excluded from the National Socialist Party!' It should come as no surprise that Goebbels changed his opinion so easily, if we bear in mind the sentence that he had confided to his diary years before: 'It doesn't matter what you believe, the important thing is belief.'[7]

Now he really did believe, and a short time afterwards, when Goebbels was personally introduced to Hitler for the first time, all the bombastic attacks on the party were forgotten, and he melted away under Hitler's smile. He was his guest for ten days in Munich Central Office. Hitler quickly recognised the talents of the little agitator, and tried to recruit him in his own service. The generous hospitality, the Munich Party's obvious access to funds, Hitler's Mercedes, all of these external factors so convinced Goebbels that he became a real vassal, convinced that the future lay with Hitler.[8] But it was not only externals that impressed him. He felt that he had been recognised by Hitler, and treated like a friend by the 'strong man'. On 17 April he captured the essence of this visit in his diary: 'Adolf Hitler, I love you, because you are both great and simple.' Hitler in turn knew very well that he needed someone like Goebbels, and a little later, in October 1926, he appointed him Gauleiter of the NSDAP in Berlin – not an easy matter, because the capital of the Reich was socialist. Most of the population voted for the Social Democratic Party, whose left wing was particularly active. The NSDAP, on the other hand, consisted only of a few hundred members who barely paid their contributions. Their rallies were more like evenings in the pub than educational soirées, and were held in beer cellars. If enough membership contributions came in, Goebbels received an income of one hundred and fifty marks a month – but that was rarely the case.[9]

A sop, just enough to fight and keep body and soul together, a challenge that could only act as a goad for Goebbels' aggression. The party had no political mandate, but it did have a marked tendency to tear itself apart. With Hitler's complete power behind him, Goebbels separated the different factions and enforced his claim to leadership. But he rapidly understood that he would have to choose different methods if he were to win Berlin: 'Berlin needs sensations as a fish needs water!' he wrote in his diary. 'This city lives off them, and any propaganda that fails to recognise this will miss its target.'[10]

Goebbels acted accordingly. He omitted nothing that could bring in headlines. He moved into the workers' districts, planned his rallies in those areas that were profoundly Communist, and deliberately provoked fights in beer halls and in the street. To this end he used his own troop of Nazi fighters, the *Sturmabteilung*, or SA. The SA was an army within the party, set up on a military model. Its members wore uniforms: the brown shirt, the swastika armband and jackboots. There were badges, belts and shoulder straps. The SA was generally unarmed, since it was Hitler's wish that it should not be a military organisation, but only resorted to force when the National Socialists found themselves in arguments. It protected the party leadership at NSDAP rallies and demonstrations, and its particular task was to cause as much trouble as possible at street demonstrations or fights at rallies. Knopp refers to one particular accompaniment to this: '"In the case of riots in which over four hundred marks in damage has been done, the riot damage law comes into power. I am only mentioning this in passing", the ringleader smugly instructed his fellow brawlers.'[11] Goebbels' SA troop consisted for the most part of heftily-built young men who, frustrated by the politics of the Weimar Republic, whose complexity they had never managed to penetrate, were unable to fit in anywhere, who couldn't find their place in society. For the first time these men felt that someone was suddenly promising them a future, giving them a sense of self-respect and offering them the chance of identification. But for the time being that identification manifested itself only in a fight against a common enemy, in this case the Communist workers.

But the verbal attacks, rabble-rousing propaganda and fights already extended to the other enemies. Even now Goebbels was projecting his hatred and frustrations upon the Jews. Berlin's vice-chief of police, Bernhard Weiss, was selected as a special target for his vituperation and mockery. Weiss embodied the democratic system of values, and introduced an order to ban Goebbels' brown-shirted hordes. Goebbels renamed him 'Isidor', and in the Nazi pamphlet *Der Angriff* he fell victim to his infamous anti-Semitic slanders. The people of Berlin laughed at Goebbels' inventive malice and broad-brushed caricatures. 'Isidor' made Goebbels famous, and the resulting libel trials were of little concern to him – they only brought him greater attention.[12]

But the actual political struggle continued in the street, because it was there that he met the disappointed and the dejected, the constantly growing army of the unemployed which the economic crisis had plunged into poverty, and which now wandered the streets, aimless and rootless. The nerves of the right and left had been laid bare, and political oppositions quickly developed into a series of bloody fights, whose echoes Goebbels then proceeded to use for propaganda purposes. He even bandaged the heads of the front rows of the storm-troopers standing in front of his podium, to point up the courage and fearlessness of his heroes.

Goebbels thought of everything. He set up 'Sturm-Lokale', soup-kitchens for the unemployed stormtroopers. For his injured brawlers he set up an SA hospital in which they could be treated for minor injuries. The hospital was tended by the 'Red Swastika German Women's Order', based on the model of the NS *Frauenschaft*, the Party Women's Association.[13] Even during this phase, the Nazi Party had a rigid organisation, and apart from the NS *Frauenschaft* there was the Hitler Youth, the NS Teachers' League, the NS industrial cell organisation and similar associations. In this way the Party and its ideology were able to enter every area of life, and afford its members a home and a resting place at a time of general collapse, but at the same time it exerted an overall control over the individual, a process that soon came to involve intrigues and denunciations.

Goebbels did everything he could to attract attention. He even used the list of his convictions for libel, disturbance of the peace and similar crimes as election propaganda. The intention was to show that the state and its laws really had no hold over him, that he was, like most people, discontented, but he turned that discontent into provocation, projecting the image that he and his party were a match for the Weimar Republic.

But he was not popular with the other members of the Nazi Party. 'I have few friends in the Party: Hitler is almost the only one. He supports me in everything. He will stand right behind me,' he wrote in his diary.[14] Many members laughed at him for his lack of resemblance to the stereotype of the blond Aryan which he preached as the elite Nordic hero. Because of his small stature and unusually large head, he was described as the 'shrunken Aryan'. But despite all these reservations he managed to build up the Nazi Party within one and a half years to the point of winning fifty thousand votes in the Berlin election. His ambition and vanity were unimpeded by the mockery of others, he continued to despise people as before, but his inner detachment and cynicism allowed him to manipulate them all the more. He did succeed in egging on the bourgeoisie against the 'Reds' so thoroughly that many overcame their reservations about the loud-mouthed and brutal Goebbels, and voted for the Nazi Party rather than risk becoming 'victims' of the Communists. His commitment and hard work during this time were immense, and as a result he was more successful than any other Gauleiter. On 20 May 1928 he was voted in as a Member of Parliament in the German Reichstag. Now he enjoyed immunity, and no longer had any need to fear legal persecution for any of his crimes. So he went on raving, pretending to the masses that he believed in his own message – when in fact all he believed in was the power of propaganda and in Adolf Hitler. Hitler had not failed to notice his success, and showed his gratitude, by appointing the venomous agitator, with his stormtroopers behind him, Reich Propaganda Leader.

Goebbels's worst period of poverty was past, and he was even renting a small apartment in the affluent area of Steglitz, but he remained true to his image. He went on playing the bogey-man to the bourgeoisie and trawled for the votes of the poor by appearing in public in shabby and proletarian clothes.

Chapter 14

After her divorce, Magda rented a tasteful and elegant seven-room apartment at number 3 Reichskanzlerplatz.[1] 'Ernst' had become her official companion, and went with Magda to dances, plays and concerts.[2] She had lost contact with Arlosoroff, who was too busy with disturbances in Palestine and whose thoughts revolved around other problems. Then another admirer of Magda's turned up: the nephew of the future American President, Herbert Hoover, whom she had met on her trip to America with Quandt. When he heard of her divorce, probably in a letter that she had written herself, he returned immediately from New York to Berlin. He was in fact a multi-millionaire, and his fortune dwarfed even that of Quandt. Henriette von Schirach mentioned that the meeting in New York had led to a 'brief and sudden love-affair'[3] (probably when Quandt was away on business), which Hoover now hoped to continue in Berlin. But Magda was cool towards him, and rejected his proposal of marriage. She had not been able to find her place in Quandt's upper-class world, so why should she fare any better in American high society?

The crucial words were uttered when she was spending an evening with Hoover on the terrace of the Wannsee Golf Club.

Hoover was disappointed and hurt by her rejection. They walked to his car in silence. On the way back he was so overwrought that he drove back to Berlin at ridiculous speed.[4] Shortly before the turn-off to the Avus race-track the car spun over onto its roof. Hoover himself was uninjured, but Magda suffered a broken bone and two fractures to the skull, and had to spend several weeks in the Westend Hospital.[5]

After her recovery Magda's life seemed even more stale than before. She no longer felt at home in Berlin's lively cultural scene, because she was worried about the tendency of many avant-garde intellectuals towards Communism, and she did not feel inclined to engage with it nor even to take part in it.[6] On the other hand, in her private life, in her relationship with 'Ernst', she had put herself beyond the bourgeois standards of the older generation. But she did not form a new circle of friends. Her divorce from Quandt was certainly seen as a stain, so that apart from her friendship with her sister-in-law, Ello Quandt, she had few acquaintances left. Her relationship with 'Ernst' was still stable, but for some time Magda had ceased to find fulfilment in it. Nevertheless during the holidays she went to his home, as promised. His family gave her a warm welcome, but she did not stay long. Meissner tells us how 'Ernst' brought her to the train, 'and, at the last moment, when the train was already in motion, he suddenly decided to leap on to the footplate – without a ticket, without a suitcase, and travelled back to Berlin with her . . .'[7]

At the beginning of term, Magda insisted that 'Ernst' should resume his neglected studies. But her own life was as unfulfilled as ever. The latest toy she had bought was a nippy little sports car, an open-top Wanderer,[8] in which she scooted around the area. But where was she to go? She had no purpose. At home a cook and a nanny looked after Harald, her mother Auguste often dropped round, and if 'Ernst' wasn't working the three of them would play Skat. But Auguste was worried. As far as she was concerned 'Ernst' had assumed the role of the head of the household to an excessive extent, and 'often raised his voice and nagged Harald'. Auguste discovered a new characteristic in her daughter: 'Is it nausea? Fatigue?' Auguste was unable to interpret it. She recalled an episode when they were playing Skat together: Magda put down her cards and groaned wearily: 'Oh my dears, how dreary it all is. How can we have more fun? Waiter, a new guest, please!'[9]

Magda was suffering from boredom, she didn't know where to put herself, seemed fed up with her own company and yawned her way through her inactive life. Her life consisted of a feeling of emptiness and frustration. George Steiner uses the word 'ennui' for this kind of boredom, to describe nervous fatigue that arises as the consequence of an unchanging routine 'A kind of marsh-gas of boredom and vacuity thickened at crucial nerve-ends of social and intellectual life . . . To me the most haunting, prophetic outcry of the nineteenth century is Théophile Gautier's *"plutôt la barbarie que l'ennui!"*'[10]

A similarly perverse longing to be jolted from one's state of lethargy by 'a bit of chaos' prevailed among a sector of the German aristocracy in the late 1920s. This desire for new sensations – however barbaric – explains why those circles had such a taste for the Nazi Party, with its upstart Hitler and his agitator Goebbels. This new Party with its brown-shirted men and its crude, coarse manners supplied the requisite frissons and sensations.

Aristocrats sympathetic to the Nazi cause early on included Princess Reuss, the wealthy Viktoria von Dirksen and the Hohenzollern Prince August Wilhelm, known by the nickname Auwi, who – rather to the disappointment of his parents – was a regular companion of Goebbels and was a high-ranking officer in the SA. They were all members of an exclusive club, the 'Nordic Ring', founded in 1909 with a view to establishing a 'new order' in every sphere. In 1926 the 'Nordic Ring',[11] having become a part of the 'Young Nordic League', re-established itself. Its head was Professor Hans F.K. Günther, who was also the publisher of the journals *Rasse* and *Norden*, and who in 1930 was given the chair of Racial Studies at Jena University.

Magda frequented this club.[12] We do not know who introduced her to it, but it was certainly not 'Ernst', and Quandt would probably not have felt at home there either. She must have been welcomed with open arms, since her outward appearance perfectly matched its ideals, and her financial situation allowed her to become a guest of such an elegant club. In addition, Magda must also have been flattered to be courted and, finally, really to belong somewhere, because until this point she had always been something of an outsider. In the Belgian Catholic convent she had been the German girl with the Jewish stepfather; after her flight from Belgium, she had been a 'refugee' at the Protestant Lyzeum in Berlin, and spoken German with a French accent; in the Zionist youth group around Arlosoroff she remained – despite all her efforts to belong – the blonde Schicksa; and to enter high society for Quandt, she was obliged both to drop her stepfather's name and to convert from Catholicism to Protestantism. She had not felt socially elevated in her marriage to Quandt. Only very gradually had she managed to achieve a degree of recognition.

The 'Nordic Ring' was probably the first time that she came into intensive contact with Nazi ideas, since its members, like Frau von Dirksen, were fascinated by Goebbels and actively supported him. In this circle Goebbels' spectacular performances were the talk of the town, especially his propaganda masterpiece, the funeral that he arranged for Horst Wessel, and which made the twenty-three-year-old brownshirt the greatest martyr of the Nazi movement. Horst Wessel lost his life in a pimps' shootout, and Goebbels turned him into a beacon among men: 'One must become an example and sacrifice oneself,' he declaimed at the open grave.[13] He took a piece of doggerel written by Horst Wessel and turned it into a hymn which would later be part of the regular fixtures of the Third Reich. Not only did the image of this very insignificant young man chime very well with Goebbels' dramatisation, but it gave the 'Nordic Ring' material for lengthy debates in which Horst Wessel was placed on a par with the Teutonic hero Siegfried, who was also murdered in an ambush in the saga.

But for the time being Magda was only a passive guest in this circle which preached Nordic superiority – and she was still bored. Auguste gives us a description of an evening in the 'Nordic Ring', which Magda clearly told her about afterwards. It was an evening that was to have serious consequences for her.

Yet again Magda complained, after consuming considerable quantities of alcohol, that she could no longer bear it, that she was afraid she was going mad, that her life repelled her and that she thought she was going to die of boredom. On this particular evening Prince Auwi was sitting at Princess Reuss' table. His narrow Hohenzollern head was tilted back slightly and, flattered, he squinted through his cigarette smoke at the excitedly chattering ladies. For a long time he had had the impression that the people around this chap Hitler were slowly becoming acceptable. For that reason he had joined them . . . Now he leant forward to Magda with a winning smile: 'Bored, my dear? – Let me make a suggestion: Come and join us! Work for the Party. Nothing too strenuous, of course, I beg you! Who would – (more laughter, and an attractive lowering of the head) – demand that so lovely a lady should exhaust herself? Just a little honorary assistance, on the side, so to speak. Time will pass, and with it so will boredom . . .' Magda had heard similar suggestions made to other friends. Now she clutched it as a drowning man clutches a straw.[14]

The first thing she did was to attend an election rally in the Palace of Sport, to give herself an idea of the Nazi programme and this fabulous orator. This kind of populist mass-meeting was not actually to her taste: neither was the choral speaking nor the noisy bands nor the garish red posters with their swastikas and exhortatory slogans, stuck to the walls of houses, to fences and even trees. For days Magda had noticed that in the wake of the election campaigns announcements were made in open squares, where thousands of torch-bearing SA men provided ghostly illumination.

She now went along, as though attending a large spectacle, although she was not really sure what she was expecting. She sat down among thousands of people whose language was generally crude and uneducated, people who smelled of sweat and leapt fanatically to their feet when Hitler's leather-jacketed agitator passed, limping slightly with one foot, through a guard of honour made up of stiff-backed brown-shirted men, and made his way to the podium. Viktor Reimann gives a vivid account of the situation:

> The crowd that has risen from its seats shouts and yells
> with enthusiasm, and then the man with the hard features
> begins to speak on the podium. He starts very quietly so
> that a very great silence falls in the auditorium. But then a
> torrent of accusations flows from him, with trembling voice
> he accuses everyone, the November criminals, the enemies
> of the people, Jewish capitalists and the bosses who keep
> the honest Germans in the strangle-hold of 'the politics of
> appeasement'. His eyes glow, and his long, nervous hands
> drum along with these dissonant phrases of irony and
> sarcasm, accusation and condemnation. But all of a sudden
> the voice changes again, this time sounding warm and
> beautiful and as full as an organ: Goebbels is speaking of
> Adolf Hitler, the man who will save the German people
> from its misery, who will lead them into the coming Reich
> of German splendour.'[15]

Magda was fascinated, as if in a trance she followed the speech of the voluble and badly dressed man. Like most people in the auditorium she was swept off her feet, although not so much by the content as by the manner and form of his oratory.[16]

His voice and the intensity that he radiated had an almost erotic effect on Magda, and cast their spell over her. Commitment to the Party also promised her release from her unreal existence.

The next day she resolved to become a Party member. The

part of the city where she lived, Berlin–Westend, had only a very small local Nazi group, consisting mostly of concierges and small employees working in the area's grocery shops. Magda was viewed with suspicion, but the membership officer gave her a warm welcome, since it showed him that the Party was beginning to move in more elegant circles. In order to stress the importance of her membership, he immediately offered her the management of the NS women's committee of the Westend local group. Magda accepted this, and seriously devoted herself to the movement. She bought Hitler's *Mein Kampf*, read it from cover to cover, and then studied the writings of Alfred Rosenberg. Despite his name Rosenberg was not Jewish, but one of the Nazis' chief ideologists, who had founded the 'Kampfbund für Deutsche Kultur' in 1928. Magda bought a copy of a Nazi newspaper, read letters about training and followed Adolf Hitler's speeches in the press. She even studied the Party programme that the membership secretary had given her.[17]

But Magda's practical commitment to her new beliefs created difficulties. In her work for the Party the other women in her local group responded to her with suspicion and envy. Her commitment was too incredible, her way of life too strange, and if Magda delivered a lecture, the women sat suspiciously in their chairs and pulled faces about her elegance and her smart appearance. Apart from this, rumours about her broken marriage to the millionaire Quandt and her relationship with her young lover were circulating, leading Magda to withdraw in disappointment from her first official post, and look for another honorary position within the Party.[18]

In September the Reichstag election campaign reached its zenith. Goebbels had led a campaign unlike anything the other parties had even dreamed of: he organised six thousand mass rallies throughout the whole of the Reich. Along with the German Nationalists, the NSDAP tried to exploit the mood of despair that had emerged among the people as the result of rising unemployment. Goebbels delivered polemics against reparation payments and roused anxieties about Bolshevism. With anti-Semitic slogans he railed against the Versailles Treaty. The legal cases against him for insult and slander he turned to his favour, and the unimaginable happened: one of the smallest parties became the second strongest party in the German Reichstag. Goebbels captured his own enthusiastic mood in his diary entry for 15 September 1930: 'Voted in the morning. SA units drove away. Many wounded. Long negotiations with police. I'm getting our prisoners out. The first election results. Fantastic. Palace of Sport full to capacity. The bourgeois parties are shattered. We have 103 mandates so far. The Palace of Sport is like a madhouse. The SA carries me through the auditorium on its shoulders.'[19]

After this unexpected Nazi victory Magda was drawn towards the man who had brought it all about, and whose passionate speech had so carried her away. After all, she was Frau Quandt, and she was well enough qualified not to waste her time with common doorkeepers' wives. So she went to the Nazi Gauleitung in the Hedemannstrasse, to offer her services, because it was here that the 'conqueror' of Berlin had his base. She was given a warm welcome, her knowledge of languages was noted, and ten days later she was given the post of secretary to the deputy Gauleiter.[20]

Now she was sitting in Central Office, and a power struggle was taking place before her eyes – but so were the attempts of some Germans to ensure that power did not fall into the hands of the loud-mouthed seducers. In October 1930 Thomas Mann delivered a thought-provoking speech, which he called 'German address: an appeal to reason.' In this speech Mann warned of the danger of National Socialism and stressed that the place of the bourgeoisie, politically speaking, was on the side of the Social Democrats. Right-wingers disturbed the meeting, but Thomas Mann was able to finish his speech.

Chapter 15

The headquarters of the Nazi Party in Hedemannstrasse looked more like a fortress than an administrative building. SA brownshirts guarded the entrances and exits, and visitors were led through closed and secured rooms to the people they wanted to talk to.

Magda had found her niche in the newspaper archive. She spotted articles and cut them out, and was able to assess foreign press reports about the NSDAP thanks to her knowledge of languages. So it was that the ex-wife of the millionaire Quandt, to the delight and amazement of Brownshirt HQ, was able to spend a few weeks working as cheap office labour. But she did so without coming any closer to the one man who, as her mother would later relate, attracted her as a woman and whom she very much wanted to meet.

However, early in November 1930, when she was going down the stairs of the Gauleitung at the end of the day, she bumped into the trench-coated 'Doktor', dragging one foot behind him, and his adjutant, Count Schimmelmann. Auguste records in her memoirs what Magda told her about this encounter at the time:

They glanced into each others' eyes for only a moment, and, ludicrous though it may sound, for that fraction of a second the spark ignited for both of them. Goebbels stopped dead in amazement while Magda walked to the exit. 'Donnerwetter, Schimmelmann,' he said, a trace of breathlessness in his voice, 'Who was that? An amazing woman!' and then climbed the stairs to his bare study. Five minutes later Goebbels knew that this jewel was working in the gem-free setting of his office. The next morning he called Magda. 'I need someone unimpeachably reliable, someone I can trust,' he told her. 'You must build me a secret archive.' Not a word of sympathy, no compliments, barely a personal remark. Only his eyes seemed to embrace Magda. 'I thought I would burst into flames beneath that purposeful gaze,' she told me much later. But by then she knew from his own lips that he had fallen in love with her at first sight. And the same was true of Magda.[1]

For a while Goebbels pretended to be uninvolved, as though he had only given the young woman an important confidential task because of her linguistic skills. She makes her first appearance in his diary entry for 7 November 1930. 'A beautiful woman by the name of Quandt is setting up a private archive for me.'[2] Magda, who at first found it hard to imagine this private archive, learned very quickly how important it was to Joseph Goebbels. It was here that he stored all the information about the NSDAP, about Hitler, and above all about himself. In this way he was able to manipulate the image of the Party both at home and abroad as he saw fit, and at the same time to exploit dark areas in the earlier life of his Party members. When Magda asked him why he didn't make this information available to the Party, he answered, 'You have a lot to learn, my dear, politics isn't like anything else. Knowledge is power, but not for the kind of people who save up their knowledge for the appropriate opportunity, and, if that opportunity doesn't turn up, make nothing of it at all.'[3]

In fact this archive was to become the crucial source for all of Goebbels' strategies. Any criticism from abroad was immediately at his fingertips, he alone knew if anyone had spoken either contemptuously or positively about the NSDAP, and where and when they had done so, and he alone knew how to respond. Magda experienced her boss's lies and manipulations at first hand. In the secret central office, she became his accomplice in his struggles and his bid for power.

A few weeks after the start of her new employment she was shown how her boss was capable of staging a political scandal and notching up one more success as a result. When, on 5 December 1930, the anti-war film *All Quiet on the Western Front*, based on the novel by Erich Maria Remarque, was shown on Nollendorfplatz, Goebbels ensured that the performance was disrupted shortly before it was due to start. He had distributed his own people all around the auditorium, to startle the rest of the audience with stink-bombs and white mice. Such was the confusion that the performance was halted. The next day the event was reported in *Der Angriff*. Over the following five evenings Goebbels repeatedly organised the SA and his party members. Thousands of people marched around the cinema, growling and roaring, 'Hitler is at the gates!' so that by the end no one dared enter the building. On 11 December 1930, by putting pressure on Nazi judges, Goebbels managed to have the film officially banned for damaging the image of Germany.[4]

Of course Magda read Goebbels's newspaper, *Der Angriff*, which now appeared every day, and in which he unleashed his sarcastic and aggressive hate-filled tirades against the Republic and above all against the Jews. So the reactions to an article by Goebbels published on 15 April 1929 could not have escaped her, particularly since the article had a legal coda. In the article Goebbels focused his attention on the unexplained death of a little boy in Bamberg. His paper expressed the opinion that one might be following a useful line of enquiry 'if we also asked the question: which religious community in Germany has for centuries been suspected of harbouring fanatics who use the blood of Christian children for ritual purposes?'[5] Clearly Magda did not object to this notorious article. Goebbels' underhand tactics didn't give her the slightest pause.

Her young friend 'Ernst', on the other hand, was distressed by her new employment. Behind Magda's admiration for her boss's flamboyant speeches, his fearless participation in beer-hall fights and so on, the young man rightly suspected that Goebbels was exerting a personal fascination on Magda, but it never occurred to him that the proletarian agitator might be of more than passing importance. 'Ernst' came from a haute-bourgeois family, he was more interested in the arts than in politics, and was to some extent reassured when Magda told him 'he was mad to think any such thing, she could never fall in love with Goebbels.'[6]

For the time being Goebbels went on acting the part of the impersonal employer, constantly on the move for the NSDAP cause. The second diary entry to mention Magda dates from 14 November 1930: 'Yesterday afternoon the lovely Frau Quandt was in my office and helped me to sort out some photographs. From the earliest days of the movement . . .'[7]

At this point, however, there were several other ladies in the Gauleiter's life: his secretary Ilse Stahl, for example, who helped out with proof-reading in the evening and stayed until six o'clock the next morning, 'a wonderful, kind, beautiful, affectionate girl. And still a virgin,'[8] or Olly Förster, the fiancée of his friend Arnolt Bronnen, a little actress determined to seduce Goebbels before her marriage to Bronnen – and Goebbels put up no resistance.

It is always difficult to imagine Goebbels as a man who exerted an erotic attraction on women, Goebbels with his small, frail, slightly crooked body, his big head with its sharp nose, with the wrinkles around his thin-lipped mouth. And he also dressed too shabbily. But Magda was disturbed neither by his appearance nor by his scruffy clothes. 'According to the memories of her sister-in-law Ello, she developed a kind of mothering, caring complex for her boss, she thought the poor man was so badly dressed because no woman cared for him as he really needed to be looked after, with his stressful life.'[9] Goebbels' addiction to work and energy were fascinating, however, and of course he expected his employees to keep the same long working-hours as he did himself. His elegant Frau Quandt, from the world of the haute-bourgeoisie, was treated no differently, so Magda often stayed until late at night. Goebbels very quickly understood that this spoiled woman was looking for something, some content to her life, to give a meaning to her empty existence, and he knew he would be able to arouse her interest by being somewhat brittle in his dealings with her. His tactic seems to have been successful. The mixture of political fanaticism, obsession with work and personal *froideur* did attract Magda, and Goebbels, who perceived her growing interest in him as a person, gained in confidence in the presence of this woman who had fascinated him from the start, but who had deeply unsettled him with her social background.

Outside her work for her new boss Magda's life had barely changed. She still maintained friendly contact with her ex-husband, but her devotion to the vulgar agitator and his party met with enormous resistance on the part of Quandt. Meissner quotes from his memoirs: ' "On my subsequent visits it struck me," regrets Günther Quandt, "that Magda was becoming an increasingly eager propagandist for the new cause, and that she was wholeheartedly behind it. At first I took this for devotion to Dr Goebbels' rhetorical gifts. But when each time I saw her she could talk of nothing else, and no arguments could distract her from it, I cut back my visits.'[10]

But for the time being nothing happened between Magda and Goebbels. When Quandt lay ill in Florence in 1930, Magda travelled to see him with their son Harald, and enjoyed Quandt's generosity during their subsequent holidays in St Moritz[11] – not the destination one might have expected for a Nazi archivist.

In February life became turbulent for Magda's boss. Goebbels' attacks on Berlin's chief of police were accumulating, and there were vituperative exchanges in the Reichstag. Goebbels did everything he could to provoke the government and ensure that the NSDAP was talked about, with interventions that were often vulgar in the extreme. Magda was not put off by this, if anything, in fact, it seemed to bring her closer to Goebbels. Thus we read in Goebbels' diary for 15 February: 'Magda Quandt comes in the evening. And stays for a very long time. And blossoms with heady blonde sweetness. How can I describe you, my queen? (1) A lovely, lovely woman! Whom I shall love very much. Today I am walking almost as though in a dream. So full of sated bliss. It is wonderful to love a beautiful woman, and to be loved by her . . .'[12]

With this entry from Goebbels' diary, his relationship with Magda appears to have begun – and that bracketed number 1 seems to suggest that it was already sexual. For the time being, however, their liaisons did not move outside the apartment in Steglitz: in Reichskanzlerplatz there was still the problem of 'Ernst'. With these parenthetical numbers Goebbels reveals himself as a would-be Don Juan, and one with rather schoolboyish tendencies.

Magda was deeply in love, she seemed to be transformed, seeing only Goebbels' rise and paying no heed to Quandt or 'Ernst' or to her mother, of whom Goebbels was not particularly fond.

The successes of the NSDAP were – thanks to Goebbels – beyond dispute, but some critical voices remained, since it was by no means yet the case that the entire German population stood behind Goebbels and Hitler. The Berlin daily press, the 'gutter press' as Goebbels called it with injured vanity, was still first and foremost Social Democratic, and the heart of most journalists beat on the left. One of the important voices, Bella Fromm, for example, wrote for the society pages of the *Vossische Zeitung* and the *Berliner Zeitung am Mittag*. She followed political developments in the diplomatic salons, had accreditation with all the foreign embassies and enjoyed their protection. As a Jew, she was a red rag to Goebbels. In 1938, by which time she had, thanks to her many contacts, acquired an exit visa, she was able to emigrate at the very last minute. Along with the published articles in her newspaper, in which – after the Nazi seizure of power – she had to adapt herself to the new regime, she took her private diary with her. It was published in New York in 1943, five years after her flight, and reflects her personal impressions and the critical stance she had maintained from the beginning. Thus she notes, on 14 October 1930 (at around the time when Magda joined the NSDAP):

At the new elections in September, one hundred and seven National Socialists obtained seats in the Reichstag. There's a touch of panic in certain quarters. Should one leave Germany and wait outside to see what will happen? Surprising how many people feel that it might be the prudent thing to do.

A handful of noisy roughnecks! They made their appearance in the chamber clad in brown, giving the Hitler salute. They shouted in chorus: 'Germany, awake!' On their way to the Reichstag they celebrated their victory by an attack on several department stores. Twenty of the delegates chose bright daylight to assault the windows of stores in Leipzigerstrasse. No one saw them. No one caught any of them.

The projectiles, casually aimed, hit only non-Aryan targets, by some odd chance. The street became a mass of splintered glass.

'The Awakening Germany', they call it.[13]

On 10 February, a few days before Magda's first visit to Goebbels' apartment in Steglitz, Bella decided to attend a session in the Reichstag. She describes it in her diary.

'The Doctor', as they call him, almost a dwarf, hobbled to the speaker's desk. But before he did so the Communists had indulged in a veritable flood of invective. Apparently that was just what he needed to start him right. You have to be impressed by the way he uses the German language,

whether you like him or not. A kind of combination of
Mephisto and Savonarola, sinister and frantic, intriguing
and fanatically obsessed. He uses his hands violently
enough for Yvonne to remark, 'Funny way of speaking for a
full-blooded Aryan.' But his voice is soft enough, and he
knows how to make the most effective use of it . . . He has
managed to snatch the wealthy industrialist Gunther
Quandt's beautiful wife right out from under her husband's
nose.

He was outright rude to the Chancellor of the Reich,
blaming him for everything. I admired Dr Bruening's
control. He listened with complete calm. Another man
might have hit the raging dwarf right across his big mouth.
But the Chancellor maintained an aloof superiority, as
though he would not contaminate himself by any possible
contact with such a dirty creature.[14]

The 'raging dwarf' was still operating in top gear. His diary
entries are almost manic, as when he talks about his SA-men carrying him on their shoulders, or people prostrating themselves
enthusiastically at his feet ('even kings have not been celebrated
so.' 21 February 1931).[15] By now the name of Magda Quandt was
making regular appearances in his diaries. On 23 February Magda
accompanied him to an election event in Weimar. He writes
about his political successes as though in a constant state of
ecstasy, but when he mentions Magda in passing, his tone changes:
'. . . Magda is beatific. Such a beautiful, charming woman . . . I sit
alone with Magda Quandt until deep in the night. She is a daz-
zlingly beautiful and gracious woman, and she loves me beyond
measure. Magda is beautiful and dreamy. I love her.'[16]

But the first clouds were appearing. On 26 February he mentions his first row with Magda in his diary.[17]

After a supposed assassination attempt on Goebbels, although
it turned out that this was probably staged by the NSDAP for
propaganda purposes, he took Magda to dinner at the Dirksens'.

He notes in his diary: 'Met the pleasant Countess Hoyos. Row and reconciliation with Magda.'[18] Might Magda have been jealous, and noticed for the first time that she had taken up with a notorious seducer?

On the following days he wrote: '15 March: yesterday was a day to cherish: . . . and in the evening a visit from dear Magda. I like her very much. Apart from anything because she is so sensible. She has a shrewd sense of life which embraces reality, and a generous way of thinking and acting. A little more training in each other's ways and we will suit each other fabulously. (4, 5) I am going to stop seeing other women and devote myself entirely to her. This afternoon I am going to go for a walk in the Zoo with Magda. It is a wonderful spring day. In spite of everything: life is lovely, my Queen!'[19]

While his relationship with Magda was developing, the law was creating problems for him. He was forbidden to deliver speeches: at an election rally in Königsberg Prince Auwi and Heydrich had to address twelve thousand people in his place, but when the event was over he was carried shoulder high in the procession once more. Then, at the station, the police unexpectedly intervened, and truncheons rained down on Goebbels and Auwi. In Berlin, Magda was ready to tend his wounds and comfort him. '22 March . . . Magda came in the evening. Lovely and sweet and radiant. I love her very much. (6, 7) Bad-tempered letters from Hella Koch and Erika Chelius . . . Now I love one woman alone.'[20]

With the decision to love Magda and no one else, we see an end to the bracketed numbers in the diary, probably representing sexual encounters, and we may assume that they become a natural part of the relationship. For the time being Goebbels urgently had to devote himself to other problems, because there were power struggles within the Party. Part of the SA was disaffected and wanted to break away. Goebbels travelled to Munich, visited Hitler and discussed the problems between his SA and Party Central Office. At the same time news came from Berlin that the government was defending itself with 'draconian' emergency measures introduced by Hindenburg against the NSDAP and its marches and rallies. As regards discord within the Nazi Party itself, Hitler's position was briefly placed in jeopardy when it was considered that the Munich section was getting above itself, and Goebbels was being put forward as a new Führer by the SA.

The Berlin SA was so disaffected because it felt neglected. Its fighters always had to do the dirty work, but within the political Party organisation they lacked both influence and money. They demanded a larger share of the lucrative parliamentary mandates, lower membership contributions and various forms of subsidy. They also felt unsettled by the increasing amount of competition and spying on the part of the SS. The political leaders of the NSDAP involved themselves in the internal matters of the SA, and saw to it that the relationship between the SA and the Party leadership became increasingly strained.[21] But Goebbels resisted the temptation to place himself at the head of an East German revolt, and sided with Hitler. Magda stood by him during these turbulent days. Then he fell ill, with a forty-degree fever. Magda left, but called him the next day, very concerned, from the Severin farm. Goebbels returned to Berlin as well, his fever returned, and old Frau von Dirksen tended to him 'like a mother'. By now Magda was in Berlin, but this time she didn't come to see him – she didn't even phone. He makes a point of noting this in his diary, and speaks of 'insane jealousy'.[22]

Chapter 16

Magda wearily opened the door to her apartment. The warmth, the familiar smell of her own world enveloped her. It was quiet, because the maid and the cook were still out for Sunday evening. Magda had returned from Severin, where Harald was to spend the rest of the week with his father and his half-brother Herbert. They had had the usual discussions, which Magda so hated. It was still hard for her to present her own arguments with the necessary confidence – particularly to Quandt. He was not pleased with her political influence on the boys. The day before, her mother had levelled the same accusations.

Magda went into the bathroom and let the hot water run into the tub. The sound was pleasingly even, relaxing. The mirror covered over with condensation, and when she looked into it she could only vaguely discern the contours of her face. That autumn she would be thirty years old. Her financial situation was secure, but what about the rest of her life? The years behind her were lively, elusive . . . and what about now? As she slid into the bathtub she remembered her discussion with Quandt. He had been criticising Hitler's ideas again, on economic grounds, and was in no way prepared to make a donation to the Party. Couldn't he see that he too was threatened by the Communists? She felt his assessment of Goebbels was unjust. So far Quandt had responded to none of her suggestions, and nor did he show any interest in seeing Goebbels at any of his events to be convinced of the uniqueness of his abilities, nor did he want to meet him privately. Certainly, in a crowd Goebbels was often rough-hewn and even vulgar. But in private he could be quite different. He alone gave her the feeling of being a queen. She admired his courage, his persistence, and by his side she was always experiencing new things. He was absolutely sure of his goal, and he was successful, people hailed him, carried him on their shoulders, leapt from their chairs with enthusiasm when he spoke – she had seen it herself, and now she was able to join in.

As she rose from the water she had little time to get herself ready. 'Ernst' wanted to come by that evening. He was forever complaining that she didn't have enough time for him. She carefully applied her makeup and put on an elegant afternoon dress. She just had enough time to light a cigarette when he rang the doorbell. As he walked into the room Magda immediately saw the mood he was in. He was annoyed, jealous, about to hurl recriminations at her. He began to remind her of their first, romantic time together, when they had been in love, and announced that she had changed for the worse, and when he went on to scorn her work in Party Central Office with the nasty little dwarf, Magda refused to rise to the bait. She hated sentimentality in others, and told him brutally that it was over between them. He couldn't imagine her preferring a man like Goebbels, but Magda remained cool and objective. He said not another word. The next day he begged Magda for one last chance to talk, and said he had a few things he wanted to collect from the apartment.

When 'Ernst' entered the apartment, he silently drew a revolver and aimed it at Magda. When she didn't move, he fired. The bullet hit the door-frame next to Magda, but she showed no emotional reaction. Instead she told him to his face that she despised that kind of nonsense, and found him merely ridiculous. From the next room she called the police, who soon appeared. 'Ernst', who had to discharge his fury and frustration somehow or other, smashed Magda's china. He was taken away by the officers, to spend the night in jail. When Magda was alone she called his father to tell him that he must attend to his son, who had clearly lost his head. His father immediately set off for Berlin on the night train, and collected his son from jail the following morning.[1]

Despite Magda's cool and collected mastery of the unexpected situation, she was so agitated that she did not immediately call Goebbels, who was still unwell and waiting for her call. Another day passed, and then Goebbels managed to contact her and drove with her to a quiet house in the forest. There Magda tearfully poured her heart out and told him that she had had to endure terrible things from her relatives and her mad lover.[2] They made an arrangement to meet the next day, but Magda pulled out of it again. By the time he came to defend himself in two trials, he was still ill and 'dog tired'. Magda sent a telegram to say she had gone to Dresden, and planned to spend an extra day there. She didn't come back to comfort him and he waited in vain. When they finally did meet up on 17 April, he was suspicious, and complained that her former lover was still coming between them. They had a vicious argument; Goebbels tried to blackmail her into spending Saturday with him instead of saying farewell to her former boyfriend. Magda wept, but refused to agree. In desperation Goebbels confided to his diary that he had resolved – in spite of his love – to end the relationship. His pride could not tolerate a rival.[3]

Throughout these days the court in Berlin-Schöneberg was hauling him over the coals for his constant polemical agitation and his direct calls to racial hatred in *Angriff*. Self-pitying, without the slightest desire to accept responsibility for his inflammatory behaviour, he complained in his diary about the fines he had to pay. But he was more tormented by his insecurity about Magda. They met for a talk in the Kaiserhof, but Magda would not show her true feelings. She kept him at arm's length, she could not deny that there was another, and Goebbels' vanity suffered from the fact that she did not love him alone.[45]

We don't know the reasons for Magda's behaviour. Perhaps she was hesitating before entrusting herself to this obsessive and unscrupulous man, having realised that by making such a decision she would be drawing a line under her earlier relationships. According to Meissner's notes, 'Ernst' had left long ago, surviving the break-up. We might wonder whether there was yet another man in her life, someone she had to see even at the risk of separating from Goebbels. Might Arlosoroff have been in Berlin? Or had 'Ernst' come back after all? It was surprising that 'Ernst', a student, should have thrown Goebbels into such a state, and remarkable that in all his desperation Goebbels didn't dare to drop in on Magda at the Reichskanlerplatz, but waited as though paralysed for her to call again.

His desperation continued. The 20 April was Hitler's birthday, but Magda remained the focus of his diary entries. He had called her a hundred times and failed to reach her, he waited and waited, and it was all 'terribly painful'. But as it was the Führer's birthday he had to go to the Palace of Sport, where the whole of the Berlin SA was marching, to congratulate Hitler. He tried to contact Magda again that evening, successfully this time. They first met in a dark street, and then she invited him to her apartment for the first time.[6]

A new phase in the relationship now began. Goebbels was in and out of the Reichskanzlerplatz, and for the first time he made plans for the future with this 'lovely, sweet woman', while at the same time she 'poured her heart out, with all its emotional inferno'.[7]

When he was back in Munich for a discussion in Party Central Office, he was arrested at dinner in the Rosengarten and brought back to Berlin under police guard in a sleeping-car. The press and photographers waiting for him at the station were full of malicious delight. He had missed another of his court appointments. He had to hand in his belongings in Berlin-Moabit, and spent the night in a cell with thieves and pimps. His lawyer managed to ensure that he was temporarily freed the next morning, until the case was heard. When he saw Magda again the next day, she was 'smiling and cheerful and chatty'.[8]

While Goebbels sensed only envy and betrayal around him in the Party, his relationship with Magda was going well. He refers to this in very stereotypical diary entries: '10 May . . . I spend the evening waiting for Magda, who doesn't come until very late. She is full of kindness, love and devotion. How happy I am to have her. Such a woman is eternal sunshine in an otherwise grey succession of days. Today the dear love is celebrating Mother's Day. Mother Magda!'[9]

But for all her 'love and kindness', Magda still preserved her independence for the time being. She was not always there for him, sometimes she made him wait, leaving no explanation. She remained mysteriously silent about her past, about which he would have liked to know a great deal more, and this goaded his jealousy even further. Nonetheless, Magda invited Goebbels to the Quandt farm at Severin for the Whitsun holidays. Goebbels was delighted to go along, but he found the shades of her past there, and they caused him great torment, however much he might have been enjoying himself. His constant shifts of mood are readily apparent in the diary entries dating from his week's holiday. We can identify the quintessence of his feelings and thoughts in the entries for the last two days:

30 May 1931
Magda gives me both joy and torment in ample quantities. She has, I think, done a great deal of living in her life, and suffered a great deal of disappointment – but she has dished it out as well. She must be formed anew. I have been dealt a very unfair hand. *Au fond* she is the best and loveliest woman alive . . . I only hope that everything goes well for us. In Berlin I have my work, and don't start having silly thoughts.

31 May 1931
   Set off this afternoon. Yesterday I had it out with
Magda. Now everything is out in the open. We gave each
other a solemn promise: when we have conquered the
Reich, we will be man and wife.[10]

Germany's situation was becoming ever more precarious. The
economic crisis was throwing international trade into confusion.
In May 1931 one of the largest Austrian banks collapsed, and
Central Europe's financial institutes came under tremendous pressure. In order at least to support the liquidity of the German banks,
President Hoover, predicting a worsening crisis, announced a one-
year interruption of reparation payments. This news was received
with some relief by the Brüning government, but with irritation by
the Nazis, who were hoping for total economic collapse so that it
would be easier to stir up the despair of the masses. But Hoover's
well-intentioned moratorium came too late. The financial crisis
had reached its peak when, on 13 July, the Danatbank (the
Darmstädter Nationalbank, one of the three largest German
banks) was forced to close its doors for want of capital. The other
banks followed its example on government orders, lest all savings
be lost. The Reich government had to intervene and shore up the
Reichsbank with financial and credit reserves.
   In the midst of this extremely difficult situation Reichskanzler
Brüning tried, with the help of the Social Democrats, to rescue
everything that could still be saved from the twin terrors of the
Swastika and the Red Flag. However he was still so dependent on
the aged President Hindenburg that it looked like weakness,
because the myth of the old Field Marshal was being abused by
other powers plotting against Brüning. While Brüning pitied the
old man whose intellectual and physical decay he saw before his
eyes, his loyalty to him remained unbroken. On more than one
occasion his political intentions collided with those of
Hindenburg's son, Oskar, and secretary of state Meissner, the
father of Hans-Otto Meissner, Magda's first biographer, who were

busy pursuing their own interests. But in spite of this disunity, Brüning needed Hindenburg's support, since the point at issue was Article 48 of the constitution of the Weimar Republic. This granted the President, Hindenburg, the right to change or even abolish laws without the consent of parliament. Brüning managed to persuade Hindenburg to use this emergency measure against both the NSDAP and the Communist Party, and thus to put some of his policies into reality. Article 48, originally conceived as a short-term emergency measure, meant that the Chancellor could govern unchecked by the Reichstag, if the Reichstag no longer had clear majorities and was thus incapable of action. For Brüning's political measures it meant salvation, but later it was to lead to the end of the parliamentary system in Germany.

In the meantime, while companies of all sizes were going bankrupt because of their inability to pay their bills, political groups – viewed with concern both at home and abroad – were becoming increasingly radical, and conflict between the SA and the Communists was becoming worse and worse. The government tried to control the growing violence both by banning Goebbels from speaking and by prohibiting the publication of the inflammatory publication *Angriff*, but without a great deal of success.

None of the many court cases that Goebbels had to attend that early summer reached notable convictions – he escaped with a few fines – because the judiciary had also been infiltrated by the National Socialists.

Throughout these weeks Magda stood by him. As a woman in love she was able to put up with Goebbels' irritable mood. His recently developed suspicion of the Party was justified, because he had discovered that Himmler's SS was spying on him. So once again he had a reason to complain to Hitler and receive assurance of his loyalty. Magda accompanied him on his travels whenever she could. She basked in his glories and comforted him during his defeats and his constantly changing moods. As the summer holidays loomed, she rented a house for them in the town of St Peter on the Baltic coast. Her grandmother, Ritschel's mother, with whom Magda clearly maintained some degree of contact, and his secretary were to join them there for a period of relaxation.

Before this planned holiday, according to Goebbels' diary, more problems arose involving Magda's former boyfriend. He turned up unexpectedly in Magda's apartment again, but this time the situation – to Goebbels' satisfaction – was different, because Magda left the apartment. And when the cavalier was still sitting there the next morning, 'he received a blunt talking-to, and the police threw him out'.[11]

So the matter of 'Ernst' seemed finally to have been put to rest, and the summer – political unrest apart – began romantically for Magda and Goebbels. Although the rain lashed the windows and the wind howled around the house all night, they led an idyllic life: they read, chatted, played music and made love, and Goebbels repeatedly stressed in his diary that Magda was a real queen of devotion. She perfectly fulfilled all female roles: she was his beloved, she looked after him like a mother, read proofs in the evening, because he made the best of the bad weather to dictate his book *The Battle for Berlin*. When the weather improved they enjoyed the garden, lying about in the sun and taking long walks on the shore. In the evening they went to the sea and watched the tide rising, 'intoxicatingly wild and impetuous'.[12]

But moods can change just as suddenly as seaside weather. The more Goebbels put Magda on a pedestal, the less well he was able to deal with the other side of her personality, what he called her 'shadow'. By this he meant everything that had happened in her life before she met him, everything that had shaped her and constituted her present personality, but which remained in darkness because she said so little about it. He confided to his diary: '17 July 1931 . . . Severe battles over our happiness with Magda. In her former life she was very frivolous and fancy free. And now both of us must pay for that. Our fate hangs on a silken thread. Pray God that her fate does not destroy us both.'[13]

Goebbels' anxiety seems to have been genuine. Could it really all have been about Quandt and the student 'Ernst'? Might something else not have been involved? What would happen if Hitler learned of Magda's past, of her stepfather Friedländer, of her membership of the Zionist youth group when she was Arlosoroff's girlfriend? Might both their fates not hang on 'a silken thread' if such a thing was to happen? Hitler's anti-Semitism was already fully apparent, and Goebbels constantly ran violent racist attacks in his paper. How could these anxieties be reconciled with his emotions?

When Magda received a critical letter from her father, in which he seemed to be expressing veiled reservations about her association with Goebbels, Goebbels reacted furiously: '24 July 1931 . . . Magda is having terrible trouble with her father who, himself a rogue and a miserable moral hypocrite, is coming over like a schoolmaster. Yesterday his fourth (!) wife, an uneducated creature two years Magda's junior, wrote Magda's grandmother an arrogant letter. That was the final straw. I gave Magda a letter to the old man, which will hardly be to his liking.'[14]

Although Goebbels had now given vent to his annoyance, the day's mood was ruined, because while Magda had obeyed his orders, she took him very subtly to task for his rough treatment of her father. She knew his Achilles heel and provoked a row by telling him something about her past.[15]

In so doing she reawakened his suspicions, and he was consumed by jealousy, his trust for her was shaken to its core.

'She has loved too much, and has only ever told me about it in fragments. And now I lie awake until the early hours, lashed by the whip of jealousy.'[16]

Although Magda tried to calm him down and make plans for the future, jealousy 'sometimes [made him] practically insane.'[17]

We don't know exactly what and how much Magda told him about her past. Some things suggest that she might have mentioned her relationship with Arlosoroff: Goebbels' jealousy for one, and also the fact that her commitment to Victor and the

Zionist movement was well known in Berlin circles, so that she might well have expected Goebbels to come to hear of it by another channel. For good or ill Goebbels was obliged to come to terms with Magda's past, with Arlosoroff's role in her life, and perhaps it was that fact that made him 'insane', because his complaint that she had 'loved too much' can not refer only to Quandt and the student. So, the 'shadow', the 'elusive' aspect of Magda went on tormenting him.

Magda herself remained the loving wife that Goebbels saw in her. She was swept away by his passionate nature, fascinated by his possessive love and his jealousy. Being so important to someone as to have power even over his moods was something utterly new to her. Arlosoroff had pursued his own desires quite independent of her. Quandt saw her more as a kind of ornamental fixture in his tidy house, and even the playful infatuation of her young student could not compare with Goebbels' emotional intensity.

At last she felt loved, desired, necessary. Goebbels needed her, he needed to communicate with her. By allowing her to participate in every area of his work, he was showing her his own path and the destination to which it led. During this period Magda adapted fully to Goebbels' needs, she lived his life. But the relationship left no room for doubt; Magda was obliged to block out some issues that arose, lest she lose her new security and find herself once more on shaky ground.

But one day they had another argument. This time the subject was Goebbels' image of women, and Magda resisted it. She felt injured by his view that woman belonged 'in the kitchen, and with the children'. He writes: '15 August 1931 . . . Heated debate about woman and her duties, or rather her capacities. I was probably too brusque, but only in principle. Magda was so furious she became abusive. We parted in a quarrel. Long, nervous telephone call in the night. Wretchedness.'[18]

Did she, that night, regret that she had given such clear expression to her views? The next day she was determined to sort things out again. She 'dropped by. A shadow had fallen between us.'[19]

Two days later all the disagreements are suppressed: 'played music with Magda at her house. She is my great star.'[20]

The summer passed. Magda abandoned more and more of her own life. Goebbels' phrases had drugged her, as indeed they had drugged a section of the German population.

From the end of August 1931 until 1 January 1934 Goebbels makes no personal entries in his diary. We must refer to other sources.

Chapter 17

In the autumn the time finally came for Magda to be introduced to Hitler, whom she had hitherto only worshipped from afar, but whose ideas she had already made entirely her own.

Hitler had by now moved his headquarters from Party Central Office in Munich to Berlin, to the elegant Hotel Kaiserhof. The reasons for this move were not purely political, although Hitler recognised the importance for Germany of the Central Office in Berlin. They were personal as well. Hitler's niece, Geli Raubal, who lived in his flat in Munich and with whom he was embroiled in an obscure relationship, had taken her own life. Even today some historians agree that this young woman played an important role in Hitler's life, and that this relationship might even supply a key to the explanation of Hitler's complexes and pathological relationships. We know from the accounts of contemporaries that after Geli's death Hitler was profoundly depressed, but even now it has never been fully explained whether Geli might not have known too much about 'Uncle Adolf' and his unusual sexual predilections, and whether for that reason she was rubbed out on Hitler's orders, or whether she really killed herself with Hitler's pistol because she was unable to continue her training as a singer –

with a supposedly Jewish teacher – without Uncle Adolf's permission.[1]

The press dealt with the various versions of this mysterious tale in such a way as to reinforce the aura and hysteria that surrounded Hitler.

One afternoon a few weeks after Geli's death Magda was taking tea in the Hotel Kaiserhof, accompanied by Harald, who was now almost ten years old. Magda had sewn together a miniature version of a Hitler Youth uniform for him, and when she heard that Hitler was on the floor above, she sent her son upstairs. Full of excitement, he pushed his way through to Hitler, who welcomed him warmly. Harald gave the greeting 'Heil Hitler', and introduced himself as the youngest member of the Hitler Youth. Also in the room was Dr Otto Wagener, who recorded detailed notes in his diary of Hitler's meeting with little Harald and, that same afternoon, with Magda, although he did not release them until 1946, in the Officers' Camp at Bridgend in Wales. Three years before the seizure of power Wagener had been a member of Hitler's closest circle. Before taking over the economic department of the Party he was Chief of Staff of the SA. Hermann Göring was then believed to have had him ousted from his role as Reichskommissar for the Economy, and he resigned before Hitler's seizure of power. But even in 1945 his hand-written notes suggest that he had no doubts about Hitler, either as a politician or as a man, and for that reason we may assume that their content is authentic, even if not necessarily recorded verbatim. He noted the course of the meeting with the boy:

'What's your name?' asked Hitler, extending his hand.

'Harald Quandt.'

'How old are you?'

'Ten!'

'Who made you this lovely uniform?'

'My mother.'

'And how do you feel in this uniform?'

At this the boy stood up rather straighter and said, 'Twice as strong!'

Hitler gave me a meaning look and said to me, 'Did you hear that: twice as strong in his uniform!', and to the boy he said, 'I think it's nice that you have come to see me. How did you know I was here?'

'My mother told me.'

'And where is your mother?'

'Down in the café having tea.'

'Then give your mother a nice greeting from me, and do come and see me again.'[2]

Shortly afterwards Goebbels came to tell Hitler he had reserved a corner table for tea at five in the hotel hall. Hitler was unsure whether or not to invite the boy's mother to his table.

Goebbels reassured him, saying that this was the innocently divorced wife of the industrialist Quandt. Hitler was interested in meeting her, and asked Goebbels to reserve a place for Frau Quandt and her son at his table. Hardly had Goebbels left than Göring arrived. When Hitler told him he planned to meet Frau Quandt over tea, Göring warned him of Goebbels' 'Pompadour', and when Hitler asked him whether there was anything wrong with sharing a table with somebody, Göring said no, but did not neglect to add: 'One must take care with a Pompadour.'

Downstairs Hitler invited Magda and her friend to the table reserved for him and his retinue, and Wagener observed:

Frau Quandt made an immediately excellent impression, and this only increased in the course of the conversation. I noticed the pleasure that Hitler took in her gay frivolity. And I also noticed the big eyes she had as she hung on Hitler's words . . .

I had to point out to Hitler that it was time to set off for the opera, so he tore himself away. Nothing particular was arranged, but there was no doubt that a close bond of friendship and respect was beginning to form between Hitler and Frau Quandt.[3]

Later, after the opera, when Wagener was alone with Hitler in the Kaiserhof, Hitler made personal confessions to him, which Wagener traced back to the meeting with Magda. He spoke quite openly to Wagener about the fact that although he had considered himself 'through with the world and with human influences', that day 'divine elements' had touched and enchanted him. He had felt something similar during his solicitous friendship with Geli '. . . but never with other women'. Since her death he had missed that, and believed that 'he had buried those feelings with her coffin. Today,' he explained to Wagener, 'they hold me once again in their thrall, as a complete surprise but with very great force.'[4]

Wagener goes on to say that shortly after midnight Hitler's driver Schaub and other Party members came home rather noisily. '"Where have you been?" asked Hitler. "With Frau Quandt," came the answer. It struck him like a thunderbolt.'[5]

Schaub explains that Magda had invited them to her apartment in Reichskanzlerplatz. When they had been gradually emptying her refrigerator, Goebbels had come home with his own house key, and they had fled. Wagener describes Hitler's reaction:

'He pulled a face and clearly wanted to laugh. But no laugh came. Schaub left, and I took my leave as well. Hitler gave me his hand with some sad words: "I was just a brief relapse. But Providence was kind to me. —"'[6]

It seems that Hitler was so attracted by Magda that, as she later told her mother, he even made cautious advances to her.[7]

A few days after this encounter there was to be a trip to Braunschweig. The day before they set off, Goebbels invited Wagener, Magda and her friend to Braunschweig in his car. Accommodation had been arranged in Braunschweig, and he would be able to sort out the ladies' return journey. Wagener happily concurred. By now Hitler had mentioned Magda several times, while Goebbels had avoided meeting Hitler since their time at the Kaiserhof. The evening before they were due to set off, Hitler spoke of Magda once again.

'"This woman could play an important part in my life, even if I was not married to her. She could play the opposite, female pole to my one-sidedly masculine instincts . . . A shame that she is not married."'[8]

The next day Wagener picked up the two ladies at around dawn, in his big chauffeur-driven Horch car. After they had stopped for a picnic he used the opportunity to take a walk with Magda, to continue a private conversation with her. He pointed out how close he was to Hitler, and how well he knew his difficult nature. He told Magda that only a woman would be able 'to help Hitler the human being make contact with life'.[9] But he went on to say that Hitler refused to marry.

Magda replied that this seemed entirely fair to her, because she could imagine that a wife would only be able to play a very subordinate role in Hitler's life, something like a piece of furniture.

Wagener was delighted that Magda could clearly feel her way so easily into Hitler's psyche, and went on to provide further explanations concerning Hitler's state of mind and sense of mission. He saw people only in terms of their usefulness, obviously not for his own person, but for the future of Germany, which he took to be his vocation. In order not to be exposed to the flatterers, the spineless, who simply parroted what he said to them, he needed someone who could keep his feet on the ground, but only a woman could do that. That woman should accompany him to the theatre, to the opera or to concerts and then drink tea with him at a well-laid table.

Wagener describes how Magda then 'looked at him with wide blue eyes. Her expression was a mixture of love and admiration.' When he said to her, 'And you could be that woman', she glanced to the floor, blushed with embarrassment and replied:

'But then I should have to be married!'

'That's right,' said Wagener, 'ideally to Goebbels.' She already knew Goebbels, Hitler liked him as well, and Goebbels was a respectable chap with whom Magda should and could undertake that difficult task for the benefit of the German people.[10]

Magda promised to think about it.

Magda must have been flattered by her conversation with Wagener. To be selected in this way as a female companion to Hitler would have meant a huge boost in her status, and at the same time given her an unexpected proximity to power and influence. In the course of this conversation she said that for Adolf Hitler she would be prepared to take anything on ('*alles auf sich zu nehmen*'). One wonders what she might have meant. Was it merely a fanatical and unreflecting declaration to stand by the 'respected Führer', to be available in the manner he wished, or did she mean that she was willing to take on board other people's reservations about Hitler? Did she perhaps have unconfessed doubts of her own about the movement, masked by her vanity and the pride that she would soon be standing at the centre of the future power?

The great SA march-past on 17 October 1931 was the spectacle for which Hitler and the Party heads had travelled to Braunschweig. The 'Führer' was demonstrating his personal power with the number of people he was able to draw to a pure display of propaganda. On the Franzsches Feld Hitler consecrated 24 SA standards with the so-called 'flag of blood'. Flags in general played an important, community-forming role in National Socialism, and the 'flag of blood' amounted to a religious symbol. Hilmar Hoffmann, who has worked on the aesthetics of flags in the Third Reich, writes:

The National Socialists imbued the concept of the flag of blood with a strong emotional significance. It was the name they gave to the swastika flag supposedly drenched in the blood of its bearer on 9 November 1923, on the legendary march to the Feldherrnhalle (the Hitler Putsch) . . . Since that time new standards and flags of the NSDAP and its subgroups were solemnly consecrated by contact with the flag of blood, always in the presence of a sworn witness from the Feldherrnhalle.[11]

The following day the theatre continued, and Hitler started a large parade in the Schlossplatz. Estimates of the numbers of participants on that day vary between 60,000 and 100,000, and the parade lasted some four to six hours. During that time the uniformed troops presented the people of the city with an image of power, discipline and solidarity; they were being marched to readiness for the total assumption of power. It was a demonstration unimaginable by any other Party at that time, not even by the German army. A sympathetic female eye-witness describes the event as follows:

> The march past Hitler lasted six hours without
> interruption. The wall of people stood densely packed; on
> chairs, ladders and railings. They had climbed up the
> lampposts. Flowers and more flowers fell from windows and
> balconies; indeed, I saw apples being thrown down, and
> chocolate. And every time a row of flags came past the
> hands were thrown up in the air: Heil. Heil. And along
> with that came all the musical bands, the fresh-voiced
> singing and shouting of Hitler's followers. The sun shone
> on everything. Such enthusiasm was hardly seen when the
> Kaiser came to Braunschweig.[12]

During these two days of quasi-religious presentations, imbued with a fascist aesthetic, there were other events related to the Nazi presence. But they were kept silent by the crowd: the first person to stand along the route wearing an SPD badge was grabbed and beaten up. Small groups of SA members left their ranks to force their way into the workers' district, and scuffles ensued as the workers furiously defended themselves. The following day the whole business was repeated, in intensified form. Two people coming from a trade union meeting fell into the hands of the SA and were murdered. It was officially claimed that the SA members had been acting in self-defence, when they were 'traitorously ambushed by Communists'. The people of the town accepted this explanation, 'although they had sufficient opportunity to learn the true course of events'.[3] Wagener accompanied Magda during these demonstrations of brown-shirted power, but we know nothing of the conversation they had had at the picnic. We may assume that Magda had been shown the importance of Hitler and the NSDAP by this display, which, with its very theatricality, satisfied the emotions of a symbol-hungry crowd. And she was gripped and swept along with the crowd by the intoxication of the spectacle, 'by sublime reality' and by the temptation to share actively in that power. The next day, saying goodbye to Wagener, she told him: 'I promise, you will be the first person to learn when I become engaged to Goebbels. Then you will know that that in itself is even greater praise.'[14]

Two weeks later Magda kept her promise and announced that she planned to visit Wagener at half past eleven the following Sunday. She appeared with Goebbels and told Wagener: 'I have come to keep my word. You and your wife are the first to learn of our engagement.'[15]

Magda had now penetrated Hitler's inner circle, and her relationship with this core of authority was like a Platonic complement to her relationship with Goebbels. Wagener writes: 'She has become like the other half of Hitler the human being, something constituted and maintained . . . by a sacred will to serve, a will to a higher duty.'[16] For that 'higher consciousness of duty' she would pay with her life.

'Love is blind,' we are told, and Magda's decision to see both Hitler and Goebbels as the object of her love, to be linked both to the 'Führer' and his right-hand man, lifted her above the crowd of followers, establishing her identification with the power she sought. Having been chosen by Hitler, she participated in the sense of being chosen that he claimed for himself and his ideas. At the same time she had been received into the inner circle of disciples; and they too were also chosen. The whole entourage of the faithful was united by a feeling of being in love with the Führer: to bend to his ideas, to subordinate her own thinking to

his was a source of pleasure for her. Many famous psychologists
have subsequently investigated this phenomenon, which gripped
almost the entire German people. Alexander Mitscherlich refers
to Freud in describing the process with which the ego blindly
hands itself over: 'The possibility of detachment from the object
is lost, the person is alienated in the truest sense of the word. In
this state of exaltation the whole of the libido flows towards the
immeasurably overestimated Führer. He occupies more or less all
routes of access to behaviour, and places himself beyond the
demands of the old super-ego and the orientation of the ego
towards reality.'[17]

From now on Magda allowed Hitler's ideals to make her decisions for her. Through her participation in his supposedly
significant life and his historically unique plans, the Führer and his
significance became a part of her; which is to say that she did not
need to develop her own personality or seek a path for herself.
That path was predetermined, and the fantasies of greatness and
power were projected on to Hitler and his aims. The connection
with Goebbels was reinforced through their shared devotion to
Hitler and his goals – even if Goebbels starkly distinguished
between what he presented as a matter of faith to the masses and
what he himself was prepared to believe – and at the same time he
did not have the slightest doubts about Adolf Hitler, judging him
not as a politician but as a religious leader. In an earlier speech,
Goebbels said: 'Whatever cannot be resolved through hard work,
knowledge and proverbs God announces through the mouths of
those whom He has chosen . . . When Hitler speaks, all resistance
succumbs to the magical effect of his words . . . Above this man's
thrilling human form we see the benevolence of fate in action, and
cling with all our hopes to his idea, and are thus connected to that
creative force that drives him and us all forwards.'[18]

Magda had now become a part of this overheated movement –
overheated not only politically but also religiously as well – and
was near to her 'redeemer'. From now on there was no turning
back.

Chapter 18

The wedding of Maria Magdalena, née Behrend, adoptive name Friedländer, known as Ritschel, former married name Quandt, to Joseph Goebbels was set for mid-December 1931.

Some of the party colleagues who knew Goebbels well maintained that the planned marriage had only come about through Hitler's intervention, that Goebbels only wanted to use it to strengthen his bond with Hitler, and would otherwise have preferred to remain single. Had this been true, it would have meant that Magda was vulnerable to manipulation in a way that hardly accords with what we know about her. In addition, Goebbels' diary entries clearly show that this was a real love affair and that the couple had forged plans for the future even before Magda's meeting with Hitler.

We have few statements from Magda about the ideology of National Socialism, and if it sometimes seems as though she had only come upon it by chance, we know that she was not blind to the meaning of the movement, having read Hitler's *Mein Kampf*, Alfred Rosenberg's *Myth of the 20th Century* and Goebbels' daily editions of *Der Angriff*. The fundamentally racist and arrogant attitude, the obsessive anti-Semitism, the paranoid fear of

Marxism and obsessive hatred of 'Jewish Bolshevism', to be eradicated at all costs, the entire violent and destructive attitude of the
movement are such a constant presence in these writings that she
must have been familiar with them, they must have corresponded
in some respect to her own ideas. We may assume that she
accepted them. But at the same time, beyond all ideology, the
Nazi movement gave Magda something else, something crucial. In
the past Magda had suffered from her own emptiness, and the
Nazi movement, which saw itself as dynamic and revolutionary,
promised her a psychological intensity that she had never known
before. As she was clearly unable to develop any enthusiasm for
her own interests, she was fascinated by the passion with which
Hitler and Goebbels were able to construct every political event,
every speech into an intense experience. As the diaries reveal,
even in his private life Goebbels was capable of psychological
intensity and a certain degree of theatricality, and this must surely
account for some of the attraction he exerted on Magda's rather
cool nature.

Among those close to her Magda continued to encounter resistance to her decision to marry Goebbels. Quandt issued another
warning, making it clear to her that when she remarried, Harald –
according to the contract they had drawn up – would be brought
up in his father's house. From Ritschel, who had no great affection
either for the party or for Goebbels himself, she received such a
disapproving letter that relations with her father temporarily
broke down. From the start, Auguste disliked Goebbels – although
he had officially asked her for Magda's hand – and described her
impression of him in her memoirs: 'His whole manner was too
demonic for me, too opaque. His very apparent charm did not
touch me, and his cynicism, which became more and more open
and cutting after 1933, often irritated and hurt me . . . For all his
indisputable intellect "Doctor" Goebbels was always an out-of-
control petty-bourgeois who wanted to escape from his origins,
who wanted to shine and dazzle and dominate.'[1]

Shortly before the wedding Auguste warned Magda once again

that it was a bad idea, and tried to make it clear to her daughter the financial security she would be giving up because Goebbels' resources were certainly not up to maintaining the apartment and the comfortable standard of living to which Magda was accustomed. But Magda coolly declared: 'I am convinced that there are only two possibilities of political development for Germany. If the red flag should fly over Berlin there will be no more capitalism, and my maintenance from Quandt will dry up. But if Hitler's movement comes to power I will be one of the first ladies of Germany.' To her friend Ello she said, less objectively, that she would travel to the ends of the earth with Goebbels. She was even ready to die with him if the party should fail. And failure was something that he would not survive.[2]

While setting her sights on the most politically radical and aggressive agitator in Berlin, Magda had, with a sure instinct, opted in favour of the rising power, even if a Nazi victory was still far from certain. Even in those days Goebbels' trademark was, quite clearly, hatred: of the Jews, of the institutions, the old aristocratic elite, the capitalists, of everyone who was doing better than he was himself, and everyone who deviated from his ideas. His attitude was not hidden from Magda. How could she say that the things happening so openly before her eyes were good? Must we not wonder whether she did not share Goebbels' fury and hatred of society, of the existing order, in which she too had found no real place? She was quite alone within her family. Her mother warned her, Quandt warned her, her biological father stopped talking to her over it. She had to make a complete break with her past, marked by the names Friedländer, Arlosoroff and Lisa, because otherwise there might be some room for doubt. She was probably aware that she was playing a dangerous game. What was she sacrificing it all for? In the explanation that she gave Ello in reply to her questions there lies a readiness to abandon herself, even to put an end to her life if the movement should fail. In saying this she was placing very little value on herself, and making her life and personality dependent on the success of the National

Socialist idea. She accepted the violence that was clearly necessary to push National Socialism and thus her own ambitions
through as radically as they needed to be, and she allowed
Goebbels to perpetrate that violence. In return she promised to
take all the consequences with him, through to self-destruction.
'All or nothing' was her attitude.

But first of all she wanted power, she wanted to 'be one of the
first ladies of Germany', and she staked everything on that one
idea. In the process she staked everything on her love of the man
who had convinced her, as he had convinced a large proportion of
the German people, through the power of his demagogic rhetoric.
It was he who had carried her along, where she had previously
been without direction. She yielded blindly to this feeling, without realising that his lack of scruple, his cynicism and his lies
would one day touch her as well. She did not understand what it
meant that Goebbels, even before they had become engaged,
should have drawn up an agreement with her which effectively
assumed and sanctioned his later infidelity. In this document he
declared to Magda that she was the queen of his life, that he
wanted to have many children with her, but at the same time he
would like to preserve his freedom to have adulterous affairs, to be
free to have encounters which he would confess to her, and which
would not affect his relationship with her. Magda agreed to this
arrangement, was not unsettled by it for a moment and did not so
much as discuss it with Goebbels. She told Ello, sympathetically,
and almost with admiration: 'Such a brilliant man, who lives three
times as intensely as normal people, can hardly be measured by the
usual standard of bourgeois morality.'[3]

In the weeks leading up to the marriage Hitler was a frequent
guest in Magda's apartment, but not only there, because Magda
allowed Goebbels to turn the farm at Severin into a kind of retreat
for the Nazi leadership. The right to live there, granted to her by
Quandt, also included the right to invite visitors, and so on some
weekends Goebbels would turn up with his adjutant Count
Schimmelmann, or Hitler and his entourage would decide to

escape the hubbub of the city for a break in the countryside. This situation was encouraged by the fact that the estate manager, Granzow, was one of Hitler's oldest devotees, and was naturally enthusiastic to be able to receive the Führer in person. Quandt was unhappy about this, but since Granzow was in other respects very efficient, he gave it no further thought. So it presumably also escaped his notice that the wedding, planned for 19 December, was to take place at Severin. Quandt later claimed to have known nothing about it, but that is highly unlikely if we bear in mind that he was invited to Magda's birthday, a good month before the marriage, where he met Goebbels in person for the first time. But he did not take to Goebbels, and the idea of Magda's relationship with this Savonarola figure was, as Magda's mother said, 'disagreeable to him'.

Magda would, according to her mother, 'have preferred to marry in Berlin, in accordance with her sense of effect, extravagance and uniqueness,'4 but she bent to Goebbels' wishes for a quiet wedding in choosing Severin. Clearly she did not consider it tasteless to marry her second husband in the home of the first. The whole wedding smacks of inconsiderateness, an insult to Quandt's feelings. Was Magda not showing him that she had no respect for his world, by which she herself had been rejected?

According to Auguste, certain difficulties had stood in the way of the church wedding that Magda had wanted. 'As a divorced woman my daughter could not marry the Catholic Goebbels according to the rites of the Roman Church. Goebbels' requests to the Bishop of Berlin, which more closely resembled the demands of an equal than the pleading of a faithful lamb, were understandably ignored.'5 So Granzow organised the appropriate ceremony in the little chapel belonging to the manor-house, and Goebbels prudently brought a Protestant vicar from Berlin. Since Goebbels and, above all, Hitler, who was present at the wedding, feared Communist demonstrations and riots in Berlin if the hated 'conqueror of Berlin' married with great pomp in the Reich capital, the village church of Severin offered a suitable way out. At the wedding ceremony, Ritter von Epp was the first and Hitler the second witness. 'The altar-cloth was a swastika flag, with the crucifix at its exact centre.'[6] In a solemn procession everyone returned to Quandt's farmhouse after the ceremony. Magda wore a black silk dress and the white shawl of Brussels lace that she had worn at her first wedding. 'Behind her walked Hitler in civilian dress, leading Magda's mother by the arm. Nine-year-old Harald, dressed in the costume of a *Pimpf*, a member of the *Jungvolk*, walked ahead of the procession.'[7] Also present at the celebration were Hitler's two adjutants, Brückner and Schaub, Frau von Dirksen, Herr and Frau Granzow, two friends of Magda's and several others. Eighteen people in all sat at Quandt's table and drank from his glasses to the health of the young couple.

'The wedding feast was curiously ill-at-ease,' Auguste recalls. 'The entire Nazi party membership seemed to have been informed about the ceremony. At least people kept turning up wanting to speak to Hitler. The Führer, who was not terribly good at making conversation, and who did his best to bore his dining companion and the whole table with his endless monologues, jumped up from the table every few minutes and hurried to join in discussions in another room. There was nothing in the way of cosiness or atmosphere.'[8] Immediately after the wedding feast the party was to return to Berlin. Magda and Goebbels left somewhat earlier, to prepare drinks in Berlin. They left in different cars: Auguste with Goebbels' mother, his sister Maria and the pastor who had performed the ceremony in the little Severin village church. Hitler sat in the car in front of them. The road was icy, and the car in which Auguste was sitting suddenly started slipping from side to side. She describes how the chauffeur frivolously accelerated and tried to overtake Hitler's car. 'Hooting the horn incessantly, and swerving dangerously, he got past him. In an extended curve, the driver of the sliding car was unable to stop. Stupidly, he tried to brake on the black ice. We turned on our own axis a few times, and crashed down the low embankment into the ditch. In my confusion I saw Hitler leaping from his car in silhouette and dashing over to us. He dragged the chalk-white driver from his seat and tore his hand open on the broken door window in the process."[9]

Magda, who had arrived in Berlin with Goebbels some time before, had grown worried, and phoned the estate manager. When she heard that the rest of the convoy had broken up two hours before, she sent a car to fetch the stranded passengers from the accident site.

In Berlin life immediately continued as hectic as before. Of course the wedding of the well-known, loudmouthed Gauleiter had not gone unremarked, and so the opposition press celebrated with the headline: 'Nazi chief weds Jewess'.[10]

At this time of political tension the honeymoon had to be called off, and Magda spent her first Christmas, a few weeks after the wedding, alone, before Goebbels finally came home after midnight from his nocturnal excursions with the SA.

Harald returned to his father's house, but very often visited his mother, who lived nearby. Goebbels had now moved in with Magda, and the anxiety of how she would keep the expensive apartment going on his income was no longer so oppressive, since Hitler had increased his income by a thousand marks. Nonetheless Magda had to do the housekeeping with half of her usual monthly sum, which was not so simple, since she had guests almost constantly, particularly Hitler and his entourage. He felt particularly at home in her surroundings, and made her apartment a kind of private headquarters for himself and his staff. Here, in Magda's apartment on Reichskanzlerplatz, Hitler also had his meals, which Magda herself prepared with the help of her old cook, because after a supposed poisoning attempt Hitler was worried about further attacks. Since he was a vegetarian, but the other guests wanted normal fare Magda had to prepare two different menus. In another way, Magda's house opened a doorway to the elegant world, because it was here that both Hitler and Goebbels picked up general etiquette and fine table manners, learning, for example, how to eat lobster or caviar, or the correct pronunciation of foreign words. On those evenings, which stretched on until late in the night, they would listen to music from the gramophone, or Hitler's close friend Putzi Hanfstaengl and Magda would perform something at the grand piano. On other evenings Hitler would deliver his endless, exhausting monologues, which no one dared to interrupt. These frequent visits from Hitler strengthened Goebbels' position, because unlike other Party members who had joined at the very beginning he had no power base, he now had Magda, who would strengthen the link between himself and Hitler in the long term.

The next few months placed heavy demands on Magda, on her abilities as a housekeeper, in that she had to learn how to keep herself financially within bounds – the occasional envelope from Hitler would be swallowed up as soon as it arrived – and on her physical strength. She was pregnant, and endured the long evenings and smoky air without a word of complaint. But her coexistence with Goebbels remained very happy for the time being. To outsiders the two newlyweds looked like a pair of turtle-doves, almost comical in their playful devotion to one another. Meissner, who knew Hanfstaengl personally, reports this mocking observation from him: 'Magda calls out, "My angel", but who should come round the corner but the black devil himself, right down to the goat's foot!'[11]

Berlin society gradually became accustomed to 'the originally plebeian National Socialist movement',[12] Bella Fromm confided in her diaries at this time. Thus, for example, the industrialist Fritz Thyssen introduced a speech of Hitler's to the Industry Club in Düsseldorf. During his address he requested support for Hitler's party. Gustav Krupp von Bohlen und Halbach and the other directors of I.G.Farben immediately made large donations. 'There was a rumour,' as Bella noted, 'that the ore and coal potentates even suggested legislation for a ten per cent tribute of their incomes to the good cause.'[13]

This discovery of polite society on the part of the NSDAP, the playing-down and camouflage of their true goals are typical of the historical moment, because no one really had an idea of how things would develop. The political situation was primarily marked by great misery and hopeless poverty, but at the same time the people felt the need for a kind of intellectual leadership to raise it up above its sense of humiliation and inferiority. And NSDAP propaganda was aimed precisely at this longing, not balking at the exploitation of misery. Chancellor Brüning might have achieved a great deal for Germany, including the end of reparation payments and a revival of German armaments, putting the country practically on a par with other European countries; but it was greatly to the advantage of the NSDAP that he was unable to satisfy the population's fundamental needs of charismatic leadership and greater affluence. He believed that because of his foreign policy successes he also had the political forces of internal politics under control, but his rather aristocratically detached style found no emotional resonance. Among the people he was known as the 'starvation chancellor', because he had further straitened the circumstances of office workers and civil servants, even if he had done so out of financial necessity.

An article in the *Vossische Zeitung* describes the situation in Germany at the time as follows:

Almost anyone strolling through the residential streets of Western Berlin, through those clean, quiet and well-tended streets, will encounter an elderly person, a man or a woman – or rather a lady or a gentleman, for they are dressed no differently from ourselves – coming up to him and asking for money. Some will approach us with a smile, as though to greet a good acquaintance; others beg mutely, their faces without expression. None has yet acquired the whining, lachrymose tone of the professional beggar . . . The worst are those who say nothing. While it is still light they sit forlornly on the benches along the wide street; later they wander along the fences of the restaurants, stop and stare at the diners without speaking, without begging, without moving.[14]

In another we read:

This morning at about ten o'clock, in front of the over-
stocked briquette warehouse of the Alwine mine, near
Halle, hundreds of unemployed men and women turned up
with handcarts, bicycles and sacks, demanding a free
handout of coal from the shocked manager. They
explained that they were freezing in their apartments
because they could buy no coal, while here in the mine
courtyard the good briquettes were weathering away and
crumbling to dust. The manager eventually gave in under
the pressure of the growing crowd, and a short time
afterwards a long procession of laden coal-carts and
bicycles with sacks made its way back to Halle. The last of
the unemployed to arrive were driven away from the
coalyard, taking their empty carts with them, by the police
squad that had arrived in the meantime.[15]

Mass misery as a result of mass unemployment, of falling wages
and deteriorating social conditions, was the harsh reality for the
man in the street. The suicide rate was, by some distance, the
highest in the world. Some days before Magda's wedding the
evening edition of the *Vossische Zeitung* of 12 December 1931
reported the suicide of a married couple. The same newspaper
reported that because of the fall in Christmas shopping in Berlin,
within a few days five businessmen had killed themselves.[16]

As early as October 1931 Hitler was introduced to the elderly
Hindenburg, although he did not make much of an impression. In
spring 1932, when Hindenburg's seven years in office came to an
end, he announced that he was standing again. At this point
Goebbels was clear that Hitler, the 'Bohemian corporal', had no
chance against the victor of the battle of Tanneberg, but nonetheless he forced the Führer to stand, so that this possibility would at
least be discussed. Predictably, Hitler lost to Hindenburg. But
since Hindenburg had no absolute majority a second round of

elections was required. Goebbels organised it with even greater doggedness. The second set of elections won the old Reich President fifty-three per cent of the votes; Hitler defeated the Communist candidate, Ernst Thälmann, thus ending up in second place. He was now able to accept the offer of forming a kind of coalition with the Brüning government and the Reichswehr, although for Goebbels this would have meant a betrayal of the 'revolution', the 'seizure of power' for which he was striving – and in this case Hitler followed Goebbels' radicalism rather than the more moderate course of Goebbels' rival, Georg Strasser, who wanted the NSDAP to participate in government.

With an absolute majority of the coalition behind him, Wilhelm Groener, the Minister of the Interior, managed to persuade Hindenburg to ban the SS, the SA and the Hitler Youth throughout the whole of the Reich, on the grounds of a threatened putsch.[17] Goebbels raged, and his only goal was to bring Reich Chancellor Brüning to book. He attacked Brüning in his speeches, pamphlets and newspapers in the most crafty and vulgar way – and unfortunately with some success. The Prussian regional election, which was held shortly after the prohibition of the NSDAP party formations, was a triumph for the National Socialists. With eight million votes the NSDAP became the strongest party in Prussia.

On 30 May Brüning and the entire cabinet stepped down. Hindenburg, to whom Brüning was bound in absolute loyalty, did not lift a finger on his behalf, instead withdrawing his trust. The old man was following the insinuations of Franz von Papen and Kurt von Schleicher, as well as his son Oskar and his Secretary of State Meissner, who were chiefly pursuing their own interests. Papen, seen as the man with Hindenburg's ear, was appointed as the new Reich Chancellor, and General von Schleicher was made Minister of the Reichswehr.

On the day of Brüning's fall Hitler, along with Göring, was once again received by Hindenburg. Hitler promised to tolerate the presidential Cabinet installed by Hindenburg, on condition that the Reichstag be dissolved and the prohibition on the SA lifted. Once the SA and the other Party formations were permitted again, the civil war continued as before. It had never really come to an end, but now the Communists resumed the fight with even greater desperation. In various parts of the city all hell broke loose. Viktor Reimann gives a vivid picture of this:

> In Moabit the Communists rehearsed an uprising in protest against the lifting of the SA ban. They systematically smashed the street-lamps to shroud the whole district in darkness, and erected barricades from concrete paving stones and rubbish bins. The police were obliged to use armoured cars to crush the revolts. Now there was fury on all sides. The democratic parties demanded that the government bring this terror to an end. Goebbels threatened the government in a speech: 'If you cannot establish order, then we will.'[18]

This gave Papen the chance to bring down the Prussian government with emergency paragraph 48. On 31 July the NSDAP became the strongest party in the Reichstag election, and even bourgeois voters had now gone over to the National Socialists. Hitler saw himself as being about to achieve his goal, because it seemed as though the leader of the strongest party should also become a member of the government. But Hindenburg would not be persuaded. However it was a further step on the road to power when Hermann Göring, because of the large majority of National Socialist votes, was elected President of the Reichstag. Hitler was only offered the title of Vice-Chancellor, which he turned down.

This constant battle for power accompanied Magda's pregnancy from start to finish. She supported all her husband's intrigues and furious, hate-filled tirades, in the hope of a political decision that would bring her the status she still yearned for. When the innermost core of NSDAP leaders met on 30 August – in her apartment, as ever – she was two days short of delivery. Only

Hitler, Goebbels, Göring and Röhm had met conspiratorially on this occasion, to decide together to bring down Papen's hated regime. Over the next few days Goebbels delivered the most heated polemics on the subject in *Der Angriff*.

Chapter 19

On 1 September, ten months after her wedding, Magda gave birth to a daughter, Helga. During her marriage to Quandt she had suffered several miscarriages, and for that reason she had undergone a minor operation before her marriage to Goebbels, to avoid any complications this time. Goebbels was happy, although he would have preferred a son.

Goebbels' strategy to bring about the fall of Papen was successful. On 12 September the Reichstag declared its lack of confidence in the Chancellor, and a new election was set for 6 November. Now, however, the coffers were empty, there were barely enough funds left for propaganda, and even those voters who had supported the nationalists at the last election had simply grown tired and given up. Even Goebbels lacked his earlier punch, and without the usual large financial donations not a great deal could be done in the election campaign. His diary entries reveal a high level of irritability, as this one from 10 October 1932 indicates: 'One editor most vilely impugned the honour of my wife in the yellow press. An SS man visited him and beat him with his riding crop until he fell to the floor drenched in blood. Then he left his visiting-card on the table and after that, unimpeded by any of the press reptiles present, he left the office. That is the only way of dealing with these reprobates who impugn one's honour.'[1]

Goebbels' furious rage referred to a series of articles that had first appeared in the paper *Bürgerspiegel*, and which were then reprinted in the 17 September 1932 issue of *Vorwärts*. Goebbels, who at this point represented the socialist wing of the NSDAP and loved to shock the bourgeoisie, had been accused in these articles of leading a 'feudal' lifestyle. The editor referred to Magda's expensive apartment in Reichskanzlerplatz, and wrote that it had been decorated by one of the best-known interior designers of the day, and had cost fifty thousand marks. He went on to refer to the fact that Goebbels, who had always ranted against 'high society', was now mingling in aristocratic circles, and that his wife was curtseying before the Crown Princess at the salon of her Excellency Viktoria von Dirksen.

The NSDAP, after rising to their strongest level of political support, suffered severe setbacks in the November elections, losing almost two million votes and thirty-four seats in the Reichstag. The mood of the party was depressed, and there were widespread speculations that this setback might be used to hamstring the party once and for all.[2] But General von Schleicher, the new Reich Chancellor, had no intention of eliminating the NSDAP, he thought very highly of George Strasser, who headed the moderate wing of the NSDAP and represented the point of view that the NSDAP might be able to reach an accommodation with a Schleicher cabinet, as a way of participating in government. Goebbels and Hitler radically rejected this idea. Schleicher himself was flirting with the idea of bringing the National Socialists into government like this because he thought he would be able to control them, because despite its setback the Party had already filtered through all social classes, as Bella Fromm points out in her account of the ball given by the 'Foreign League of German Women'. She was dismayed to see that the NSDAP had found many friends among the old aristocracy, and that even among the élite circles of Potsdam and Berlin the SA uniform was replacing the dinner jacket. Of the 'Auslandsbund Deutscher Frauen' and their ball she writes:

December 16, 1932
. . . This organisation of German women abroad is becoming a sort of sounding board for radical propaganda. You hear a great deal of talk there about Lebensraum, and about the abolition of the treaty of Versailles . . . A great many diplomats appeared at the Ball yesterday.[3]

At this ball she also met Magda, and notes in her diary what was said about her in this company: that Magda, as Frau Günther Quandt, had not valued her secure and luxurious life, but had made life hard for her husband with her moods, or that she was interested in contradictory ideas and theories, such as Buddhism and National Socialism. Bella Fromm describes how the National Socialist ideology had captured Magda's imagination, but was mixed with vestiges of the Zionistic doctrine that her old friend, Arlosoroff, had taught her. She also knew that Magda's friendship with Arlosoroff went back a long way.

When Magda entered the dining room with Viktoria von Dirksen, Bella's companion spoke of Magda's past. He remarked; "'If rich Günther Quandt had not come along . . . who knows where she'd be now? Probably doing sentinel duty in front of a Palestine Kibutz, rifle on shoulder and an Old Testament password on her lips.'"

Bella describes her own impression.

Tonight at the ball, Magda was lovely. No jewels except the string of real pearls around her neck. Her golden hair owes nothing to any drug store or chemist. It, too, is real. Her big eyes, iridescent and ranging from dark blue to steel grey, radiate icy determination and inordinate ambition. 'How do you like her?' asked François-Poncet. And without waiting for my answer, he added: 'I never saw such ice-cold eyes in a woman.'[4]

Bella Fromm's diary entries suggest that the press, and thus Berlin society in general, was well informed about Magda's earlier life. For Bella Fromm herself, the diary was also to have dramatic consequences. Goebbels' hatred would later, after her emigration, pursue her across the Atlantic. In 1943, when she published her diary under the title *Blood and Banquets*, she felt persecuted by American Nazis working for Goebbels, and was therefore shadowed by the FBI.

The French ambassador François-Poncet, the man struck by Magda's cold eyes, was an alert observer. For power-hungry Magda, the political uncertainty of the NSDAP must have been hard to bear. She had experienced enough dashed hopes, but she was at least as ambitious as Goebbels himself. That was something that even her maternal devotion to baby Helga could do nothing to conceal.

But for the time being she had to content herself with the social opportunities that she was about to outgrow. Bella Fromm met her three days after the ball mentioned above, at the benefit ball for the 'Cecilienwerk' in the Hotel Esplanade. This was an event normally overseen by the Crown Princess. In the past, only the most elegant members had been invited, but this time the tickets were on public sale, so that the party seemed less exclusive than usual. Bella Fromm observes that Frau von Dirksen had brought Magda once again, and reluctantly noted 'how people were abasing themselves to enter her good graces.'[5]

While Magda was displaying her charm at social occasions, Goebbels travelled throughout the Reich to inject new life into the fading NSDAP. This was not an easy matter, as the party had debts of around eight million marks. The organisation was in a state of despondency, and on 9 December 1932 Goebbels wrote: 'Hitler says that if the party collapses he's going to close it down in three minutes.'[6]

For Goebbels this whole period was a test of nerve, and Magda herself was well aware of this, since Goebbels continued to discuss all his plans with her.

The extent to which her hopes and expectations were bound up with politics is revealed in an anecdote related by her mother:

> One evening we met Magda sitting with a half-empty
> bottle of cognac. Her eyes were rather glittery, and her
> words flowed more slowly than usual. She had decided to
> use strong liquor to fight off a cold she had caught while
> doing the spring-cleaning. For my daughter had an
> obsession about cleaning in general. Every few weeks she
> had to turn the whole apartment upside down, shift
> furniture, re-hang pictures and go around the place with
> her scrubbing brush and her bar of soap, like the most
> stalwart of charladies. Magda twinkled at us, smiled and
> raised her index finger: 'I've checked it very precisely. The
> stars don't lie! 1933 will be victory year!' Maria (Goebbels'
> sister, who was living in their house at the time) and I
> looked at her, baffled. We knew that my daughter had
> pursued astrology as a hobby for some time, but this was
> the first time she had expressed her views in such
> forthright terms.[7]

But despite her belief in astrology Magda's nerves were on edge, and one morning when Goebbels didn't come home until five o'clock after a night with his comrades in the Kaiserhof, according to Auguste she hurled imprecations at him.[8] One day before Christmas, in the middle of the holiday preparations, she suddenly fell ill. As we have seen with the pressures of her marriage with Quandt and the heart problems that ensued, Magda tended to have psychosomatic reactions in difficult personal situations. Her mental life, which she herself was unable to express in words, and of which she would not even have thought in those terms, seemed to find physical expression. Goebbels was desperate, as his diary entry shows: 'Magda does not feel well. Severe pains. Stoeckel comes and immediately orders that she be taken to the clinic . . . 1932 is one long string of bad luck. It will have to be shattered into pieces. I sit and brood until late in the night. Everything is so empty and bleak. When Magda isn't there, it is as though the house had died.'[9] The next day he drove to the clinic with Harald. 'We light a Christmas tree outside in the corridor, and put Magda's presents on it. Then we push everything into her room, and the sweet creature laughs and cries. We all stay for an hour, our hearts quite heavy.'[10]

Magda recovered, and Goebbels decided to accept Hitler's invitation to Berchtesgaden with Harald. His sister Maria would stay temporarily with Magda and come with Magda for New Year's Eve. But on 30 December the news came that Magda was feeling ill. Goebbels was worried about her, and wanted to go back to Berlin straight away. Then Maria called later to say that she was much better. Magda had had a miscarriage.[11]

Goebbels stayed in the mountains to spend his first New Year with Hitler. In the meantime Magda's condition had worsened. She had developed an infected wound. Goebbels noted: '1 January 1933 . . . Magda is seriously unwell. Very high fever, refusing to eat. I am very worried. It is approaching 12. The ceremonial cannon are being fired downstairs. A hellish noise, like a great battle . . . The old year is over! In with the new. We want to fight. To win or to die! I give Hitler a firm handshake: "I wish you power!"'[12]

He received a telephone call from Berlin, telling him that Magda was being fed artificially. Beside himself with anxiety he took the train back to Munich with Harald. His sister rang again to tell him that Magda was calling out for him and for her son. Hitler came to the hotel to comfort him.

Goebbels had to wait for the night train in Munich, and while he was waiting and during the journey he wrote down his anxiety, from the depths of his soul: 'It took this anxiety to tell me how deeply I love this woman, and how infinitely I need her . . . Finally the train departed. To bed. And trembled and prayed all night: may God save my wife for me. I cannot live without her.'[13]

These stammered assurances from Goebbels were probably authentic, and indicated that this really was a loving relationship, and that at this point in time he really did need Magda. He needed her like a mother, and his anxiety is like that of a child fearing abandonment. Magda slowly recovered, happy that Goebbels was with her. The fever gradually subsided. Hitler also phoned to inquire about her condition.[14] Further attacks of weakness followed, and Magda had become pale and drawn, but Goebbels was able to turn his attention once more to the politics of the day.

While Magda was slowly returning to health, a Hitler Youth was murdered. For Goebbels this was an opportunity to demonstrate the macabre side of his talents: the celebration of the cult of death. His gift for staging party funerals as emotionally charged mass events runs through the history of the NSDAP, and would later, in the war, reach its climax with the glorification of the mythical heroic death. Viktor Reimann writes that he buried Hitler Youth Wagnitz 'as though he was a king'. For three hours, from noon until dusk, he drove the body of the murdered boy through the Berlin suburbs: 'The time had been calculated so that the procession reached the cemetery as darkness was falling, and Goebbels delivered the funeral address in the midst of a fiery sea of ten thousand torches'[15] before 'returning him to the earth's maternal womb', and then he held a vigil in the cemetery until midnight.[16]

This sole purpose of this dramatised event was to impress people, to win them over emotionally to the party, because Goebbels knew very well that the NSDAP would only achieve its breakthrough among the masses if he were to sweep the people along with him. If he could not do that now, it would mean the death of the organisation. And that would also mean the failure of his life. Events worked in Hitler's favour: Papen, Secretary of State Meissner and Oskar von Hindenburg were plotting with the senile

Reich President against Chancellor Schleicher. They brought about Schleicher's resignation on 28 January 1933. Hindenburg did not support him, and appointed Hitler Reich Chancellor in his place on 30 January. Bella Fromm notes; 'At 11.10 this morning Hitler was made Chancellor of the Reich. It took him another ten minutes to form his cabinet . . . Hitler certainly loses no time. This afternoon he had already convened his first cabinet session. It seems an ironic foreboding that the new Hitler cabinet should start off without a Minister of Justice.'[17]

This sealed the fate of parliamentary democracy in Germany. As a result of the global economic crisis a 'practically pathological intensification of the revisionist syndrome' had developed, and 'nothing was to remain as it had been conceived in 1918–19. The revision of the Weimar constitution did not merely encompass a few individual components, but aimed at a fundamentally different system of government. Internal revisionism corresponded to revisionism in foreign policy.'[18] The belief in a messianic Führer, a redeemer bringing salvation where reason apparently failed, had carried the day. On 30 January Goebbels noted in his diary:

The time has come. Hitler is Reich Chancellor. We shake Hitler's hand. Great jubilation. The people are rampaging down below. Straight to work. The Reichstag is dissolved. New elections in four weeks . . . Called Magda. She practically hit the ceiling . . . Hitler fantastic. He goes to his cabinet meeting. With Anni and Hanfst, to Magda's. She almost explodes with delight. She'll be free tomorrow . . . At 7 o'clock Berlin looks like a startled anthill. And then the torch-lit procession begins. Endless, endless, from 7 o'clock in the evening until 1 o'clock in the morning the people march past the Reich Chancellery . . . A few metres from the Reich Chancellery the Reich President stands at his window, a towering heroic figure, venerable and swathed in an aura of mythic enchantment. Every now and again he taps out the beat of

the military marches . . . When, long after midnight, the
procession comes close to an end, tens of thousands of
people stand before the Reich Chancellery and sing the
Horst Wessel song . . . The new Reich has come about. It
has been consecrated with blood. We have reached our
goal. The German revolution is beginning.[19]

Considering the events of 1932 as a whole, the impression
arises that Hitler himself did not have to do a great deal to seize
power. Until January events had turned against the NSDAP. In
the end, a small group of conspirators around the senile Reich
President, a group pursuing its own aims, persuaded Hindenburg to
appoint the 'Bohemian corporal', whom he despised for his unsuccessful military career, as Reich Chancellor.

The idea of a new Reich, the 'Third Reich' had already been
repeatedly evoked by Goebbels. It achieved a mythical resonance
among the masses, leading away from the supposedly coldly cal-
culating and purposeful negotiations of the Weimar Republic, and
instead promising 'to give the Reich of the Germans a new historical form, its third, which would last for all eternity.

'The Third Reich was also the last German Reich. In both
thought and deed.'[20]

Chapter 20

On 2 February Magda finally left the clinic. Goebbels notes: 'Still very pale. Hitler so sweet with her, Frau Raubal there as well. Welcoming party at home. I am so happy. Magda is the best I have.'[1]

But the joy of reunion was tinged with bitterness. There was no post for Goebbels in the new cabinet. It had eight non-nationalist ministers sitting on it, with Papen as Vice-Chancellor, and only three National Socialists: Hitler as Reich Chancellor, Frick as Reich Minister of the Interior, and – Goebbels' eternal rival – Hermann Göring as Minister without Portfolio. This made him responsible for the police – and whoever has the police has the power.

The Reichstag election, which was to bring the definitive majority they were hoping for, was fixed for 5 March. For the NSDAP the new election was already beginning. This time their strategy lay in provoking an attempted revolution on the part of the Communists, so that, with the support of the masses behind them, they could attack. When street battles escalated between the Communists and the SA, and when the National Socialists had suffered four fatalities, it was once again down to Goebbels to stage a funeral that would celebrate the cult of death and a readiness to make sacrifices to the Führer.

Otherwise, Goebbels' self-confidence was severely shaken. He felt he had been passed over in the distribution of the ministry posts, and 'pushed into the corner'.[2] When he heard rumours that he was to be given the position of Radio Commissar, he described it as 'disgusting'.[3] But he had to organise the next election. He had a month to bring his propaganda back up to its peak. He knew that this was his final opportunity to demonstrate his importance for the success of the coming battle. But as his diary entries for 3 and 6 February reveal, he was profoundly hurt – as was Magda – that he had been boycotted when the jobs were being handed out. His wife was unhappy, spent much of the time in tears and seemed unable to come to terms with the situation. Her nerves were still on edge, of course, since she had only just recovered from her life-threatening illness. But the need for power and attention was a constant in her life. If this was unsatisfied, she, like Goebbels, stood by an abyss of which she seemed fully aware.

During these days Goebbels alternated between depression and last-ditch efforts – enjoying minor triumphs, before he too succumbed to a wave of influenza that had afflicted the Party. Magda too fell victim to it.

But Goebbels recovered, and in any case he had a new propaganda medium: radio. In giving him the post of Radio Commissar, Hitler had ensured that the National Socialists had one more means of influencing the masses, and that it was closed to all other participants in the election. And Hitler and Goebbels made use of it, as the following entry by Goebbels clearly shows: '11 February . . . first I brush aside the press. Then I speak on all the channels. It goes splendidly. I don't have stage fright. I deliver my report and do my introduction. Hitler delivers a fantastic speech. All against Marxism. Very dramatic at the close.'[4]

The mood in the Goebbels household – Magda irritable and dissatisfied, Goebbels himself 'tired and listless, with no purpose and no pleasure in my work'[5] – only changed when an unforeseen event took place, which the National Socialists immediately capitalised upon. On 27 February 1933 the Reichstag burned down.

The news came like a bombshell. This was arson, and the Communists were immediately blamed in furious polemics in all the NSDAP organs. Some Berliners suspected the National Socialists, with Göring or Goebbels as their ringleader, but there was no proof, although it would have been entirely in line with the tactics of the Party. A young Dutch tramp and anarchist was arrested; there was no connection with the Communist party. And yet Göring immediately seized the opportunity to ban the entire Communist and Social Democratic press. Prominent Communists were arrested the same night and dragged from their homes by the SA. Many of them were beaten up. Beneath the headline 'Hundreds of Arrests', the next day's *Vossische Zeitung* reported on the arrest of Werner Scholem, whose brother, Gershom Scholem, already lived in Jerusalem, where he had made a name for himself as an interpreter of the Kabbala. His mother, who still lived in Berlin with the rest of the family, wrote to Gershom on 28 February:

I am so excited today that I can barely write. Werner was arrested again during the night! You will have read that a madman set fire to the Reichstag; one might almost imagine that he was paid to do it, so stupid is such a deed. As a result the government had all former Communist Party members of both the Reichstag and the Landtag arrested, along with Communist lawyers and some who are not even Communists, but who have merely defended them! A chill wind is blowing! Today at 1/2 past four a policeman and 2 men came to the door and when we didn't answer when they rang the bell they opened the door with a skeleton key, isn't that nice? They searched the house for an hour, even in the child's room, where they didn't find anything, because Werner has no prohibited material in his apartment, but they took him off anyway, because they were ordered to do so.[6]

The opportunities to exploit the Reichstag fire, and to use aggression and hatred against the falsely suspected Communists during the final days of the election campaign, rekindled Goebbels' joy in life. He had complete control of the press and radio, the Communists were constantly under attack in all the media, and most of them were in any case in jail. All the more disappointing for Goebbels was the election result of 5 March. In comparison with the massive NSDAP propaganda campaign, the result was rather thin. Hitler's party received forty-four per cent of the votes, but not the absolute majority they hoped for. Despite placing the most intense handicaps on the other parties, despite the use of terror and the press ban, fifty-six per cent of the German people voted against Hitler. The NSDAP had to form a coalition, and, along with the German National Party, won a total of 340 seats in the Reichstag, which gave them only a small majority of eighteen mandates. But that was enough to deal the final blow to democracy, already in its death throes.

Goebbels and Magda spent the Sunday evening after the election at the opera listening to Wagner's *Die Walküre*. Afterwards Goebbels wrote: 'When we returned from the performance to the Reich Chancellery, the glorious victory had been won . . . We are the masters in the Reich and in Prussia.'[7]

But not all contemporaries had recognised how dangerous the NSDAP actually was. They were unable to see what the regime was really striving for, and even the head of the Central Union of German Citizens of the Jewish Faith closed his official address with the words: 'Today more than ever we must heed the slogan: wait and see.'[8] Goebbels did not wait for long. He put the bourgeois parties under such intense pressure that they eventually caved in, recommending that their own voters support Hitler. By doing this he managed to enforce the so-called Enabling Act in the Reichstag on 23 March 1933. As the Communist members of parliament were in prison, had been driven underground, or were otherwise prevented from participating, the Social Democrats alone rejected the bill, with eighty-four votes against forty-one. The Enabling Act gave Reich Chancellor Adolf Hitler unlimited legislative and executive powers. Germany had legally placed itself in the hands of a dictator.

Goebbels leaves hardly any private diary entries about this period, only notes originally destined for publication in his book *From Imperial Court to Reich Chancellery*. But we may nonetheless assume that he and Magda were content, because on 13 March he was awarded the ministerial post for which he had been waiting for so long. He was now responsible for the Reich Ministry of National Information and Propaganda.

Chapter 21

Hitler did not need much more than this to consolidate and extend his power. The *Länder*, the regions of the country, were brought into line with Nazi policy. Most organisations, institutions, associations, parties, media and universities followed; the two most powerful groups, the army and heavy industry, readily joined with the new regime, which promised them both rapid rearmament and the crushing of the trade unions, which were actually dissolved in May 1933 and replaced by the 'German Labour Front'. In the spring of 1933 the cult of the Führer assumed unimagined proportions among the people: 'the support of the population for the activities and constant demonstrations of power of the NSDAP grew like an avalanche, and by mid-July there was no other party in the Reich.'[1]

During these months Goebbels' diary entries indicate that he no longer saw his position as secure. Despite the ministry of which he had been assured, he continued to deliver sweeping verbal assaults, and at the same time he felt he was himself being unjustly attacked, particularly from abroad. He reacted with random arrests.

After the Reichstag fire and the subsequent mass arrests of some ten thousand people, it no longer made any sense to talk of a 'Communist threat' in Germany. Political prisoners were transported to specially created concentration camps: Dachau was set up on 20 March 1933, and on 1 April officially opened by SS head Heinrich Himmler.[2] The terror was now being directed more intensely against the Jews; they were being deprived of their livelihoods, and at this point the plan was for them to leave the country – on condition that they leave their possessions behind.

Criticism abroad was growing, and Jews who emigrated from Germany were reporting on the reasons for their flight, and what was happening in Germany. Goebbels foamed: 'We will only be a match for this anti-German propaganda from abroad if we can get hold of its originators, or at least those who are exploiting it, the Jews living in Germany who have so far gone unchecked. So we must move towards a large-scale boycott of all Jewish shops in Germany. Perhaps the Jews abroad will have second thoughts when their racial fellows in Germany are facing ruin.'[3]

This opened the most shameful chapter in the history of the Third Reich: the systematic expulsion and subsequent destruction of the Jewish population. Most Jewish and left-wing artists and intellectuals had already left Germany. They included the literary critic Walter Benjamin and the composers Otto Klemperer and Bruno Walter, who was forced to flee by being mistreated in a particularly underhand manner: when Walter was about to conduct a special concert by the Berlin Philharmonic, he was told that there were rumours that the Philharmonic Hall was going to be burned down if he did not pull out.[4] The 'de-Jewification of the arts and sciences' stopped at no one. Theatre director Max Reinhardt fled, Albert Einstein was stripped of his German citizenship, and even the eighty-six-year-old painter Max Liebermann, honorary president of the German Academy of Arts, and bearer of the highest German honour, the Order of Merit, was put under such pressure that he declared his resignation from the Academy. Saul Friedländer casts light on the situation: 'As the painter Oskar Kokoschka writes from Paris in a letter to a newspaper, none of Liebermann's colleagues deemed it necessary to say a single word of acknowledgement or sympathy. Isolated and ostracised, Liebermann died in 1935; only three "Aryan" artists attended the funeral. His wife survived him. In March 1943, when the police arrived with a stretcher to collect the bedridden eighty-five-year-old to be transported to the east, she committed suicide by swallowing an overdose of Veronal.'[5]

In his hatred Goebbels ensured that the cultural sphere was the first to be rendered barren by systematically expelling from it the Jews and 'left-wingers'.

Victor Klemperer, Professor of Romantic Philology at the Technische Hochschule in Dresden, wanted to 'bear witness to the last' in his diary. On 30 March 1933, when Goebbels had already officially announced his boycott of the Jews, Klemperer wrote:

Yesterday evening at the Blumenfelds with the Dembers. Mood as before a pogrom in the depths of the Middle Ages or in deepest Tsarist Russia. During the day the National Socialists' boycott call had been announced for the evening. We are hostages. The dominant feeling . . . that this reign of terror can hardly last long, but that its fall will bury us. Fantastic Middle Ages: 'We' – threatened Jewry. In fact I feel shame more than fear, shame for Germany. I have always imagined: the 20th century and Mitteleuropa was different from the 14th century and Romania. Mistake.[6]

And, on 31 March: 'Ever more hopeless. The boycott begins tomorrow. Yellow placards, men on guard. Pressure to pay Christian employees two months salary, to dismiss Jewish ones: No reply to the impressive letter of the Jews to the President of the Reich and to the government. Murders are carried out in cold blood or "with delays". No "hair is harmed" – they are just starved.'[7]

The boycott went peacefully. It was as though the population was not taking part in it terribly enthusiastically, and many small shops brought down their blinds and remained closed, so that Goebbels called it off after a day.

The American Jews and the Jewish leadership in Palestine were uncertain how they should react: should they protest and boycott German goods? Or would such a reaction merely provoke further retaliations against the German Jews? They decided to wait and see for the time being.

At Hitler's behest, Goebbels set up the former Palace of Prince Leopold on the Wilhelmsplatz, opposite the Reich Chancellery, as the Reich Ministry for National Information and Propaganda. Goethe had dined in this Schinkel-designed building, and Queen Luise had danced at a costume ball, but Goebbels decided to rebuild the whole thing. He didn't like the stucco ornaments and the stuffy plush curtains, and when the rebuilding did not happen quickly enough he brought in the SA: 'They knocked off the plaster, ripped out the wooden fittings and hurled newspapers and files down the stairs with a terrible racket.'[8]

By now Magda's apartment on the Reichskanzlerplatz had become too small for her duties as a political hostess. Not far from the new ministry, in an overgrown garden, stood the magnificent villa of a Prussian Lord Chamberlain, built one hundred years previously.[9] As expense was no longer an issue, the old building was turned overnight into a 'white palace'.[10] Both the villa and the park were renovated; heated greenhouses were built, a winter garden was planned, and at last Magda was able to draw on unlimited resources to achieve this transformation. An extra storey was built on to the palace, a private cinema was installed, the rooms were decorated with carpets, paintings and Gobelin tapestries from museums, and a commode owned by Frederick the Great was even installed in the drawing-room. According to contemporaries, however, everything remained on the level of a cultivated private household, because Magda was careful not to succumb to the pomp and bombast that very rapidly afflicted some leading Nazi households.

In mid-April Goebbels travelled with Magda to Cologne.

Clearly they had become estranged over the past few months. Perhaps, after the successful seizure of power, Goebbels no longer needed his companion's maternal support quite so urgently as he had in the days of the depression, but he was thoroughly aware that their relationship had cooled off, as his diary makes clear.

The journey continued along the Rhine to Heidelberg, Freiburg – memories of his student days – and then on to Lake Constance and Berchtesgaden, where Hitler and some of the other faithful were already waiting. Here Goebbels discussed the plan for the mass demonstration on 1 May. He notes: 'We will turn 1 May into a grandiose demonstration of the German national will. On 2 May the trade union buildings will be occupied. They too will be brought into line with party policy. There may be trouble for a few days, but then they will belong to us. Caution must be thrown to the winds.'[11]

'*Gleichschaltung*', the policy of bringing institutions into line with the Party, was Goebbels' great concern. But once he had, at breakneck speed, brought all the organisations in the Reich into line, within a matter of weeks he had no enemies left to fight. The only ones remaining were the Jews. And now he concentrated all his loathing on them, spurred on by Hitler's own feelings of hatred. And what about Magda? Had she really forgotten or repressed the whole of her own past? Or was she worried that Hitler might come to hear of it? Hitler, whose anti-Semitism touched every area of his life, and who might turn away from her if she spoke out of line? Her mother Auguste had been divorced for a long time and now bore the name of Behrend, but before restrictions had been imposed, the press had on several occasions referred to Magda's past. Did Hitler know of her history, or had Magda successfully denied it? Should she not, in any case, have been worrying about what was happening around her, or what might at least happen to her old stepfather? We do not know whether she had already severed contact with him, or whether she knew that during this time Friedländer had been called to Goebbels' office. We only know that friends of Friedländer's, who managed to emigrate to Palestine before things became impossible, told a journalist in the 1960s that after being summoned to the Ministry of Propaganda Friedländer was never seen again. There were as yet no mass deportations in Germany, only individual arrests. The 'Book of Tears' displayed by the Jewish community in Berlin's Fasanenstrasse records the deportation of a Max Friedländer who later died in Sachsenhausen concentration camp. This man's details might well match up with those of Magda's stepfather, in which case the journalist's statements would appear credible. According to the other version, reported by Hans-Otto Meissner's widow, Magda was able and willing to protect her stepfather, who was supposedly not forced to wear the Yellow Star, and who survived the Nazi regime. What makes this version appear dubious is the fact that it is not mentioned anywhere else, in oral or written testament, neither by Auguste in her memoirs nor by Meissner himself in his biography of Magda. At the same time this would have been an opportunity to add a positive, human quality to their rather apologetic image of Magda. Meissner only mentions in very general terms what Ello Quandt had told him. When she asked Magda about her attitude towards the campaign of hatred and the boycott of the Jews, Magda is supposed to have replied that Joseph had explained it all in terms of *raison d'état*. The Third Reich was opposed to the Jews, and it was his duty as propaganda minister to take action against them in the press and on the radio. 'That was what the Führer wants, and Joseph must obey.'[12]

Magda, who had been torn from her inner emptiness and apathy by National Socialism, who, under the influence of Goebbels' powers of persuasion, believed in Hitler and his ideology – like much of the rest of the country, which had felt humiliated and inferior since the defeat of 1918 – identified her own deficits, needs and desires with the 'Thousand Year Reich', and thus rescued herself from her own insignificance. She was not in a position to question that generally accepted ideal. If she had taken account of the destructive and barbaric powers underlying it, particularly where the persecution of the Jews was concerned, she could not have clung to her desire to be part of this fantastic realm. What was her alternative? It was safer to remain on the path that she had chosen. Like many other Germans she felt protected in her devotion to the collective ideal, and the question of Friedländer's subsequent fate had no place in this.

Of course the shock-waves of the Nazi regime's measures reached Palestine. Ships filled with families, often three generations of the same one, were arriving every day. They hoped to start a new life in Palestine, they were desperate people whose livelihoods had been stripped from them. Gershom Scholem observed what was going on around him, and in April 1933 he wrote to his mother in Berlin:

> But what makes the greatest impression is the confirmed report about the expulsion of the Jews from their posts, the prohibition on Jewish lawyers appearing in court and the restriction of their numbers, about the plans afoot against Jewish doctors, all things, in short, that people can read in any permitted and dependable German newspaper. People abroad are very well aware that the Jews could be destroyed, and that it would not have to take the form of an actual attack, that the Jews are now being excluded from the professions that earned them their living, when the economic crisis had long since destroyed important Jewish positions, and anti-Semitism had for years threatened the future of young Jews in Germany. The exclusion of the Jews from their most important source of income, the liberal professions, is being seen here as evidence that they can be destroyed without bloodshed, by starving them to death. No one abroad can believe that a large nation such as the Germans has been forced to proceed with such methods against one per cent of its population . . . [13]

These events prompted a mixed mood in Palestine. All of a sudden the new inhabitants saw themselves confronted by people who had left Germany out of fear and poverty, but who were far from prepared for the harsh lifestyle of pioneers, and who had not until now given political support to Zionism. What awaited the immigrants was certainly not a country flowing with milk and honey. It was a young, wild country, torn, both politically and religiously, by terrible internal tensions.

In 1931 Chaim Weizmann lost his position as President of the Zionist World Congress as a result of the agitation of the Misrahi. Arlosoroff, who was treated in political circles as a successor of Weizmann and bore the nickname Chaim II, had for some time been a favourite target of the extreme right, because he embodied the majority of the moderate young Zionists, who still believed in a general and cautious colonisation of Palestine. The revisionists, on the other hand, wanted to develop structures which would lead on the spot to an independent state – even if that involved armed violence against the British sovereign power. This conflict at the leadership level of the Jewish politicians in Palestine was intensified once Hitler held the reins of power in Germany.

In 1933 Arlosoroff bore the title of Head of the Political Department of the Jewish Agency, the equivalent of today's Foreign Minister. He was one of the first Zionist leaders far-sighted enough to observe the fate of the Jews in Germany with deep concern, since, after all, he knew life in Germany better than most. At the same time he was linked to German culture, poetry and music by his own life history and the love and enthusiasms of his youth. The British government's restrictions on immigration, the so-called 'White Book', seemed less justified than ever, since in many cases these immigrants were Jews whose lives would be endangered if they were returned to Germany. Arlosoroff, who had advocated moderation and understanding throughout his political career, was so enraged by the situation that he described the desperate state of affairs in secret letters to Weizmann, mentioning the possibility of a temporary uprising against the British. When the next Zionist Congress was planned in Warsaw, Arlosoroff planned to travel via Berlin to seek ways of improving conditions of emigration for German Jews. Both the extreme right and the ultra-orthodox spoke out violently against this idea, accusing him of cuddling up to Hitler's Germany.

1 Magda Goebbels (11 November 1901 – 1 May 1945)

2 Victor Chaim Arlosoroff, born on 23 February 1899 in the Ukraine, spent his childhood and youth in Königsberg and Berlin. In 1924 he emigrated to Palestine. He was one of the most important leaders of the Zionist Workers' Movement. At the time of his murder on the beach at Tel Aviv (on 16 June 1933), he held the office of Foreign Minister for the 'Jewish Agency' of Palestine.

3 Joseph Goebbels (29 October 1897 – 1 May 1945), the future 'conqueror' of Berlin, at the NSDAP election in 1928. In the background an SS bodyguard.

4 The industrialist Günther Quandt was thirty-eight when Magda met him. She was married to him from 1921 until 1929. Even after their divorce he remained generous towards Magda.

5 Magda, her ex-husband Quandt, and Joseph Goebbels at the register office for their marriage in December 1931. Hitler was their witness.

6 Magda's marriage on 19 December 1931 with Goebbels at Quandt's Severin Farm near Parchim in Mecklenburg. Beside the couple, Harald Quandt, Magda's son from her first marriage. In the background, their witness, Adolf Hitler.

7 Magda Goebbels accompanies Hitler on an election trip in summer 1932.

8 1932, during the Reichstag elections in Berlin: Gauleiter Goebbels leaves the voting centre with Magda, greeted enthusiastically by placard-carrying Nazis.

9 1932: Hitler at home with Magda and Joseph Goebbels in Magda's Berlin apartment on Reichskanzlerplatz. At the piano sits Ernst 'Putzi' Hanfstaengl.

10 Magda and Joseph Goebbels during a trip to Italy in May 1937.

11 Magda and the newly appointed Minister for Information and Propaganda, Joseph Goebbels, 1933.

12 Family photograph around 1935 (*left to right*): Magda's son from her first marriage, Harald Quandt, daughter Hilde (b. 1934), Magda Goebbels, Joseph Goebbels, daughter Helga (b. 1932)

13 1934, at the coffee table in the garden of the Reich Chancellery (*left to right*): Economics Minister Walter Funk, Hitler, Magda Goebbels, Joseph Goebbels, Viktoria von Dirksen.

14 Journalist Bella Fromm, who escaped into exile in 1938. Her diaries contain numerous observations about Magda Goebbels.

15 Magda Goebbels during a reception in the Reich Propaganda Ministery for the International Automobile Exhibition in Berlin 1936. She took her representative duties very seriously.

16 20 April 1936: congratulations for Hitler's birthday (*left to right*): Hitler, Hilde and Helga Goebbels, Joseph and Magda Goebbels.

17 Hitler salutes to honour the victors at the Avus racetrack in May 1937. In the box of honour (*left to right*): Joseph Goebbels, Magda Goebbels, Minister Graf Schwerin-Krosigk.

18 Karl Hanke, permanent secretary at the Propaganda Ministery. Hanke stood at Magda's side as her companion and 'knight in shining armour' when she was considering divorce.

19 Werner Naumann, Hanke's successor as permanent secretary in the Propaganda Ministery, April 1944. He was Magda's last love, and she wrote him poems.

20 Lida Baarova, with actor Gustav Fröhlich and Joseph Goebbels, around 1936 (*left to right*)

21 The Goebbels family with the children Hilde, Helmut and Helga (*left to right*) visiting Hitler in the Obersalzberg around 1938.

22 Christmas 1940: Magda Goebbels gives presents to soldiers' children in the auditorium of the Propaganda Ministry.

23 On Goebbels' yacht *Baldur* with Magda's sister-in-law and best friend Ello Quandt (*left*), who had divorced from Walter Quandt, Günther Quandt's brother.

24 Joseph Goebbels with Magda and their children on his forty-fifth birthday, 29 October 1942: Helmut (b. 1935). Holde (b. 1937), Heide (b. 1940), Hedda (b. 1938) (*front from left*); (*back*) Hilde (b. 1934), Harald Quandt (b. 1921), Magda's son from her first marriage to Günther Quandt, and Helga (b. 1932).

25 February 1943: Magda Goebbels with her daughters Helga and Hilde, in the audience at the Berlin Palace of Sport. It was here that Goebbels called for his listeners' agreement with 'total war'.

26 Magda Goebbels always stressed the importance of dressing elegantly. Even shortly before the collapse of the Nazi regime, she was still ordering made-to-measure shoes and hats.

Chapter 22

On 27 April 1933 Arlosoroff arrived by boat in Trieste, travelled on to Vienna and, after a short stop, to London. Negotiations with the British were not very successful. The restrictions on immigration were not lifted, and no one could understand Arlosoroff's anxieties about the Nazi regime. But they were ready to allow the transfer of Jewish funds via an English bank connection if Arlosoroff was able to set in motion the relevant arrangements in Berlin, either with the new Economics Minister or with a bank. Arlosoroff attempted to make the appropriate contacts from London.

On 9 May he left London to continue his mission in Berlin. The channel crossing took place without a hitch, and there were not too many passengers on the ferry. Arlosoroff boarded a train at the Hook of Holland. At first he was alone in the compartment, and he was then joined by a well-dressed, agreeable gentleman from Amsterdam. Since this man spoke German as well, they chatted about unimportant matters. But once they had crossed the Dutch border his fellow-passenger grew noticeably silent. The German border guards boarded the train, and immediately the tone of passport control changed. Both guards were the kind of person who grows in stature when he dons a uniform. They derived their self-importance from their insignias of power – in this case the swastika stamp. In as abrupt a fashion as they thought their position demanded, they demanded Arlosoroff's and his companion's passports. Arlosoroff took startled note of the brusque tone, when one of them turned to him: 'Aha, born in Russia, British passport, issued in Jerusalem. Interesting. And what brings you to Germany?' Arlosoroff had difficulties restraining his annoyance at the complacent hostility of the man's tone, and said he was only passing through. When he sensed the contemptuous gaze of the official he could no longer contain himself, and added that the reason for his journey had nothing to do with the man, since all his papers were in order. Still holding Arlosoroff's passport in his hand, the young man smiled, pointed to the mandate stamp, and said, 'That isn't going to help you for much longer.' Arlosoroff maintained a furious silence. He was annoyed at almost allowing himself to be provoked, but he choked back his displeasure and was relieved to be holding his passport again. After the border guards had left the compartment Arlosoroff tried to resume his conversation with his fellow-passenger, partly to calm himself down, but also to make a joke of the matter, because rude border guards are a universal fact of life. But his neighbour was clearly intimidated and said nothing.

When Arlosoroff reached Anhalt station in Berlin, everything appeared at first glance to be the same as before: the thundering noise of the station hall, with the hissing of the locomotives, the rhythm of the trains pulling into the station or setting off again, the hubbub of the people, their confusion of greetings, farewells and advice, the occasional cry of joy. The background noise was intensified by the size and height of the hall, with white clouds of steam rising and dispersing among the sooty iron girders. But while much that he saw was familiar, Arlosoroff immediately registered all the changes: the sayings and swastikas of the Nazis were draped everywhere. Clearly the Nazis had brought out the old national colours, black, white and red, to distinguish themselves from the 'shame of the Weimar Republic' with its black, red and gold. Now he saw policemen and self-important brownshirts, arrogant SA men marching up and down in pairs or larger groups, or simply standing around watching. Although Arlosoroff was inwardly prepared, he was shaken by the sight, and happy when he recognised his old friend Robert Weltsch, the editor of the newspaper *Jüdische Rundschau*, who had come to collect him. Robert suggested they leave on foot, as the offices were not far away. Once again Arlosoroff felt like a foreigner in a city that had once been so familiar to him. Robert chattered away quietly beside him, and when a troop of brownshirts came towards them he pulled Arlosoroff on to the opposite side of the street: 'You have to be very careful,' he said, 'they have spies everywhere, and enough people have disappeared already. I don't think it's entirely safe for you, either.' Arlosoroff reassured his friend by referring to his British passport.

Shortly after this they witnessed an event that was incomprehensible to Arlosoroff: they heard shouts emerging from a little restaurant, followed by crashing and breaking of wood. Shortly after this the owner stepped furiously into the street and showed a handful of hooligans to the door. Half-drunk, and bellowing insults, they had started to demolish the restaurant from outside with their boots. The owner called loudly for the police, and four brownshirts suddenly appeared as if from nowhere. They didn't arrest the hooligans, but instead insulted the owner as a 'filthy old Jew', and said he should be happy not to be treated the same way as his building. Arlosoroff was furious, and wanted to get involved, but Robert energetically pulled him aside. 'You've got to know,' he explained to his friend, 'there's no law in something like this, ever since they made the call to boycott Jewish shops. Jews and Communists have been carted away in broad daylight, to places like the SA barracks on General-Pape-Strasse. And then they wait in vain for the case to come to court. Sometimes it's days before their relatives find out where they are. Whole families have been torn apart, children are left at home with no way of contacting their parents. Jewish teachers are being fired, and they want to make a drastic reduction in the numbers of Jewish pupils, even now grants for Jewish schoolchildren have been stopped. And of course you can never find a lawyer to represent these cases. No one trusts anyone any more, because die-hard Nazis want to curry favour by making denunciations . . . Sometimes Jewish families who have been denounced come to my office and tell me their stories. They expect me to help them, but there's not much I can do for them. At the same time it wouldn't be true to say that everyone is against the Jews all of a sudden, but the population is apathetic, it's every man for himself, and in any case the people who know what's going on are frightened as well.' He went on to tell his friend that letters were being censored, and that he had already had unexpected visits in his office at night, and people had been going through his desk-drawers. But, he added, he didn't want to give up: the *Jüdische Rundschau* was now more important than ever, and after all he did have a Czech passport.

Arlosoroff found it hard to walk calmly through the streets while Robert walked next to him telling such stories. Robert's accounts suggested that things were worse than he had feared, and at the same time he remembered the past: what had become of his former schoolmates, his old German teacher who had taught them the poems of Rilke, Goethe, Heine and Hölderlin?

The symbols of the Nazi regime were present everywhere. Arlosoroff was horrified to notice that they even adorned the shop-window displays. He recalled a bookshop, it must have been on the next corner, which had belonged to the Sterns, friends of his mother's. The bookshop seemed still to exist, but it had clearly changed hands. Arlosoroff curiously stepped closer: then he caught his breath. No, he was not mistaken. In the display, against the background of the swastika, stood a picture, the photograph of a lovely young woman on the arm of her bridegroom – and the young woman was Magda! The former love of his youth, Magda Friedländer, his unhappily married friend, who had considered leaving her wealthy husband to emigrate with him to Palestine.

Remarried! Of course Arlosoroff recognised the man at her side, it was Joseph Goebbels, the new government's Propaganda Minister, without whose rabble-rousing Hitler would never have come to power. He felt dizzy, his heart seemed to skip a few beats, and he could not breathe. Concerned, Robert supported his friend, who could hardly stand upright. By the time they reached the newspaper office, Arlosoroff was still short of breath. Robert fetched help. The old doctor, who was quickly on the spot, gave him an injection, and Arlosoroff slowly calmed down. He knew Robert's doctor from before. The old man wasn't quite as busy these days, and so he was happy to stop and chat. Many of his former patients had emigrated as quickly as they could, and his non-Jewish patients were worried about visiting his practice during the day. Nonetheless, the old doctor felt secure in Germany. After all, he had been awarded the gold Iron Cross in the First World War. Back then he had served at the front as a young doctor, doing practically nothing but performing amputations. He saw the current situation as an intensified form of anti-Semitism, and thought it would pass. After all, there had always been waves of persecution against the Jews, and Germany was not Russia. In Germany you could rely on a certain degree of culture.

After the doctor had left and Arlosoroff's condition had improved, he explained to Robert the reason for his unease, unable to credit what he had just seen. He told Robert of his former friendship with the young Magda, their adolescence together, the 'Tikvat' group, he talked about her plan to emigrate to Palestine with him. While he was bringing his memories to life for Robert like this, an idea occurred to him: Magda might be able to arrange an interview with Goebbels. The financial transfer agreement for which he had come to Berlin – perhaps that was something she could bring about. He had to get in touch with her again! Robert urgently warned him against taking such a course of action, but Arlosoroff would not be dissuaded. If he were to ask Magda for help, of course he would not be able to mention anything intimate, anything about the past, but he was on a political mission here, and in his position as 'Foreign Minister' he felt entirely on a par with Goebbels. A private discussion could not be entirely ruled out. If it could be arranged, his task would be made a great deal easier. Magda had once been very close to him, after all, and shared his goals. How could she now be completely indifferent to his situation and that of the German Jews? Surely she would have to help him?

He actually did manage to talk to Magda. She promised to meet him, although only after his return from the Zionist Congress in Warsaw, in about four weeks' time.[1]

The same evening as Arlosoroff succeeded in making contact with Magda, Berlin and other cities in Germany saw further demonstrations of the anti-Semitism that was spreading throughout the country: the notorious book-burnings. On 10 May 1933, 'as a reaction to world Jewry's "shameless provocation" of Hitler' there was to be 'a "public burning of disruptive Jewish writing" by university students'.[2] The propaganda campaign relating to this had begun on 12 April, and was designed to extend the anti-Jewish action, begun on 1 April with the boycott of Jewish businesses, from the economic to the cultural level. The campaign was not aimed solely at the Jewish spirit, however, but also at Marxism, pacifism and the 'soul-shredding overestimation of the life of the instincts', in other words Freudian psychoanalysis. 'In Berlin more than twenty thousand books were burned, and in all other large German cities two to three thousand. In Berlin an enormous fire was lit at the Staatsoper, and Goebbels was one of the speakers.'[3]

Goebbels' diary entries about the auto-da-fé that he himself had staged overflow with complacency. '. . .late evening speech Opera Square. By the pyre of filthy, shameful books burned by the students. I'm in the best of form. Enormous crowd.' But the same evening he notes: '10 May . . . row with Magda.'[4] Had they had another discussion about her past? Had the name Arlosoroff been mentioned? By now Goebbels was no longer as open about his feelings as he had been. There might have been other reasons for the 'row with Magda', namely that Magda had discovered that her former husband, Günther Quandt, had been arrested, and had been in custody since 3 May, a week previously, supposedly over some tax affairs.

In his memoirs Quandt would later write that he was imprisoned for four months, on no legal grounds. He never learned of the reasons for his arrest. So here, too, lawlessness prevailed.[5] After the book-burnings the foreign press reacted with unusually high levels of criticism to the Nazis' ritual exorcisms, and this annoyed Goebbels, leading him to impose even stricter controls on domestic press and radio.

Magda had other concerns. We do not know how disturbed she was by Arlosoroff's unexpected appearance. She was chiefly concerned with herself, and thought the moment had come to present herself in public and create an image for herself. On Sunday 14 May, Mother's Day, she gave a radio talk on the subject of 'The German Mother'. 'Very sweet and good. The form was perfect,'[6] as Goebbels was pleased to note.

Magda had clearly yielded to Goebbels' opinion that women had no business in politics, although some days earlier she had still insisted, to his annoyance, that she wanted to assume overall charge of the National Socialist charities.

Despite all the events that he had experienced at first hand during his short visit, Arlosoroff found it was very difficult to understand how much the situation in Germany had changed. For the first time since 1871 the Jewish population no longer had any support in law; instead, step by step, the new government was promoting discrimination against the Jews. It was becoming clearer and clearer to him that he could not depend on Magda's possible support to find access to senior Party members. So he immediately tried, in tough negotiations with Schacht and other government representatives, to alleviate economic conditions for Jewish emigrants. He actually managed to make preparations for what would later be known as the Ha'vara Agreement, finally ratified in August 1933.[7] But for the time being this success was not yet on the horizon, and despite all his doubts Arlosoroff wanted to seize the opportunity of a meeting with Magda, which might be his final chance.

With a heavy heart he set off for Prague for a few days, to deliver further lectures on the subject of Zionism, and from there he wrote to Sima and his sister Lisa in Palestine, for fear that his letters from Berlin might be opened by the censors – and this turned out to be the case. He sent Lisa a small brochure containing a photograph of Magda and Goebbels, writing in Hebrew: 'Magda's bridegroom'.[8]

From Prague he travelled on to the Zionist Congress in Warsaw, where violent tumults awaited him. The Zionist Workers' Party, of which Arlosoroff was a member, and the revisionists were at each other's throats. Arlosoroff's speech was interrupted by repeated heckling, rebuking him for his diplomatic activities, his attempts to help the Jews by holding discussions with the Nazis, and accusing him of caring only for the German Jews and of taking an unnecessarily gloomy view of the situation. When he walked with Ben Gurion through the medieval streets, deeply disappointed, to discuss their common concerns, he mentioned to his friend that he planned to meet Magda. He described his earlier relationship with her, and spoke of how they had grown up together, how fond Magda had been of her stepfather Friedländer, and how committed to Zionism she had been as a girl. But Ben-Gurion was horrified by Arlosoroff's plan. He tried to explain to him that Goebbels was, along with Hitler, the worst anti-Semite of all, that all current anti-Semitic measures had been introduced on his initiative, and that Magda must surely agree with those measures or she would not have become Frau Goebbels.[9]

While Arlosoroff succumbed to gloomy thoughts in Warsaw, on 26 May Magda had set off with Goebbels and Hitler and the entire Nazi entourage, including Leni Riefenstal, from whom Goebbels hoped to commission a film about Hitler, to the Baltic resort of Heiligendamm. The weather was splendid, but a planned picnic was a disaster. Bella Fromm had also been hoping to enjoy the fresh sea air there. 'Apparently there is a brown curse on me,' she wrote in her diary, 'Adolf Hitler, Dr Goebbels, different staffs and inevitable "secretaries" of the chief of propaganda had unfortunately also chosen my place of seclusion for a merry holiday interlude from their work. The solitary Kurhaus was spotted with the Brown beetles. The beach, the boulevards and the cafés rang out with *Heil Hitlers . . .*'

The German edition adds the following: 'Pretty Hela Strehl, a fashion editor with Scherl, was part of Goebbels' "team". Her relationship with Magda Goebbels was fairly tense, of course, but no one apart from Magda seemed terribly bothered about that.'[10]

According to Bella Fromm's diaries, Magda was fully aware that Goebbels had already begun to take a keen interest in other women. Magda presumably knew that the happiest part of her marriage was already behind her, and she was suffering as a result.

Three days later, on 29 May, Arlosoroff arrived in Berlin once again, but Magda was no longer there, having set off for Rome with Goebbels the day before. We do not know for sure whether it was her intention to avoid seeing him again, or whether Goebbels had decided to travel to Rome at short notice because he was jealous of Göring, who had been in negotiations with Mussolini over the fate of Austria a month before, and who had been fêted and entertained by the Duce. Once again Goebbels could not bear the fact that it was his rival who was in the limelight rather than himself. Now it was his turn to cut a fine figure in Rome, and he was treated like a prince in the Eternal City. Magda enjoyed this, and shone by his side.

> Everybody in Rome turned up. The king is very pleasant. And Balbo. Magda is making great conquests . . . Dinner given by Mussolini at Grand Hotel. Magnificent gala. Mussolini presents Magda. She performs wonderfully well. He looks dazzling. Charming to Magda. Beautiful women. Music and chatter. Groups after that. Myself and Mussolini. Continued conversation . . . We agree about

everything. 'The German revolution is the greatest of all time' . . . He soars alone into the lofty heights. A Caesar. He says some fabulous things about Magda.[11]

The entries from Rome continue in similar vein. Goebbels was celebrated and basked in the attention heaped upon Magda for her looks and her knowledge of languages, since as well as her perfect French she spoke Italian and English. On the way home they travelled via Munich and saw Hitler, and still basking in the brilliance of their performance they decided that 'they wanted to have another baby. A boy, this time.'[12]

Magda had regained her place in the marriage.

Before the Roman trip, however, Magda had conveyed another message to Arlosoroff, in which she stated that a meeting would also be too dangerous for her, and that he should leave Germany as quickly as possible.

Arlosoroff wrote an agitated reply to his sister Lisa. His letter would never arrive, and we know about it only through his second letter, which a Zionist friend in Prague personally brought to Palestine. In this second letter Arlosoroff wrote that Magda had told him she feared for her life. He himself, he confided in Lisa, had committed the greatest mistake of his life. He did not know whether he would ever see his loved ones in Palestine again.[13]

This was a desperate letter from a man on the run. The very next day, after failing to meet Magda, he left Berlin. Up until this point we can follow his journey very closely, but from now on he seems to obliterate all his traces. Two weeks later, having travelled via London, Paris and several other stops along the way, on 14 June he finally reached Palestine.

Chapter 23

Arlosoroff spent the first evening after his return to Tel Aviv dining with his wife Sima at the Kate Dan hotel. After dinner they took a walk on the beach. The evening was warm, and the air was heavy with the scents of the orient. The dusk slipped quickly into the velvety darkness of night. Arlosoroff and Sima took a walk by the Moslem cemetery. A camel being led by a sleepy Bedouin broke away from him. Arab curses and cries rang out in the night, and some little boys tried to recapture the beast.

Sima and Arlosoroff strolled along the beach, Sima walking a few steps ahead of her husband. Suddenly two men walked towards him out of the gloom. When they had reached him they stopped, and the shorter one shone a torch into Arlosoroff's face. 'Are you Dr Arlosoroff?' he asked in Hebrew. When Arlosoroff replied that he was, he continued, 'What time is it?' Arlosoroff awkwardly took his watch from his pocket. Before he could reply, the second man pulled a revolver and fired at him. Arlosoroff collapsed, and the two men disappeared silently into the night.

Sima stopped and immediately ran back to her husband. 'They've shot Chaim,' she called in German. 'Jews have killed a Jew!' 'No, Sima, don't say that,' Arlosoroff said weakly. Two passers-by, Moshe Weiser and Jaakov Zlibanski, who happened to be coming along the beach, gave the wounded man first aid and carried him back to the side of the road to flag down a car and take him to the hospital. But it was Friday evening, and it was twenty minutes before a driver prepared to break the Sabbath rule finally came along.

In the Hadassah Hospital four doctors fought for the patient's life. News of the attack spread through the city like wildfire, and a crowd gathered in front of the hospital. Arlosoroff's family and the mayor of Tel Aviv rushed to his bed before he was wheeled into the operating theatre. A few minutes later he lost consciousness, and the doctors were unable to save him.

A terrible grief settled on the square in front of the hospital and spread through the city. People were deeply moved by the death of their young, charismatic leader.

The very next day, telegrams arrived from all over the world, lamenting Arlosoroff's sudden death. Suspicion first fell on the revisionists, who had always considered him a thorn in their side. This theory was hotly defended by the Socialist Workers' Party, because such a slur meant that the revisionists would surely lose the next election. Three suspects were arrested, of whom one was freed without trial and the second sentenced to death, but later acquitted by the high court for want of evidence, as was the third.

Arlosoroff's unexplained assassination left a bitter taste among Israel's Jewish community, and one which was to last for years afterwards. It was a traumatic experience, and when proceedings were reopened at various times the revisionists tried to shake off the terrible suspicion attaching to them, but they were only partially successful. Despite other suspects and contradictory eye-witness statements, the suspicion of this political assassination lingered around them, and may well have had a crucial effect on the politics of the next forty years, intensifying the irreconcilable hostility between the Workers' Party and the revisionists. Even today no actual perpetrator has ever been identified, and papers and police records have disappeared in the meantime.

For political reasons some clues were left unexamined, such as the statements of the lawyer Max Seligman. The British had condemned Seligman to a period of imprisonment for assisting illegal immigrations at the time of the persecutions of the Jews in Germany. With him in prison were two Arabs, professional killers, one of whom boasted of assassinating Arlosoroff. The names of these two potential murderers were well known, but no one knew who might have been responsible for hiring them. The hearings produced little, and in any case the two Arabs were involved in other murder cases. The younger of the two spoke good Hebrew and made a statement to the effect that on the Friday evening in question he had visited a large number of Jewish cafés in Tel Aviv with his older companion, who had not told him why they were doing this, when in fact they were searching for Arlosoroff. The younger man also stated that the other man had fired the gun to frighten Arlosoroff into letting him have the woman. But why then would he have shone the torch into Arlosoroff's face and asked him his name, to be certain that this was the young head of the Jewish Agency? To judge by the sequence of events, it seems clear that he fired in order to kill Dr Chaim Arlosoroff. But under whose orders? The flight of the two Arabs after the event seems curious, if we bear in mind that the shortest way to the Arab district of Jaffo would have led along the beach, while the two fled via Sarona, to the north of Tel Aviv – as though they were reporting back to the Nazi settlement there.

After the younger man had listed all these details in his statement, he later withdrew his confession in response to unexplained pressure from an unknown quarter.

One other possibility, not unrelated to this account of events, was not further pursued because it led straight to the heart of the Nazi Reich, and was consequently taboo.

In the mid-seventies the serious Israeli newspaper *Ha'aretz* suggested a new version of the unexplained murder. The late journalist Haviv Kanaan published a thoroughly-researched article under the headline 'Goebbels gave the order'.[1] In this he refers to the fact that two Nazi agents, Grönda and Korth, were living in Palestine at the time of Arlosoroff's assassination. They had been sent on Goebbels' orders to Palestine by the Prussian Gauleiter Koch, officially in search of buried gold.

In 1918 a German sergeant, Karl Todt, had buried the treasure in a valley in the Djenin, on the road to Nazareth, when British troops led by General Allenby had surrounded the Germans and the Turks. The treasure had remained untouched since the collapse of the Ottoman Empire. Since 1930 Todt, who after his release from a British prisoner-of-war camp had lived in Germany, where he ran a small bicycle shop in Duisburg, had tried to get an expedition going. He confided his plans to Richard Kunze,[2] who was at first keen to go along himself but later pulled out of the project. Finally, before the Nazis came to power, he found a travelling companion in an adventurer, Baron von Bolschwing, and a translator who was to be made leader of the enterprise. All the preparations had been made, and the necessary diplomatic steps had been taken. These still remained valid after the Nazi seizure of power, since Foreign Office staff did not change as rapidly as government positions within the Reich itself. So the treasure hunters had all the proper accreditation they needed by the time they set off in their car. They reported to the consulates in Athens and Istanbul. There, to their surprise, they found a telegram from Karl Todt's wife, telling her husband that two other people, Theo Korth and Heinz Grönda, were on their way to Palestine, and would arrive ahead of their own expedition. Through various channels, including Kunze, who was by now a member of the Reichstag, the matter had come to the attention of Goebbels. At Goebbels' initiative the two NSDAP agents, Korth and Grönda, were secretly dispatched to Israel by Gauleiter Koch. Their plan was to dig up the treasure themselves. Officially Goebbels explained their journey by saying that he did not want to make common cause with the British authorities, but hoped that with the help of those two selected Party members and an NSDAP cell in Palestine, he would be able secretly to rescue the gold. But the two agents' unofficial mission, their real reason for travelling to Israel, was to do away with Arlosoroff, of whom Goebbels had been terribly jealous since Magda had told him of her past.

On 5 April 1933, according to German Foreign Office files, the two Nazi agents Grönda and Korth introduced themselves to the German Consul Dr Friedrich Wolf. Wolf was clearly not informed about the purpose of their visit, because he sent various telegrams to the Foreign Office asking for instructions, since he could not tell exactly what was going on. Todt had abandoned his plans and returned to Germany, but the adventurer von Bolschwing was in Sofia, planning to travel on to Palestine and in the meantime he was demanding information from the Foreign Office.

According to witnesses, the two Nazi agents had never been to Djenin before, and had no interest in the buried treasure. They avoided ever coming into contact with the authorities of the British Mandate. They spent their time almost exclusively in Sarona and Jaffo, where the local Nazi Party had members within the Templar settlements. They were probably in search of paid killers whom they might persuade to eliminate Arlosoroff, as they would have been unable to carry out the task themselves – and in any case they had already attracted too much attention. What they had not reckoned with was the fact that Arlosoroff had unexpectedly set off for Europe on 27 April. This surprise departure clearly speeded up the two agents' plans. Five days later they paid another visit to Consul Wolf, to tell him they had found the hiding-place of the gold, their mission was at an end and they could travel back to Germany. Wolf's wife was Jewish, and she knew about the anti-Semitism prevailing in Germany, and secretly listened in on the conversation. The whole business struck her as very curious, but Wolf asked no questions, for fear of falling out of favour with the new government in Berlin. Grönda and Korth assured the unsuspecting consul that they would be back shortly to set up a repair workshop in Djenin. But as Wolf observed with some surprise in a letter to the Foreign Office, they never came back.

If we imagine ourselves back in Berlin at this time, we may assume that Goebbels was told about Arlosoroff's presence in Berlin, since he had come on an official mission. It remains probable that he also knew about Arlosoroff's attempt to resume contact with Magda, and that this had heightened his jealousy. As a result, Magda's message to Arlosoroff – as conveyed to us by Lisa – in which she said she feared for her own life and advised him to leave Germany as quickly as possible, might have had some justification.

In his article in *Ha'aretz* Kanaan refers to an interview with Robert Weltsch, who had escaped the Nazis in 1938 by emigrating to Palestine. In the early seventies he was still living in Israel, and Kanaan owed a great deal of his information to him. Weltsch could still clearly remember the shock that Arlosoroff had felt when he caught a glimpse of Magda in the photograph with Goebbels, and the subsequent conversation in which Arlosoroff had told him about Magda. But by his own account Weltsch had warned him against seeing Magda again. Nevertheless, he added to Kanaan that his wife had thought otherwise, as she could only see the romantic side of the affair, the love story. In his article Kanaan further develops the hypothesis that Arlosoroff, who was protected in Germany by his British Mandate passport, could only be eliminated via middle-men in Palestine, and that this was prepared for by contact with the Nazi agents. If we follow this hypothesis, it does seem possible that Goebbels really was behind the assassination of Arlosoroff, and the murderers, as Kanaan describes, were put up to it by the Nazi agents.[3]

There is, however, no conclusive proof of this. Goebbels' diaries, understandably enough, contain no reference to the murder. In Israel, files dealing with the case have disappeared over the years, and the British Mandate government lost documents dealing with the murder when a British ship sank with all papers aboard after the foundation of the state of Israel.

Arlosoroff's younger sister, Lisa Arlosoroff-Steinberg, confided the whole story to her brother's school-friend, Dr Max Flesch, on the understanding that he would not discuss the matter until after her death, because she was frightened of what might happen. Her suspicion that Goebbels might be behind her brother's murder was based both on the circumstances of his death and on her personal knowledge of the relationship between Magda and Arlosoroff, and the knowledge that Goebbels was a very jealous man.

Lisa's fear seems understandable if we examine the biographies of the figures involved in the Arlosoroff affair. Gauleiter Koch, who had dispatched the two Nazi agents, later became Reichskommissar to the Ukraine. Baron von Bolschwing became a spy for the Nazi government in the Middle East, and was later involved in a Romanian pogrom in which Jews were tortured to death with unimaginable cruelty.[4]

Chapter 24

On 20 June 1933, in bold print, the *Jüdische Rundschau* carried the headline 'Chaim Arlosoroff murdered'.[1] This was followed by a lengthy obituary, paying detailed homage to Arlosoroff's work, and his various efforts to achieve a progressive Palestine, which he imagined in harmony with the culturally awakening Arabism of the Middle East. Memorial services were held for him everywhere, in Jerusalem, in Tel Aviv and London. Even some Bedouin chiefs expressed their sympathy.

The Berlin memorial service was held on 26 June in the Philharmonie: '. . . it was organised as an imposing, profoundly moving testimony of friendship and attachment to the dead man. The great hall was so full that long before it began the floods of mourners had to be turned away for lack of space . . . Very many of the assembled are young people.'[2]

Magda and Goebbels had stopped talking to one another again during this time. By now their disagreements – according to his diary entries – were a daily event. Much had changed for Goebbels. He had achieved something for which he had striven throughout the years of his political struggle, but some of his energies, which could clearly be properly expressed only in aggression, now went unused. He was mostly left with administrative tasks, the control and manipulation of press, film and radio, the staging of mass events and marches – and his polemics against the Jews. A fundamental change had taken place in his relationship with Magda, despite the assurances they had given one another. He no longer needed Magda, or her belief in his goals, as much as he had. He now sought confirmation outside the marriage, but at the same time he still wanted to make Magda the mother of his children. She was to be his understanding companion, and she was still the strongest bond linking him to Hitler.

He had totally changed in his outward appearance too, having abandoned the 'proletarian look' that had been so effective in the workers' districts of Berlin. 'A barber attended to his hair. The best tailor in Berlin made his suits, while a specialist in orthopaedic shoes successfully ensured that his limping walk was less conspicuous than before.'[3] The manicurist came to his house, because the Reich Minister for Public Information and Propaganda also placed considerable value on well-tended hands. His mother-in-law relates that he spent an hour a day under the sun-ray lamp, that he often polished his shoes himself 'because no one else did it well enough. And if his trousers had to be ironed, the whole staff trembled, because the Doctor tended to hold them up to the light to check that a double crease hadn't been ironed into the fabric.'[4] Rumour had it that he possessed more than a hundred suits; with them he preferred to wear cream silk shirts. Even under his brown uniform coat he chose to wear dress trousers with silk stripes and patent shoes.

But if at first sight he appeared to have shed his vulgar behaviour, his complexes and inhibitions remained the same as before. Despite the fact that he was happy to bellow his slogans to crowds of thousands, Goebbels found it difficult to make conversation in a small circle, particularly in the society of people he barely knew, or who came from another social class, the haute-bourgeoisie or the aristocracy. His relations with other Party members were frosty, and he had such a need for admiration that he could not bear anyone else being the focus of attention. This is made especially clear in his relations with Göring, of whom he had always been jealous because of 'fat Hermann's' extraordinary popularity among the people. Magda, too, was dismissive of him and his rather jolly companion, later his wife, Emmy Sonnemann.

Still no one apart from Hitler really stood behind Goebbels. Goebbels was convinced that he would be liquidated if anything were to happen to Hitler, and that the end of Hitler would also be his own. But for the time being Hitler remained a frequent guest at the home of Magda and Goebbels, where he found a kind of 'extended family', and he remained in a sense the centre of both their lives until the bitter end. In the first years after 1933 Hitler tended to arrive at around eight in the evening, accompanied only by an adjutant and the director of the Mercedes car factory, Werlin, who was at the time the president of the Reich Association of the German Automobile Industry. 'He greeted Magda very sweetly, and my daughter served him a caramel pudding, of which he was very fond.'[5] According to statements by intimates of the household, Magda gazed at Hitler with loving eyes, attending to his every need. She was transformed in his presence: her usually relaxed style vanished, she became nervous and frantically tried to be charming.

One day Goebbels mentioned a man who had made an insulting remark about the regime. Hitler remained relatively calm, and simply said that the man should be locked up. But Magda, her blonde hair parted in the middle, her blue eyes opened wide and her hands folded in her lap – the very picture of a Madonna – said, 'I think they should cut his head off!' and Hitler smiled calmly at her. She was by no means so fanatical in reality, and as far as she was concerned the enemies of the regime could have gone on living quite happily, but on that day she thought that Hitler might be pleased by the violence of her opinion, and she wanted to please her idol at any price.

Goebbels continued to listen to a great deal of music, and kept company with composers and performers of light music, as Auguste recalled: 'In the years after 1933 Paul Lincke, a prominent representative of the world of light entertainment, was often a guest in the Goebbels household. The grey eminence of *Berliner Luft* was an excellent skat player, and this interested Magda almost more than his compositions.'[7]

Of the classical composers Magda loved above all Wagner and Chopin. '"Mozart is too sweet for me", she would always say if I wanted to hear something from *The Magic Flute* or *Don Giovanni*. Goebbels was a virtuoso pianist. His greatest musical enthusiasm was Liszt. But, like Magda, he was not averse to a little light entertainment . . . One of his favourite composers was Peter Kreuder. Which did not, incidentally, prevent him from calling Kreuder in to see him in about 1943, to give him a terrible time about having a half-Jewish wife.'[8]

Magda had decorated the new house in Hermann Göring Strasse entirely to Goebbels' liking, but then he expected her to be perfect in ways that she could not always live up to. Meissner writes on the subject: 'Where her parties were concerned, it was often the luck of the draw. Often the tea wasn't quite ready by the time the guests were sitting down. Sometimes the soup was served cold, or the cutlery was in the wrong order . . . But Magda always acted as though it was the most natural thing in the world, even if the most embarrassing things happened. She once told Ello one could tell a real lady by the way she continued her conversation with her guests without so much as a flicker even if the gas oven was exploding in the kitchen.'[9]

However much money Goebbels spent on himself, the household was run on an almost miserly basis. Goebbels did not much care about food, and unlike many of his colleagues in the party he was not a great drinker. Guests to the Goebbels home were often still hungry when they left the dinner table. People from the film world, who often dined frugally in the Goebbels household, tried to make sure they grabbed a snack before it was time to turn up. Magda herself was also extraordinarily thrifty, and all the family's servants confirm that only absolutely necessary foodstuffs were kept in the larder.

Magda was generous with her staff, however, and gave them free rein. But they did change remarkably quickly, and Magda was forever in search of new nannies and cooks.

Meissner, who had first-hand knowledge of Magda, writes that she was not a soft-hearted person, not a tender woman. She held any lack of self-control in the utmost contempt. He bears this out with the following story: 'Once she had a maid who forgot everything and, if she didn't forget it, got it wrong. Magda scolded the girl and threatened to give her the sack. The unhappy creature went to the kitchen, turned on the gas-tap and lay down under it. Fortunately the girl was soon found. Magda ordered her to pack her bags immediately and go: "If a person's so out of control that she wants to kill herself for a justified scolding, I have no sympathy. It's practically unnatural." The girl fell on her knees and wept, but Magda was resolutely unsympathetic and insisted on firing her.'[9]

This kind of reaction does seem to suggest that Magda was rather short of empathy, that she could not easily imagine her way into other people's feelings.

The daily life of Herr and Frau Goebbels ran on extremely regular lines. Goebbels' manservant came into his bedroom at 7.30 to wake him up. He trundled a little tea-trolley with a cup of black coffee into the room. On a plate were three different vitamin tablets and two slices of whole-wheat bread, each cut into quarters. It took Goebbels exactly forty-five minutes to get ready.[10]

Magda, too, had iron self-discipline. She lived according to a rhythm regulated almost to the minute. She got up each day at exactly the same time, even when she had gone to bed very late or felt unwell. Her morning preparations followed a precisely ordered plan, counting even the strokes of her hairbrush and spending the same number of minutes brushing her teeth from right to left and from bottom to top.

In this way Magda was able to get herself ready or get dressed in an astonishingly short time, and even her closest family members never saw her other than perfectly coiffed and manicured. Magda hated the slightest sign of negligence. She changed her clothes for lunch, and reapplied all her make-up.[11] One might wonder whether Magda's extreme discipline, which she devoted to her outward appearance, was not based on a sense of insecurity, as though she could not even be herself 'unmade-up' in her closest domestic surroundings, and only felt secure once she had put on her mask.

Magda was certainly an intelligent woman, but her contemporaries never describe her as witty or quick. She liked to laugh at other people's jokes, but she herself was incapable of creating a cheerful mood. She seemed to be more of an empty vessel, absorbing the atmosphere of those around her and reflecting it as best she could. She was by no means a match for Goebbels' sarcasm and the cynical remarks that he liked to make at her expense. Meissner describes her judgement of people as 'intolerant, even impatient. Sometimes Magda was quick to drop people about whom she has been annoyed or disappointed for no real reason, but she showed unswerving loyalty to those to whom she was really close.'[12] Her relationship with Quandt was informed by this loyalty. When, in the second half of the war, Goebbels heard that Quandt was supposed to have said, 'Hitler is leading Germany straight into the most terrible catastrophe in its history,' he was so furious that he wanted to bring him before the courts on grounds of defeatism. That would have meant Quandt's death. As Meissner reports, Magda had secret meetings with Quandt and advised him to come up with a number of excuses. 'Then she managed to calm Goebbels down somewhat.'[13]

Meissner points out that 'Magda was superstitious. She often had her fortune told by gypsies who agreed in prophesying that she would die an unnatural death between the age of forty and forty-five. She didn't believe it, but she often thought about it. When the end approached, Magda remembered that prediction, and talked about it.'[14]

Goebbels emphasised the importance of cutting a fine figure abroad. He was able to claim his trip to Rome in June as a personal success. In September 1933 Hitler sent him to Geneva, where he took part in the meeting of the Plenary Group of the League of Nations, to correct the negative image that other countries had of Germany. Hitler and Goebbels felt that the League of Nations, of which Germany was still a member, was not a friendly or a neutral organisation, but one that was actively hostile. Viktor Reimann describes his arrival in Geneva:

... he acted the gentleman for the people in Geneva. He was wearing a Stresemann, a stiff black hat and gloves ... In a press conference held in the hall of the Carlton Hotel, despite being initially rejected, he enjoyed personal success. He began his speech with a lament about the suspicion with which foreign countries were treating the new Germany. He spoke out on the Jewish question: 'I cannot but admit that in the course of the National Revolution in Germany assaults by uncontrollable elements have indeed occurred. But it strikes us as incomprehensible that other countries should refuse to take the surplus of Jewish emigrants.' He invited the journalists to visit the concentration camps in Germany, in which the 'most humane and loyal methods were applied.' Then he emphasised that Germany wanted to work for peace, and that it had 'the greatest success of its life' on its side.[15]

The mendacity of his words came to light two weeks later, when Germany left the League of Nations. Hitler announced that Germany considered that it had been forced into taking such an action, since, despite Hitler's peacemaking speech, it was not recognised as an equal partner. On 12 November there was to be a referendum on the issue, at the same time as the Reichstag election, and Goebbels had made Germany's withdrawal from the League of Nations the main plank of the election campaign. The National Socialists were the only party to stand in this election, and exerted strong pressure on those who diverged from their opinion. Victor Klemperer describes the preparations for the election in his diary:

The extravagant propaganda for a 'Yes' vote. On every commercial vehicle, post office van, postman's bicycle, on every house and shop window, on broad banners, which are stretched across the street – quotations from Hitler are everywhere and always 'Yes' for peace! It is the most monstrous of hypocrisies . . . Demonstrations and chanting into the night, loudspeakers on the streets . . . Yesterday from one until two the 'festive hour'. 'At the thirteenth hour Adolf Hitler will come to the workers.' The language of the Gospels exactly. The Redeemer comes to the poor.[16]

Klemperer listened to Hitler's and Goebbels' speeches on the radio:

From the engine shop at Siemenstadt. For several minutes one heard the whistling, squealing, hammering, then the siren and the humming of the switched-off wheels. A very skilful, calmly delivered evocation of the atmosphere by Goebbels, then more than forty minutes of Hitler. A mostly hoarse, strained, agitated voice, long passages in the whining tone of the sectarian preacher. Content: I know no intellectuals, bourgeois, proletarians – only the people. Why have millions of my opponents remained in the country? The emigrants are 'scoundrels' . . . And a couple of hundred thousand rootless internationalists – interruption: 'Jews!' – want to set nations of millions at one another's throats. I want only peace. I have risen from the common people, I want nothing for myself . . . You should say yes for your own sake. Etc.[17]

As the masses were being duped for weeks with this kind of dis-honest peace propaganda, the result can hardly come as a surprise: ninety-three per cent of votes for Hitler. Goebbels basked once again in the victory of his propaganda, which seemed to have exceeded all bounds, as Klemperer observes: 'And since then we have been told in every possible key: this "election" is recognised abroad, "all of Germany" is seen to be behind Hitler, [the foreign powers] admire Germany's unity, will be conciliatory towards it, etc. etc. . . . On top of everything else "London says": what especially commanded admiration was that even in the concentration camps most had voted "Yes". But that is undoubtedly either a matter of falsification or compulsion.'[18]

Chapter 25

New Year 1934 opened with tensions between Magda and Goebbels. After their reception with Reich President Hindenburg they had to attend to the task of 'congratulations' at home. Magda, who was already several months pregnant, received her guests in a negligée. Goebbels was furious. Magda shouted back. The situation between them became so tense that he refused to go to see Hitler 'until she gave in and admitted she was wrong'.[1]

Magda's behaviour during this reception at their home comes as a surprise, since she is usually described as extraordinarily correct. Was her intention to provoke Goebbels, attract his attention because she did not want to express the real reasons for her annoyance with him?

As ever, things temporarily sorted themselves out. At the end of March, shortly before the baby was due, the Goebbels rented a little house in Kladow, on the shores of the Wannsee. Goebbels had a motor yacht brought to the lake. It was named after the Nordic god of light, Baldur. He learned to sail and, at much the same time, to drive a car. In this he was something of a late starter, especially if we bear in mind that Magda was already driving her own car by the time they met, although after she became Frau

Goebbels she was no longer allowed to do this. Kladow was close enough to Berlin for Goebbels to be able to commute between the summer house and the city on weekdays. He saw Hela Strehl and Petra Fiedler, later inviting them to his Wannsee house and going on boat-trips with his family and guests. When Magda began to go into labour, he noted: 'I hope it's a boy!'[2] But the pains passed this time, and Magda was brought to the clinic on 12 April. Then, on 13 April 1934 a little girl, Hilde, was born. Magda's mother Auguste describes Goebbels' reaction to a second daughter, as the story was told to her by Prince Schaumburg: 'When the birth became known in the Ministry, the whole company of adjutants became nervously excited. Who would be man enough to be the first to congratulate the Doctor on his second daughter? Schaumburg expressed his congratulations in extremely cautious terms. Goebbels rallied, with sparkling eyes: "If fate believes it has done me wrong, then I will teach fate some manners!"'[3]

Perhaps because she had not had the son and heir that Goebbels longed for, Magda urged her husband to re-establish her custody of Harald, whom she missed. Since Magda's remarriage Harald had lived with his father, in accordance with the divorce contract. To change that Goebbels was prepared to exploit his position of power for Magda's purposes; it must also have been a personal pleasure for him to show the big industrialist Quandt, who was of good and well-established family, who held the whip hand. Before he did that he checked that he had Hitler's support, and then called Quandt to a meeting in the Propaganda Ministry. Here he accused the industrialist of bringing up his son in ways critical of the Nazi regime, and stated that for that reason it was appropriate for him to return to his mother. Quandt insisted that he had signed a legal contract with Magda, according to which he had sole custody of Harald.

Goebbels made his position clearer, and threatened him with an order from the Führer.

Quandt, who could not see what the Chancellor had to do with his young son, replied that he would defend his rights before the custody court. Goebbels in turn replied that he was quite free to do this if he wished, but he would end up a ruined man.

'So I will be bowing to force,' Harald's father said, rising to his feet.

'No!' Goebbels explained, standing up as well: 'No, you'll be bowing to your own intelligence!'[4]

After the birth of Hilde, Magda stayed in the clinic for a little while longer. Hitler came to congratulate her, and Goebbels came to terms with the 'fate' of being the father of two daughters. The constant arguments with Magda made way for what he called a 'cease-fire'. But not for long. In June 1934 Magda made another scene, so violently this time that he was truly shaken by it. As far as we can tell, the reason for this was a young baroness with whom he had gone walking in the Grunewald, and whom he had invited to private film screenings.

While Magda was conducting her private battle with Goebbels, the whole of Germany had been brought into line with Nazi policies. The regional governments had been dissolved, and the Law for the Rebuilding of the Reich was passed on 30 January 1934. Anyone wishing to work as a teacher had to join the National Socialist Teachers' League. But although by now all the institutions, professions, schools and universities, press and radio were under Party control, Hitler still perceived an element of instability in the 'Reich': the chief of staff of the SA and Minister without Portfolio, Ernst Röhm.

Since 1933 the SA had encompassed a militia of some four and a half million soldiers. In itself it did not pose a direct problem for Hitler, but a threat was posed by its leader, Ernst Röhm. While at the beginning of his regime Hitler had had to establish a delicate political equilibrium, on the one hand making sure to avoid terrifying the conservatives, reassuring the bankers and industrialists that Germany was on the way to an economic recovery and the Nazi revolution had come to an end, at the same time he had to suggest to radical forces that the revolution had lost none of its impetus. This revolutionary side of the Party, to which Goebbels had belonged, and which he still represented – in his attacks against the aristocracy or the church, for example – was embodied in Ernst Röhm. The historian Fritz Stern writes that throughout the whole of Hitler's career only this one man, Ernst Röhm, dared to stand up to Hitler, negotiating with him on equal terms. Röhm was prepared to preserve the interests of his left wing within the NSDAP in order to risk a conflict with the Reichswehr, and Hitler was opposed to this because the Reichswehr, which was supported by the conservative elements within the state and headed by the weak von Blomberg, was prepared to co-operate with Himmler and the SS. Hitler preferred this possibility because it enabled him to put the conservative wing at its ease.

Discontent had been bubbling within the SA for some time, because the brown-shirted fighting troops of the early days were now earning less money and had less prestige than before, despite the fact that it had been they who had conquered Berlin with Goebbels. Playing a clever game, the Nazi leadership managed to surprise the chief of staff of the SA, Röhm, accusing him of plotting a putsch. Hitler interrupted a visit to the Ruhr valley, and flew with Sepp Dietrich and Goebbels to Munich, landing there at four o'clock on the morning of Sunday 30 June. The SA officers who had turned up to welcome him were stripped of their party insignia, and arrested by the police. A column of black Mercedes limousines then dashed to Wiessee. Hitler insisted on being present at the planned murders. At eight o'clock in the morning the homosexual Röhm and his circle, some of them with young male lovers, were chased from their beds, and the bloodbath began. Most of them put up little resistance. Over the next three days about two hundred people lost their lives, some taking the option of suicide. Among those murdered was Goebbels' old rival, Georg Strasser, along with General von Schleicher and his wife. The massacre entered the annals as the 'Night of the Long Knives', but the bloodbath remained without legal consequences, because on 3 July a law was passed declaring 'St Bartholomew's Day' a legal measure taken for the defence of the state. On Friday 13 July

Hitler himself addressed the Reichstag on the subject. The American journalist William L. Shirer noted in his Berlin diary: 'When he screamed: "The supreme court of the German people during those twenty-four hours consisted of myself!" the deputies rose and cheered.'[5]

During these days Goebbels stayed close to Hitler, as though it was only there that he could feel safe. Was he afraid something similar might happen to him? He did not get on well with Himmler, while Ernst Röhm had been a regular house-guest at Reichskanzlerplatz. And what about Magda, who also knew Röhm, and who must have put two and two together after the bloodbath? Was she repelled by the events, scared perhaps? It is well known that she did not like Röhm, since she had once noticed him making drunken advances on press chief Sepp Deitrich. During the massacre Goebbels had also been concerned with her safety, because he called her back with the children from Kladow to the ministerial villa in Berlin, where she was placed under police guard.

After the foreign press had reacted with horror to the events, and Goebbels had responded with counter-attacks in which he talked about sensationalism and gun-barrel journalism, he returned to Magda. She had by now returned to Kladow, but was suddenly – despite the presence of her staff – frightened and alone in the lakeside house. She must have been struck by the horror of the events, and was plagued by states of anxiety, fearing that she too was going to be killed. Later in the year she would give generous Christmas presents to the widows of the murdered SA leadership.

Hitler's triumph over law and justice was now complete. He no longer presented events as being merely politically necessary – because of the supposed risks of a putsch– but stressed his own moral superiority by stressing the homosexuality of Röhm and his circle, although he had, of course, known about it for a long time.

During the Weimar Republic there had been a certain liberalisation in the laws on homosexuality, but after the liquidation of

Röhm, according to Friedländer, 'homophobia in the SS became particularly shrill. A 1935 article demanded the death penalty for homosexual behaviour, and during the Nazi period 10 to 15,000 homosexuals were imprisoned. We do not know how many died in the camps, but according to a prisoner from Dachau "the prisoners with the pink triangle never lasted long, they were quickly and systematically annihilated by the SS."'[6]

While Hitler was planning his next coup, the *Anschluss* of Austria, Magda spent the rest of the summer in Kladow. Goebbels and Hitler were frequent visitors, they enjoyed their boat-trips and sunbathing, and Goebbels played with his little daughter Helga, whom he idolised. After 21 July Goebbels and Hitler set off together for Bayreuth, to the Wagner Festival. They amused themselves in the home of Winifred Wanger, one of Hitler's most ardent devotees, and during the performance of *Rheingold* they waited for news from Vienna, because behind the scenes the Nazis had been pulling every available string to get rid of Chancellor Dollfuss. On 25 July 1934 the news came that Dollfuss had been murdered: yet another victim of the Nazis, who had occupied the State Chancellery and the radio; however they did not manage to achieve a complete coup, because Schuschnigg, his replacement, had the situation under control. 'I do not like murder, and Nazi murder least of all,' writes William L. Shirer. 'But I cannot weep for Dollfuss after his cold-blooded slaughter of the Social Democrats last February.'[7]

Mussolini, who had a keen interest in the disappearance of Dollfuss from the scene, reacted with rage and sent soldiers to the Austrian border. There was a temporary break in diplomatic relations with Germany. The murderers of Dollfuss were publicly hanged, and died with the words 'Heil Hitler' on their lips as the rope tightened around their necks. From now on, the rise of the Nazis to power could clearly no longer be stopped.

When Hindenburg died on 2 August 1934, a law was passed by the Reich government an hour later, bearing the previous day's date. According to this law, the office of the President and that of the Chancellor were united in the person of Hitler, and the Wehrmacht swore its allegiance to him the same evening. While hymns were being played for Hindenburg all over Germany, millions of people were presumably unaware that the Nazi government had just pulled off another perfect coup, and one which had been prepared long in advance.

The referendum on the unification of the offices of the Reich President and the Reich Chancellor on 19 August was nothing but a farce. The results had been fixed long before the vote was held. But there were still five million negative and spoiled votes as against a total of thirty-eight million votes in favour, and as Klemperer points out, in an ethical sense these meant 'a great deal more than merely a ninth of the whole'.[8] Of course the voters had previously – as usual – been drugged with slogans and intoxicated with the noise of parties.

In the autumn, after the spectacle of the Nuremberg Rally, which brought Hitler's devotees together in a mood of hysteria, social life in Berlin resumed. There was plenty of gossip about Joseph and Magda Goebbels. Word had got around about their marital difficulties, and Goebbels could not stop bragging about his relationships with the stars and starlets of the film industry. After a party which Bella Fromm attended, she wrote the following observations in her diary: 'Goebbels has dreamed up something new for his girls in the Ministry of Propaganda. He has come up with a system for getting rid of them before they grow tiresome. He seeks out a good-looking young man, encourages him and then marries him off to his latest mistress. He honours the boy and his abandoned sweetheart by coming to the marriage ceremony which is taking place on his orders. The most recent case is young, blonde Maria Stahl, who is marrying Josef Terboven, the Gauleiter of Essen, today.'[9]

Of course this kind of gossip also reached Magda's ears, and the attempt to keep Goebbels' affection at all costs, as though she would be lost without him, now runs like a thread through her life. Since autumn 1934 she was no longer only lighting down a constant suspicion, but had learned by chance that he really was betraying her, and that he did not shrink from bringing his girl-friends to his own house.

One stormy autumn night Magda lay awake. She was sleeping badly, as she often did by now. Too many thoughts oppressed her. How would her life and the lives of her children continue? Her trust for her husband had been shattered by all his little lies. Socially she had achieved what she wanted – she was the first lady of the Reich, and Hitler was still a frequent guest, even taking an interest in the children – but Goebbels' interest in her as a woman had vanished, as she was keenly aware. He went to parties on his own, and took no interest in taking her to the theatre or to film premières. She now suffered from frequent migraine attacks, but she knew that she could not mention the fact, as she would get nothing from Goebbels but yet another cynical remark.

Goebbels and she had slept in separate bedrooms since she had the house renovated. The two rooms were separated by a hall and a bathroom. That noise she had just heard must have been the bathroom door banging on its hinges. The wind would not let Magda sleep. Finally she got up to close the door properly. Then she discovered to her great surprise that the door leading from her own bedroom to the bathroom had been locked on the other side. She had to cross the corridor to close the banging door from that side. Magda was shocked, although she did not try to go into Joseph's room to speak her mind, but she could still not get back to sleep. Towards morning she heard Goebbels quietly approach-ing the locked door and carefully turning the key to open it again.

In the morning, when Goebbels tenderly inquired why she looked so dreadful, Magda explained that she had a headache. He believed her, and set off unconcerned for the Ministry.

At breakfast, Magda sat alone with her house-guest of the pre-vious night. But she passed no remarks, swallowed back her anger and irritation, and instead tried to be extraordinarily charming, telling the lady: 'My car will take you to the tram . . . you don't have much time to pack.'[10]

While Magda endured her husband's injuries with apparent resignation, she still tried to take her small revenge by making his life difficult for him in her own way, either through moodiness or through social snubs. When there was another row in the Goebbels household about a new secretary, it had typical effects on a dinner party. Bella Fromm, who understood the background to the unsuccessful evening, describes a conversation with a member of the old, aristocratic society, Frau von Neurath, whose husband, Baron Konstantin von Neurath, was Foreign Minister: 'She was in a state: "It's a shame how the Goebbels behave! The last dinner at the Italian Embassy was scheduled for seven thirty. He cancelled his invitation at seven o'clock! She was to come alone. The entire seating order had to be changed. At seven forty she had not shown up. Cerruti had somebody phone her house. The maid reported: "Madam has gone to bed with a headache." Such rudeness from people who are supposed to have equal rank with my husband!'[11]

This event also shows how Magda, following the example of the Nazi leadership, infringed the social rules of the old elite, and how conservative society thought it might reach an accommodation with the Nazis as a means of appeasing them and maintaining their own privileged position. The 'von Neuraths' failed to understand that this was not merely tactlessness or childish behaviour on the Nazis' part, but that their behaviour was actually based on a profound contempt for the old aristocratic elite.

Chapter 26

Joseph and Magda spent New Year in the Black Forest with their children and a large circle including Magda's sister-in-law Ello Quandt. Magda skied and played skat, while Goebbels chatted with the ladies. After their return to Berlin Magda discovered that she was pregnant again. The many disagreements and permanent tensions between Magda and Goebbels, based on the fact that he was constantly involved with other women, clearly didn't mean a complete loss of physical attraction. Since they needed more room for their growing family, they planned to renovate the city villa by adding on a large residential hall to be designed by Hitler's favourite architect, Albert Speer. The expensive enterprise was financed with taxpayers' money. Goebbels also had a small apartment in his ministry, which he used for private purposes: it consisted of a drawing-room, a bedroom and a bath, and when he stayed there he had a complicated system to ensure that he could not be surprised or disturbed.

Although Goebbels had, like Göring and Ammann and various other notables within the Party, yielded to luxury, it galled him to see the Görings' extravagance when, on the wishes of Hitler, who wanted to see the relationship given legal status, he married his long-term companion, the actress Emmy Sonnemann. The city of Berlin came to a standstill and thirty thousand troops lined the streets, apart from anything because the actress was very popular. Bella Fromm wrote: 'Emmy is no feminine intriguer. The witty Berliners already call her Landesmutter. She is a sympathetic, motherly woman. The Valkyrie type. Her lovely blonde hair frames her brow in a large braid. Her big blue eyes are soft and serene. She loves to wear floating gowns which make her look even plumper and rounder . . . The Reich's First Lady is the exact opposite of skinny, sour-tempered, mean Magda Goebbels.'[1]

Faith in Hitler, and in a re-establishment of Germany's greatness, were constantly growing, particularly when the Saarland decided, after a costly campaign followed by a referendum, to 'return to the Reich'. Until then this region had been under the protectorate of the League of Nations, and a referendum scheduled for this time had been guaranteed by the Versailles Treaty. Now Hitler saw the decision as a great personal success on the part of his policies.

On 16 March he prepared for his next strike. In direct contravention of the Treaty of Versailles he decided to abandon military restrictions, and instead to reintroduce universal military service. Even prior to this, the party leadership had put huge amounts of energy into bringing young people into what were called 'sporting' organisations, although these were run along paramilitary lines. After the official reintroduction of military service there was no longer any need to rearm on the sly. The new army was presented the following day: the Wehrmacht. From now on, within Germany, enthusiasm for Hitler appeared boundless, and no foreign power dared to react to this massive transgression of the Versailles Treaty. 'It is a terrible blow to the Allies,' noted the journalist William Shirer, 'to France, Britain, Italy, who fought the War and wrote the peace to destroy Germany's military power and to keep it down. What will London and Paris do? They could fight a "preventive" war, and that would be the end of Hitler. But first reactions tonight . . . are all against it. We shall see.'[2]

During this time Magda devoted most of her time to her children. In the summer, Hitler often came to Kladow. Trips on the yacht were his frequent distractions, and in the meantime Goebbels organised film screenings for him. Young actresses and successful film-stars were invited to Kladow, where they were paid lavish attention by Goebbels – and the young ladies, hoping for a part or a contract, flirted back. In his diary Goebbels noted the names of these various visitors, but he also took the time to play with his little daughter Helga, whom he loved, and whom he repeatedly describes in his diary as 'simply sweet'. But Magda's tensions continued.[3]

As autumn began, the Goebbels household returned to the city, and while Magda waited to learn when her baby was due, her husband prepared for the next Nuremberg Rally.

For some time now, alongside Bolshevists and Jews Goebbels had also been attacking the churches, both Catholic and Protestant, since to a large extent they seemed resistant to a takeover by Hitler, although not enough to stand in the way of the general development. In the churches, in spite of everything that might have repelled active Christianity, there were enough committees and fellow-travellers to withdraw shrewdly from open conflict or – in the spirit of the First World War – to preach national pride and Germany's new greatness from the pulpit.

Since the beginning of 1935 the attacks on the Jews had also become more aggressive. There was severe rioting, particularly in Munich, and then, from mid-July, along the Kurfürstendamm in Berlin, where there were still some elegant shops belonging to Jews. Friedländer quotes Jochen Klepper, a profoundly religious Protestant author, whose wife was Jewish: '"Anti-Semitic riots on the Kurfürstendamm. Threats of the cleansing of the Jews from Berlin."' Friedländer reports: 'Jewish women were struck in the face; Jewish men behaved courageously. No one came to their aid, because everyone feared arrest.' On 7 September Klepper, who had lost his position in radio in 1933 because of his Jewish wife, was fired from the recently 'Aryanised' Ullstein publishing house, where he had found employment. That day he noted that the signs banning the Jews from access to the swimming pool had been put up, and that even in the little street where he went walking with his wife, the same warning hung on one of the fences.[4]

Anti-Jewish discrimination spread to every sphere. In spite of everything there were still some Jews who clung to their German nationalism, and after the foundation of the Wehrmacht wanted to volunteer for service. But by 21 May, only a few weeks after the official reintroduction of Germany as a military power, a declaration was made banning Jews from military service.

In this anti-Semitic climate, Goebbels, in his capacity as Propaganda Minister with responsibility for culture, refused to back down, and shortly afterwards announced that all Jews were excluded from membership of the Reich Culture Chamber.

But in doing this, particularly as regards the Reich Music Chamber, which was a subdivision of the Reich Culture Chamber, he had set himself a task of Herculean proportions. Its total 'cleansing' took significantly longer than he had imagined, because he found himself fighting on two fronts: against the people concerned, and against their tunes. The battle against light entertainment, against the popular songs of the day or favourite operetta tunes, turned out to be particularly difficult, because once something has entered the popular mind and is being whistled by boys in the street, it becomes difficult to eliminate.

Almost all contemporary Jewish interpreters and composers had fled the country, but even 'historical' artists threw up problems. The libretti of the three Mozart operas *The Marriage of Figaro*, *Cosi fan tutte* and *Don Giovanni*, were written by the Jew Lorenzo da Ponte, so that the libretti had to be retranslated or reworked.

Anti-Semitism was not restricted to certain spheres, however, but increasingly spilled over into daily life. In the summer of 1935 'the rage of the radical Nazis was inflamed particularly against Jews who dared to use public swimming pools, Jewish shops, Jews in market-places and, of course, racially polluting Jews.'[5] All these demonstrations of 'popular anger' were officially desirable, but not as yet authorised by law – that was still to come.

On 15 September 1935 the annual Nuremberg Rally came to an end. The same evening, in the auditorium of the Nuremberg League of Culture, an extraordinary meeting of the Reichstag was held. At this meeting, Hitler declared that the provocative behaviour of the Jews demanded spontaneous defensive reactions among the enraged population, which could only be regulated by laws. After this he had Hermann Göring read out the laws that were to be passed by the Reichstag.

While the first law, the Reich Flag Law, defined the swastika as the national flag, the second, the Reich Citizenship Law, established the fundamental distinction between Reich citizens, who enjoyed full political rights of citizenship, and state subjects, who were now robbed of those rights. Only those with German or related blood were eligible for citizenship. From that moment onwards, the Jews had the approximate status of foreigners.

The third, the Blood Law, forbade marriages and extra-marital relationships between Jews and non-Jews – for the 'protection of German blood' – a law that would have made the marriage of Magda's mother Auguste and Friedländer impossible, if she had not been divorced long since. Magda's relationship with Arlosoroff would also have counted as 'racial pollution'.

The law also forbade Jews from employing German staff under the age of forty-five. Klemperer, who had by now lost his professorship, describes how the Jews must have felt after these official declarations: 'The Jew-baiting has become so extreme, far worse than during the first boycott, there are the beginnings of a pogrom here and there, and we expect to be beaten to death at any moment. Not by neighbours, but by purgers who are deployed now here, now there as the "soul of the people". On the tram stop signs on Prager Strasse: "Who buys from the Jew, is a traitor to the nation."'[6]

To the population at large, the 'man in the street', these measures were sold as a reaction to the healthy 'popular feeling', which was more highly valued than the citizens' rights pertaining up to this point. This supposedly healthy popular feeling defined as a right anything that benefited the German people, and anything that harmed it as a wrong. This perversion of legal language and justice brought with it a general distortion and falsification of values and concepts. Hitler, for example, changed the function of central Christian concepts for the purposes of his ideology by identifying the party's victims as 'martyrs', who had been 'resurrected in the Third Reich'. We may assume that Goebbels had a hand in this language.

While we know that the new racial laws caused consternation both at home and abroad, we do not know how Magda reacted. She was pregnant once again, and her due date was drawing near. Two weeks before this, 15 September, the day of the announcement of the racial laws, she went to the clinic. 'Please God may everything go well, and may it be a boy,'[7] noted Goebbels in his diary, but it was only a false alarm. On 19 September Magda came back home, was sent back to the clinic, and came home once again. On 23 September, when Goebbels returned home from an excursion, 'things seemed to be starting with Magda. We are all very excited. Back to the clinic. Anxious waiting! But nothing happens, our waiting is in vain. Stoeckel is considering the possibility of a Caesarian.'[8] On 25 September Goebbels visited Magda in the clinic, and they had a terrible row.

Ello Quandt, who was very loyal to Magda, had probably told her best friend that during her stay in the clinic Goebbels had found comfort in the company of Hela Strehl. And Erika Chelius, an old flame who had married in the meantime, also makes an appearance in Goebbels' diary, and makes him wallow in 'blissful memories'.[9] But finally, on 2 October 1935, the time finally arrived: Goebbels was in his car when the police stopped him on the street to tell him he must call Magda's doctor. Court Councillor Stoeckel congratulated him on the telephone: The boy has arrived! Goebbels dashed to the clinic and found Magda weeping tears of joy. He was 'happier than could be imagined', as he later confided to his diary, 'the face of a Goebbels!'[10]

Goebbels was so beside himself with joy that he forgot his usual thrift, and bought sparkling wine for his entire staff. The boy was to be called Helmut; Magda had chosen the name after her unfulfilled love, her stepson who had died so young.

Later on there was a great deal of puzzlement over the names of the Goebbels children. Since they all began with H, it was assumed that Magda had chosen the names in honour of Hitler – but this has never been proven. Auguste has a different theory: 'It was pure coincidence that the name "Helga" was chosen for the first child, agreeing with the first letter of the first name of Magda's son from her first marriage. When this was noticed, the search for Christian names beginning with H almost became a family hobby. And chance played a considerable role in that.'[11]

Herr and Frau Goebbels' contentment continued to grow over the next few weeks, and we find only benevolent entries about Magda in Goebbels' diary. For the time being she was once again 'kind', 'sweet' and 'dear'. We can tell that Goebbels thought having a large number of children was politically desirable from one of his diary entries: at a farmers' reception at a rally in Hanover Goebbels found himself sitting next to a man 'with twenty-two children. I am thoroughly ashamed. I have a lot of catching up to do.'[12]

A large family as a duty to the state – Goebbels hints at it here, and in all likelihood Magda was also aware of her merits as the mother of many children.

Hitler went on rearming, but not in such a way as to arouse the suspicions of the European powers. By now Mussolini had begun to conquer Abyssinia – supposedly to avert a possible threat from that country. This development was thoroughly welcomed by the Nazis, as the American journalist Shirer conjectured. Either Mussolini would stumble in this war of conquest, thus weakening his position in Europe, which would mean that Hitler could take Austria, currently under the protection of the 'Duce', or else Mussolini would win, in which case he would make an interesting confederate for Hitler, which would in turn present a challenge to the western democracies.[13]

Magda seemed to take little interest in political events abroad, but as well as her role as mother to her family she enjoyed playing the part of the 'mother of the country'. She received so much post that she employed a number of private secretaries, under the tutelage of Frau Freybe, who had been a fellow-pupil at her boarding school. The many letters sent to Magda reveal that she enjoyed a great deal of popularity, chiefly based on her maternal role. This must have something to do with the fact that she came so close to the ideal of motherhood propagated by the party. Thus, for example, she received begging letters from women who found themselves in financial difficulties, and whose partners refused to help with the maintenance of the children; she was asked to resolve marital difficulties, she had letters from companies hoping for commissions to decorate the ministerial household. All letters received replies, all requests were examined, and the political attitudes of those requesting help, the length of time they had belonged to the party, were more important than their actual needs.

After November 1934 we see a lengthy correspondence with the Romatzki fashion house on the Kurfürstendamm. It appeared that the umbrella organisation of film suppliers and craftsmen had demanded proof of Aryan status from Hilda Romatzki, after an NSDAP denunciation. Since the relevant department was not in a position to make a decision about Frau Romatzki's Aryan status, when she saw her livelihood threatened Hilda Romatzki turned to Magda, and the documents dealing with the case were actually passed on to 'Frau Reich Minister'. Magda, who had had work done for her by Frau Romatzki, took responsibility for the affair, and it turned out that Hilda Romatzki still officially bore the name of her Jewish husband, Schulen-Gossel, and had temporarily converted to the Jewish faith, but at the wishes of her customers had declared herself prepared to sever her Jewish connections and give any Jewish staff the sack. She also promised to revert to her maiden name.[14]

We can also tell something about how the system of denunciations in the Nazi state worked, and how people were corrupted by it, from what subsequently happened to the Romatzki fashion house. In 1937 Hilda Romatzki registered a complaint with the 'German Labour Front', which answered to the Gau Authorities in Berlin, about the Jewish fashion salon Grete, which, only a few doors away from her own business, was competing with her. Once again she was advised to apply to 'Frau Dr Goebbels', and once again Magda personally helped her to 'put a stop to unfair competition' by the Jewish salon. In all likelihood both fashion houses were rented from a Jewish proprietor, who could only be eliminated in this way. Magda's letter to the 'German Labour Front' in defence of Hilda Romatzki's position reads as follows: ' . . . Apart from the fact that I think it non-National-Socialist to allow such damage to be done to an Aryan company, and to make life so difficult for a woman on her own, it is also personally disagreeable to me, and unbearable to be suspected of being dressed by a Jewish fashion house . . .'[15] This letter was personally signed by Magda Goebbels.

Magda, who had been so helpful on behalf of the Romatzki fashion house, clearly imagined that she had earned some kind of price reduction. In her correspondence the name of the Romatzki fashion house pops up a number of times, as when Frau Freybe requests a price reduction for 'Frau Reich Minister'. Magda was clearly of the opinion that her silk summer dresses were too expensive at two hundred Reichsmark, and that alterations and cleaning were beyond her purse.

Chapter 27

The more secure the Nazi regime became, the more claustro-phobic and oppressive was the intellectual atmosphere in Germany. But the web of the totalitarian state was not only tight-ening around culture, but around every single area. The fact that significant artists like Furtwängler or Richard Strauss had stayed in the country was deceptive. No one could escape the system of espionage and control, even in their private lives. Hitler, who had repeatedly stated that he wanted to protect the family, in fact did precisely the opposite. Children and adolescents were made members of the Hitler Youth and League of German Girls, the Bund Deutscher Mädchen (BDM), and thus removed from the influence of their families, but also indoctrinated with the NSDAP ideology, and even inveigled into denouncing their own parents if their parents were critical of them.

Goebbels and Magda, however, brought up their daughters in the manner of the haute-bourgeoisie – at least outwardly. The photographs that remain show unusually pretty little girls in white dresses, with white socks and patent shoes, with big wide hair-bands. Goebbels declared his eldest daughter, Helga, to be his favourite. She was to remain so until the very end. In Goebbels' diary we find repeated references to the fact that Helga was also Hitler's favourite, because her father often took her to see Hitler. He was flattered when Hitler publicly treated the Goebbels children as if they were his own. Goebbels' only son, however, did not fulfil his father's hopes for him, and grew over the years into a dreamy, rather slow boy, who, unlike his sisters, also had learning difficulties.

Where Magda was concerned, we do not know whether she preferred any of her children to the others. She described her children's different temperaments to her friend Ello, even going so far as to imagine them all grown and married, and aware of betrayal by their partners: Helga, she thought, would take a revolver and try to blow her adulterous husband's brains out. Hilde would collapse in sobs and tears, but come round when her husband swore his fidelity. Helmut would be unable to believe that his wife was betraying him. Holde would never come to terms with the adultery, but would be too proud to level any accusations at her husband, and would then have a nervous breakdown. Hedda would get over it with a laugh and demand a kiss.[1]

Goebbels was considered a good father; he could only be accused of political indoctrination where his stepson Harald was concerned. None of the girls had to join the BDM, at a time when almost all children in Germany were obliged to become members of the National Socialist youth organisations. There was a Nazi influence in the parental home, of course, and the children all attended public schools whose curricula were in such conformity with the ideas of the Party that Goebbels evidently didn't consider it necessary to become further involved. According to his diary the children were important to him, although of course we do not know exactly what would have happened if his children had talked back to him or put forward views of their own, because he could not bear being criticised. At this point, though, the children were still small, and admired him. In Goebbels' diary it is repeatedly made clear that his children flattered his vanity – both before Hitler and in public – since in a sense they guaranteed his continuation, and bore testimony to his vitality. But his treatment of the children did not always meet with the approval of Magda, who liked to work according to a regular timetable. She found it hard when Goebbels – even if he came home late – took the little ones from their beds to the drawing-room, where, wrapped in blankets and pyjamas, they were allowed to watch films with him. 'Afterwards he would ask each child what they had liked about the film.'[2] We know little of Magda's relationship with her children. But the children were, according to all the contemporary accounts, happy and well brought-up, and not unnaturally well-behaved. Of course the ministerial household had maids to deal with practical matters, and Magda was happy to hand her children over to the relevant staff if she wished to go travelling or fulfil her social obligations.

Goebbels, who had always preferred planning on a grand scale, was now able to delegate the detailed work to his colleagues, which meant that he now had more time than ever before. He used that time to improve his relations with the worlds of film and theatre, which meant in concrete terms that he liked to surround himself with ambitious young talent. Hitherto it had not been customary in Germany for the government élite to consort with actors, or to introduce them to society in this way – even the little starlets. At most, singers might have been present at smart aristocratic receptions, or a famous theatre actor might have been invited to dinner – film people, on the other hand, were not socially acceptable. But Goebbels and Hitler felt at home with artists, more relaxed than they did with members of the old Prussian aristocracy or up-and-coming industrialists. They preferred the company of the stars, and this in itself did them no harm with the masses.

To put these encounters into their proper context, Goebbels founded the 'Kameradschaftshaus der deutschen Künstler' (K.d.d.K, the Comradeship Club for German Artists) in the old Rathenau villa on Skagerakplatz. According to Hans-Otto Meissner, who was a regular visitor to the building as a young diplomat, the Artists' Club consisted of social rooms, a dimly-lit bar, a winter-garden, a dance floor and a drinking room in the cellar. Access was permitted to anyone who was reasonably well known from the worlds of 'stage, film and press', or to people with contacts. Goebbels often came here alone late in the evening. If he was at all interested in one of the well-known actresses or rising starlets, he would introduce himself. He would be charming on such occasions, and while a little band played jazz from Broadway, he would chat and joke with the ladies. 'An outside visitor, who knew nothing about the German situation behind the scenes, and who knew nothing of the nightly arrests, would hardly have been able to imagine an image more international than this.'[3]

Magda went there extremely seldom, instead giving tea-parties at home, to which she invited her favourite artists or celebrities like the Swiss author John Knittel, whose *Via Mala* was her favourite book. General Rommel, too, liked to drop in when he was in Berlin, as did Crown Prince Umberto of Italy and Count Ciano, the Italian Foreign Minister and Mussolini's son-in-law. His wife, Countess Edda Ciano, Mussolini's favourite daughter, became a close friend of Magda's after they had spent holidays together in Switzerland. Bella Fromm wrote of Edda Ciano, on the occasion of a dinner at the Italian Ambassador's:

> Mussolini's daughter is in her early thirties, neither pretty nor plain, not too feminine . . . like her father, she is quite immoderate in her consumption of lovers . . . She is said to direct her father politically, and to settle his private affairs, getting rid of the women for him . . . Edda taught [Magda] that there was no reason to be miserable about a faithless husband, and that wedlock was only one of the states of man. Magda was most demonstrative about her friendship with Edda, and has carefully manoeuvred to keep 'those climbers', the Ribbentrops, as far away from her as possible.[4]

Germany was rearming. Although Hitler presented himself as a man of peace in his dealings with other countries, giving repeated assurances that he did not want war, it could not have escaped anyone that he was really pursuing militaristic policies. Even in February 1936, as Bella Fromm observes, '"Air Raid" is the watch-word of the day. Air raid shelters have to be built into every house. Very frequently there is an air raid alarm tryout. Sirens shriek and fire alarms whistle between 6.0 and 7.0 a.m.. The block warden counts his sheep. If one of the flock has not turned up in the shel-ter, he dashes to the apartment, knocks, rings the bell, and shouts until the missing lamb is roused..'[5]

In these manoeuvres Jews and non-Jews were kept strictly sep-arate, and the Jews had to go to the most vulnerable part of the cellar.

Air raid spaces were equipped for lengthy stays, and the govern-ment regularly organised nocturnal air raid exercises, ensuring, for example, that windows were covered with sheets of black-out paper.

There were good reasons for these measures. When France signed a treaty with Russia, Hitler took this as an excuse for declaring the Locarno Pact non-binding, and sent thirty thou-sand soldiers into the de-militarised zone of the Rhineland. Despite condemnation by the League of Nations and the proposal of an international police force for the Rhine zone, this step was another great triumph for Hitler. At the Reichstag session in Berlin that followed this German aggression, Hitler once again pulled out all the stops, talking for the umpteenth time about the shame of Versailles and feeding fears about Bolshevik world dom-ination and what he called the destructive 'Asiatic view of the world'. According to Bella Fromm's account, the session in the Kroll Opera was like a noisy pageant. 'With flags, Hitler Maidens, lanes of SS and SA, crowds of onlookers, radio cars, movie trucks, and, of course, a multitude of loudspeakers. They multiply every-thing in the Third Reich, just as a person with an inferiority complex magnifies his aggressive mannerisms. A people with a national inferiority complex.'[6]

After this new 'act of liberation' on Hitler's part, the people continued to cheer him on, while all kinds of threatening gestures were tried abroad – but in the end nothing happened. 'Now Hitler knows he can dare anything.'[7]

Magda almost always took part in demonstrations of National Socialist power, and she was happy and often moved to tears when the regime was successful. It was as though she continued to identify with the aims of the party, as though she felt secure in the sense that she was part of this power, and that she was able to exert some of that power in her own right. This sense of belonging to the movement, along with her own personal power – and of course the luxurious lifestyle that she was able to afford – made it easier for her to bear Goebbels' insults.

Magda and Goebbels had greatly enjoyed the summer months of the past year in their rented house in Kladow, and toyed with the idea of buying a property of their own nearby. When they found an English-style country house that matched their ideas they leapt upon it. It was on a peninsula in the Wannsee, Schwanenwerder, which slopes gently down to the reedy shores of the Havel. To the rear of the property there was a wood. Goebbels was able to buy the land cheaply, for only 350,000 marks. Magda added her settlement with Quandt; the rest was given to him by the Eher Verlag as an advance for his book, and Hitler contributed a further 70,000 marks. 'On the property stood three buildings, the main house, the "Kavaliershaus" – an annex for guests – and the farm building with stables and store-rooms. Part of the farm building was turned into a cinema . . . Children, ponies and sheep-dogs scampered around the garden, and the white motorised yacht, the *Baldur*, was moored by the jetty.'[8] The Kavaliershaus was set aside for guests who were not family members. On the ground floor there was only a pretty hall with a fireplace, while upstairs there were four guest rooms and a bathroom.

During the Easter holidays Magda managed to get the house in such good order that the family was able to spend the holidays there, and in his diary Goebbels records the image of an idyll whose delights he fully enjoyed. But in public the purchase of the magnificent property aroused envy, particularly since Goebbels – probably out of mere vanity – had allowed his family life in Schwanenwerder to be filmed and shown as part of a weekly news-reel in the cinemas.

Magda was not able to enjoy this time quite so completely, because she had constant rows with Goebbels, as a series of Goebbels' diary entries reveal; such as this one from 3 May 1936: 'depressed mood row with Magda . . .'[9]

Or this, from 5 May 1936: 'Schwanenwerder . . . Early to bed. Another row with Magda.'[10]

And the following day: 'Not a word out of Magda.'[11] The next day, a Friday, he set off for Schwanenwerder from his office: 'Magda is not here, I am alone with the children. It's wonderful. Magda comes back later, and I immediately set off again. I have no home when she is there.'[12]

For the next day he had brought his colleagues out to Schwanenwerder, to do some work.

'10 May . . . More rows at home . . . It's nauseating! . . . In the evening, talk things out with Magda. Pointless, though, as she is completely unreasonable. She is sometimes very remote from me.'

'11 May . . . Talk things out with Magda. She weeps and is ter-ribly sad. I am quite moved. Sometimes I don't treat her well. Must devote myself more to her. She is so kind underneath. But sometimes she has her moods; like all women. Then you have to show her your teeth.'[13]

Magda had often been profoundly hurt during her relationship with Goebbels. And then there were the everyday vexations, as when the upkeep of the two households proved to be more expen-sive than Goebbels had imagined, or when Magda lacked the money to pay some of her bills. In such cases she would make scenes. But she did not voice her true concerns about the estrange-ment that existed between herself and Goebbels, because she knew and feared his cynicism. When he writes that she is unrea-sonable during a discussion, he is referring to the arrangement that he had made before their marriage, in which he had insisted on a guarantee of his later freedom from her. She might have passed breezily over that at the time, perhaps because it had been simply unimaginable back then that this man's passionate love for her could ever cool. By now their roles were out of kilter with one another. He was the one who was desired, the minister who was fawned over and flirted with by beautiful women, while she stayed at home and made sure that everything ran smoothly – and on top of that, one pregnancy followed hot on the heels of another. Only the children gave her a certain degree of security, keeping her feet on the ground, and allowing her to hold on to Goebbels despite all his extra-curricular activities.

Her friend Ello said, in conversation with Meissner, that Magda had started to look a bit homely, she had filled out a bit and started to look motherly, and that Goebbels acted as though it was enough for her to appear by his side at official occasions. In reality, however – according to Ello – Magda was already an unhappy woman.

In July 1936 the Olympic Games were held in Berlin, and once again the Nazis managed one of their greatest propaganda coups. 'Visitors coming to Germany for the Olympic Games found a Reich that looked powerful, orderly and contented.' Thus wrote the liberal American magazine *The Nation* on 1 August 1936: 'No one sees Jewish heads being smashed in, or even Jews being given a good thrashing . . . The people smile, they are friendly and sing enthusiastically in beer-gardens. Accommodation and catering are good, cheap and lavish, and no one is swindled by grasping hoteliers or shopkeepers. Everything is terribly clean, and the visitor likes it all.'[14]

Magda, who was not otherwise interested in sport, and who played no sport herself, took the games as an excuse to appear in public almost every day, alongside Hitler and famous guests from abroad. Some of these she also invited privately to Schwanenwerder, such as the King of Bulgaria, a wealthy Indian prince and Crown Prince Umberto of Italy.

To complete the good impression with these guests, all the Nazi dignitaries gave intimate dinners, expensive receptions and intoxicating parties. Ribbentrop and Göring competed with massive parties in their own homes. Journalist Bella Fromm: '"Rib" [Ribbentrop] had an ox roasted whole over a roaring fire. Göring presented his guests with the spectacle of Ernst Udet looping the loop over the startled heads of the foreigners . . . Goebbels outdid the two of them, running a party with two thousand guests at the Pfauen Island, near Potsdam.'[15]

But Goebbels' swanky party on the Pfaueninsel, which had previously been the arena for the hospitality and pride of the Prussian kings, was a fiasco: along with the Greek King and Queen, the Prince of the Netherlands, the Prussian aristocracy and international diplomats, Goebbels had invited many well-known personalities from the theatre, opera, concerts and film. Among them mingled guests from the senior ranks of the party, and others who formed its grass roots, and who had won their colours – along with Goebbels – in the bar-room brawls of the Berlin workers' district. At the start of the evening, Magda, in a brightly-coloured organdie dress, as elegant as ever, sat at the King of Bulgaria's table and seemed to be calmly watching the evening develop.

This time Goebbels had spared no expense, and the tables were lavishly laden, there was no shortage of alcohol, and young girls disguised as pages stood in rows bearing flaming torches while the old trees were illuminated with thousands of little lights. Various bands played uninterrupted dance music.

But the idyll did not last long. Over the course of the evening, with increasing consumption of alcohol, some of the guests started to behave in an outlandish manner. Coarse young men disappeared into the bushes with shrieking girls who had been torch-bearers a moment before. Goebbels' adjutants tried to keep the situation under control, but fist-fights ensued, and tables were tipped over, bottles were broken and Goebbels ran helplessly back and forth while Magda withdrew in terror. 'Squeaks emerged from the bushes, girls howled and glasses shattered. Dawn was rising, but they saw it was midday before the last drunk was carted away . . . And that was the end of the great party on the Pfaueninsel . . . Magda wept with shame, and her husband was furious.'[16]

During this time Goebbels' constant affairs, lies and adulteries reached their peak in a new affair. But where his other relationships had been superficial, this time Goebbels was seriously in love.

Chapter 28

The Czech actress Lida Baarova came originally from Prague, but decided to try for a film career in Germany, where the highly developed German film industry meant that her prospects were rather better. She was a beautiful woman: dark and delicate, with an expressive face – and she was very young. By the time Goebbels made her acquaintance she had just celebrated her twenty-second birthday.

Goebbels, who, in his capacity as Propaganda Minister, was also in charge of German cinema, and who was involved in all reasonably important works, to be sure that nothing escaped his control, met the young Baarova at the Ufa studios in Babelsberg, when he was watching some sequences from Paul Wegener's film *Hour of Temptation*. She played the lead, next to the popular actor Gustav Fröhlich. Friends and colleagues saw Fröhlich and Baarova as a couple. They lived together in Fröhlich's big villa in Schwanenwerder, very close to the Goebbels' property. The 'Fröhlichs' had, naturally, been invited to the party on the Pfaueninsel. Seeing her again, Goebbels was more aroused than ever. But this time he had to be careful. He was obviously looking for more than an erotic adventure. So over the next few days he invited her first to the Ministry, to discuss film matters, and then he invited her on little outings in the summery countryside. He began to act like a courtly lover – he was taking his time.

After the party on the Pfaueninsel, Magda's health began to suffer. She was in the early stages of a new pregnancy, and spent some time being cared for at the elegant 'White Hart' sanatorium in Dresden. At the weekend Goebbels flew to Dresden with the children to visit her. Magda briefly interrupted her cure to accompany Goebbels to the Venice film festival, but then she returned to Dresden. Goebbels was left alone in Berlin, and in his free time he travelled to Schwanenwerder to play with the children, delivered various speeches and attended the Nuremberg Rally. Lida Baarova, who was taking a spa cure in Franzensbad with her mother, came to listen to him. There was nothing unusual about this, since other artists, such as composer Paul Hartmann, actor Gustaf Gründgens and conductor Wilhelm Furtwängler had also been invited as guests. But we can tell that it was unusual from Reimann's account: 'Shortly before his speech Goebbels arranged a rendezvous with the actress to talk to her about her plans for the future. At the end he gave her a kiss. She had to wipe the lipstick from his lips with her handkerchief. But he told her that if he took his watch off during his speech, she would know that he was thinking about her. And he would frequently take out his handkerchief to dry his lips, and that too would be a sign of love. He did all this during his speech, always glancing towards Lida, who was sitting right at the front among the dignitaries.'[1]

After his speech he went to lunch with Lida, as his diary records. From now on Goebbels's diary entries concerning the young actress are in code; he avoided talking about her directly or mentioning her name, but the general tone changes, as does his mood. He closes his old diary with the words: '14 September . . . Life is beautiful. It is struggle, pain and happiness.'[2] A day later he opens the new one: '15 September . . . The wildest life is the finest.'[3]

Some days later Magda was in Berlin to clean the house. Once again they were irritable with each other. 'Disgusting,' as he notes.

The evening in Schwanenwerder did not go much better, 'Magda nags'[4]. On 19 September: 'Endless complaining. It's repellent.'[5] Despite the bad atmosphere they set off together for a trip to Greece. Magda impressed the Greeks with her elegance and her knowledge of languages, but her mood had clearly not improved. She was unable to go on some of the outings, and suffered from the heat. By the end of September Joseph and Magda were back in Berlin.

At the beginning of October, Goebbels set off for Schwanenwerder once again for little Helmut's first birthday, bringing flowers for Magda and giving her a pretty ring. But in the evening she did not go back to Berlin with him, instead staying in autumnal Schwanenwerder. Had she perhaps sensed that Goebbels was now seriously involved with someone?

When he went to Baden-Baden, Lida Baarova went with him, but according to his diary for 13 October, not everything went according to plan. 'Didn't come down from room. I am so sad.'[6]

Back in Berlin, Goebbels made little effort to conceal his new love. Lida went walking up and down in front of his Ministry while he looked down at her; and from now on they met almost every day for little outings around Berlin. He obviously remained 'quite cavalier', as Lida Baarova said in an interview she gave some years ago. In that interview she was still full of praise for her admirer, saying that he behaved entirely properly towards her, they had simply been in love.

Magda, who knew nothing of the new affair – for years she had been used to her husband going his own way – was almost always in a bad mood, but tried to find some distraction in Berlin's social life, and as usual she also accepted invitations alone. Bella Fromm met her at a soirée given by the Italian Embassy: '23 October . . . The Italians never entertain without a musicale. Count Ciano attempting to be arrogantly condescending, which makes him, with his singular carriage, somewhat ridiculous. His manner was not haughty towards Magda Goebbels, however, who kept her ermine wrap on her shoulders during the entire evening, in complete disregard of good manners. She and her devoted Italian sat in

a corner flirting ardently. I was amused to see him offering a cigarette to Magda out of one of Goering's cigarette cases – solid gold,
with genuine jewels . . . the best edition, of course.'[7]

In some respects Magda failed to match up to the Nazi ideal,
and maintained a certain degree of individuality. She was smoking
and drinking rather more than usual, even at this point in her
marriage, and had her darkened hair dyed to the desirable Nordic
blonde. She smiled at National Socialist institutions, despised
many of the lower Party officials, and rejected the Party's insis-
tence on conformism and loss of individuality. 'When our
generation has passed, there will be no culture, no merriment and
no real joy in life in Germany. Instead there will be only discipline, blind obedience, prescriptions, orders, the *Bund deutscher
Mädchen* and the Strength through Joy movement,'[8] she said to
her friend Ello Quandt. In conversation with Ello Magda sometimes voiced personal and critical opinions about National
Socialism, but she didn't dare to speak in this way in front of
Goebbels or the rest of her circle. Clearly she avoided conflict lest
she be isolated among her closest associates. Goebbels, too, maintained the view that the German woman did not smoke or wear
make-up. But he seemed to pay no more attention to his wife's
independent attitude in this respect than he did to the cosmetic
extravagances of his young girlfriends.

After a while the country house in Schwanenwerder was no
longer enough for Goebbels. In his need for the magnificent display of power, which he shared with other senior Nazis, such as
Hermann Göring, he was keeping his eye out for a large landed
property, a baronial manor. Since the tenth anniversary of his
appointment as Berlin Gauleiter fell towards the end of October,
and his birthday was just around the corner, the city of Berlin
came up with a special present for him: Lanke Castle on the
Bogensee. The Old Prussian aristocratic property had been bought
by the coal magnate Friedländer-Fuld, who had been ennobled by
Wilhelm II. 'The Reich capital bought the property at reasonable
"Aryanisation" prices, and now gave it to its Gauleiter and Citizen

of Honour in perpetuity. The country house lay in the middle of lovely fir, pine and beech woods, near the village of Lanke in the district of Barnim. The road leading past the property led to the Schorfheide, where Göring had set up his magnificent castle, Karinhall.'⁹

Magda prepared the little farmhouse for Goebbels' birthday. She travelled out there with Hanke, Goebbels' permanent secretary, to decorate it. Meanwhile Goebbels visited Schwanenwerder, because next to it was the Fröhlichs' house, where Lida was staying. Then came an event that has never been proven, but which is probably more than a mere legend. Meissner relates that Fröhlich, who, like everyone else, knew that Goebbels was courting his girlfriend, wanted to find out exactly what was going on, and waited one evening in the darkness outside the front door of the Goebbels' villa. 'When Fröhlich saw the first enthusiastic embrace with which his fiancée bade farewell to Goebbels, he was overcome with fury. He dashed across, tore open the car door, which had been closed until then, pulled the horrified actress out and slapped her face in punishment. All this in quick succession, while the Minister and his chauffeur looked on and did nothing . . .'¹⁰

The only one who knew nothing about the whole story was Magda. When, some weeks later, she came to hear of it and asked Goebbels about it, he admitted that he found Baarova very attractive, but he assured her that he had resisted the temptation, since his beloved partner was expecting another child. Magda fell for this story once again, and told her friend: 'Joseph and I are closer than ever before. It makes me so happy that he can resist seduction and remain true to me.'¹¹

After his birthday, celebrated with great expense and a visit from Hitler, he set off with Magda for Lanke, the house on the Bogensee. '2 November . . . Out with Magda after dinner. It is wonderful. Very peaceful. We sit and chat, make it all nice, re-hang paintings, play music, sing Schubert Lieder. What an afternoon! In the middle of the forest. The quiet develops a voice of its own. Back to Berlin in the fog.'¹²

Time and again, Goebbels could demonstrate a special capacity to convince Magda of the intensity of his feelings. Even if it was utterly fake, he nevertheless gave her a sense of being important to him, a sense that he needed her to share her life with him, to be his lodestar. And by this means he gave her a confirmation of herself, and that confirmation in turn gave her the security she needed to live. And so she forgave him time and again.

On 3 November Goebbels set off once more and began a separate diary at the Bogensee, which he would only write there, under the motto: 'To relax is to prepare for greater tension.' Although his diary tried to suggest that he was alone – 'I work, read, write and am happy. All around me is woodland, faded leaves, fog, rain. An idyll in loneliness . . . left entirely to my own devices' – the next sentence, 'We cook something for ourselves, outside the forest rustles, the rain lashes, the fog builds up. Early to bed,'[13] reveals that Lida was sharing his loneliness.

In the morning he complained about how hard it was for him to leave the Bogensee and travel back to Berlin.

While Goebbels and the rest of the Nazi elite enjoyed their power and their life of luxury, Germany was secretly preparing for the next war. After the practice air raid drills, the people also had to learn to tighten their belts. Bella Fromm explains what that meant in practice: 'We live as though at war. Substitutes for all kinds of goods, practically no butter. The one-fifth, or, if one is lucky, one-fourth of a pound per head per week is only obtainable on food ration tickets. As for myself, I have never had such an abundance of butter as just now. The foreigners a long time ago stopped eating the miserable stuff we call butter here. They obtain real, genuine, creamy butter from Denmark and Holland. With the introduction of butter tickets a flow of butter from the legations and embassies has been coming to my house. Foreign friends are sending me "fatty regards" now instead of flowers. I accept gladly. The senders know I am sharing it with my sick and needy protégés.'[14]

In Germany the threatening approach of the coming war was

sensed by everyone, but officially it was never mentioned, while at the same time the Nazi government carefully followed the civil war that was tearing Spain apart. General Franco and his followers were trying to set up a nationalist and fascist system in Spain – against the republicans, who were made up of different elements but were united in their desire to fight the military dictatorship. Germany secretly sent troops to support Franco, but the public was better informed than the government would have liked. Bella Fromm notes on 10 November 1936: 'Elsa, my help, came to me in tears today. Three months ago her husband was called up for a "military exercise". Today she received news of his death. He had died for Germany's honour, the message said. "Spain," she told me, "I had to sign a document to say that I wouldn't speak about it or wear mourning."'[15]

Germany did not only give Franco the armed assistance that he needed; Goebbels also promised to help him with propaganda. German anti-Communist films aimed against Russia, which was sending volunteers to Spain for this conflict, were dubbed into Spanish, to associate the atrocities of the 'reds' with the freedom struggle of the Spaniards.

On 11 November Magda celebrated her thirty-fifth birthday. By now she was a mature and elegant woman. She had given birth to four children and was expecting a fifth. She had achieved everything she had dreamed of as a girl: social status, wonderful houses, a life of luxury. The words of the old clairvoyant in the Berlin boarding-house had become 'reality'. Every day she lived the life of a queen, and yet today we know that in reality– like most women in those days – she felt powerless: her inner equilibrium and well-being depended on Goebbels and the externals of her lifestyle. Apart from a certain elegance, and the ability to present herself well in public, she had developed none of her skills.

She received lots of presents on her birthday, many guests were invited and Hitler himself came to congratulate her. She was particularly delighted by Hitler's presence, because it proved that she could still feel she was the first lady of the Reich. Magda was overjoyed to be at the centre of attention. 'She is so changeable,'[16] Goebbels notes in his diary.

The Goebbels also celebrated the first Advent with friends at home, including Ello, Lida Baarova and Fröhlich. Magda still knew nothing about the affair. Ten days later the party came back to their house for pre-Christmas tea. This time Goebbels brought home a propaganda film about the mentally handicapped, on the occasion of the law passed on 18 October 1936, according to which the bearers of hereditary illnesses and the so-called feeble-minded were to be sterilised. In order to create the 'correct attitude' towards these unfortunates, the Nazi government spared no efforts and shot films in psychiatric institutions, which were to show the public what a financial burden these people were for the state and the economy. The group to whom Goebbels showed the serious cases from an institution was shocked, but no one dared speak out against this law, which amounted to a systematic preparation for the subsequent euthanasia programme. It was clear even at this point what the Nazi government's intentions were. Why did no one say anything? Was it fear of falling out of line, helplessness or tacit agreement?

During these days, Goebbels tried to ensure that the last feeble attempts on the part of the press to preserve a certain degree of freedom could no longer be tolerated. In his diary of 12 December he writes: 'Licked the moaning-Minnie editors-in-chief into shape. Spoke to the depths of their consciences. Rubbed their nose in their irresponsibility with countless examples. And now that's it. I'm preparing severe punishments. I want order and conformity. I'm no longer tolerating outsiders. I don't care what's behind it. I think they understand me. If they don't, they'll learn it from their punishments.'[17] The punishments that Goebbels had in mind for such cases could mean concentration camps for the journalists.

As she did every year, Magda hurled herself into the Christmas preparations. She chose the presents for the domestic staff herself. They could not cost more than eighty to ninety marks, but each member of the staff was to receive a Christmas box of 400 marks. Magda had also become used to giving presents to orphans and families who had fallen into poverty through no fault of their own. Here we find the beginnings of a kind of social commitment in Magda: 'She had set up a real donation fund for this purpose, which she filled over the course of the year, asking leading men from the state and the party for donations of between 500 and 1000 marks.' According to her mother, 'she did not simply find people with money, but tried to understand the situation of each individual and find out what was most urgently required. "I don't want to hand out alms," she insisted in many conversations with me, "but to give people real help. They shouldn't feel they're being given something for the sake of peace of mind, but rather that the gift comes from a heart that really understands their misery!"'[18]

Christmas was – as it should be – celebrated within the family, but on 23 December and then again on 29 December Goebbels set off for the Bogensee, supposedly alone. Once again, however, his diary reveals something else. 'To Bogensee. It is cold and sunny. A glorious afternoon and evening. Magda is at home clearing up after Christmas. I stay overnight at the Bogensee. Chatted until late evening, much music and reading. Slept rather late today.'[19] In early January the whole family went to visit Hitler on the Obersalzberg. On the night train from Berlin to Munich, when the children were already asleep, Magda and Goebbels went on chatting. 'About love, marriage and so on. She is so kind and clever. I feel more and more close to her. When we are alone and there's no one between us we get on wonderfully well.'[20] One might wonder whether Magda's advanced pregnancy reduced the tensions between them; the more of a 'mother' she was, the less urgently Goebbels felt pressed to engage with her as a woman. After several days in Hitler's company, Goebbels had to travel back to Berlin. Magda stayed in the mountains with Hitler and her children to recover. The state of her health was far from stable, and she sometimes suffered from heart complaints. Meanwhile, in Berlin, Goebbels was preoccupied with Baarova's latest film, *Patriots*. The script wasn't yet patriotic enough for him, and he wanted to rework it on his own. During Magda's absence, he enjoyed his freedom, going out a great deal and seeing Baarova, but he still missed Magda. When he spoke to her on the telephone he missed 'both of them, Magda and Helga'.[21] A week later he collected Magda and the children from the station, but Magda's health remained such a cause for concern that on 6 February she went to the clinic. She was suffering from heart pains again, and if she knew nothing precise about Goebbels' affair with Baarova, it seemed almost as though her heart was better informed than she was. Goebbels was ill at this time, too, having problems with influenza or an inflammation of the kidneys, but he was also under a great deal of mental pressure, because he could not simply keep his relationship with Lida hidden away, as he had his other numerous affairs. He was agitated, he felt as though he was torn in two, and wrote that he too had 'pains in the heart'.[22] But he was also worried about Magda: 'With Magda in the clinic. She has had a few serious heart attacks. Stoeckel pulls a worried face. I feel so sorry for the poor, sweet thing. I spend half an hour at her bedside, comforting her. She weeps such bitter tears . . . I can no longer imagine a life without Magda. May God protect her! Work at home, terribly tired. I can barely read or write. And I miss Magda wherever I am . . . The Führer is very concerned about Magda's illness.'[23] These expressions of emotion sound just as authentic as his feelings the first time Magda was seriously ill in hospital, in 1932–33. Once again he was as scared as a child, afraid that she might leave him alone in his emotional turmoil. At the same time his diary entries reveal that he too was dependent in this relationship. Without Magda he had no safe haven, he was lost.

On 19 February 1937 the time had come: Magda gave birth to her fifth child, two months premature. The baby was small, but healthy and very sweet, and when the doctor – Court Councillor Stoeckel – bent over the child, he said: '*Das ist eine Holde* – That's a pretty one!' so Magda called the little girl 'Holde'. Goebbels notes: 'We are all so happy. How I suffered the previous day. Not to mention Magda. I was with her at half past three. She was in pain and feverish. Red and irritable with sleeplessness. And then, all of a sudden, the baby came. Thanks to dear, good, brave Magda! I'm about to visit her. She is lying blissful and happy in her pillows. With big dreamy eyes. And the little one: just like Helga. We are all as happy as can be. Magda weeps with joy. We hug and kiss. What a joyful day!'[24]

Chapter 29

Holde, the premature baby, made a quick recovery, but Magda was in poor shape. The quick succession of births had taken too much of a toll on her strength. Apart from that, she had breast-fed each of her children for several weeks, then taken a series of injections to make it easier for her to lose weight, and finally gone on a draconian diet. After this last birth Dr Stoeckel urgently advised her against becoming pregnant again too soon, instead telling her that she must look after herself and take another cure in May. The children stayed, as ever, in Schwanenwerder. They were given a pony and a little cart, and Goebbels was very contented. He speaks of the two little girls as 'two little angels',[1] although he is not so affectionate in his treatment of Helmut. We find very few direct entries about Helmut, only mentioning that he must be brought up rather harshly, or, elsewhere, that the boy would have to be taught a lesson.[2]

While Goebbels was playing in the garden with his children, and the German population was living as though in a bell-jar, with only a very distorted perception of what was going on beyond the country's borders, the civil war in Spain continued to rage. Idealists from all over the world joined the International Brigades, led and organised by the Communists, and made up of young people whose common goal lay in fighting Fascism. They included many authors, including Ernest Hemingway, George Orwell, André Malraux and Arthur Koestler. One of the first to die for his convictions was the young poet Federico Garcia Lorca, who was arrested and secretly shot in Granada by the Phalangists.

Joseph and Magda continued to maintain the image of the happy family in the weekly newsreels. Magda's health was still a problem, in spite of the fact that she had taken the cure, but she tried, with her usual self-discipline, not to make a fuss. Goebbels visited only rarely, chiefly to see the children. During this time he usually spent the night in his little apartment attached to the Ministry, or else he stayed away in Lanke, in the house on the Bogensee – or with Lida. By now, with her patron behind her, she had made a very satisfactory career, and could afford to rent a small villa in the Grunewald. When Goebbels visited her there he left his car, whose number was known to everyone in Berlin, parked outside without a care. And he had also given Lida the key to the back gate of the fence that surrounded his property in Lanke, so that she always had unhindered access to his house.

Magda had few opportunities – unlike during the 'time of struggle', when she had been Goebbels' enthusiastic companion – to take part in his life. His anti-Semitic rants and attacks against 'Bolshevism' she took as given. Goebbels' chief interest at this time was in the film industry, which was also strongly connected with the name of Lida Baarova.

Although Magda's life was concentrated more and more on the house and the children, without so much as noticing, Magda had herself acquired a loyal admirer, who had seen for a long time what Goebbels was up to, and who felt very sorry for her. Karl Hanke, Goebbels' closest colleague, had occupied a senior Party position since 1931. In 1933, with the seizure of power, he became Goebbels' adjutant and personal advisor. Goebbels later appointed him permanent secretary. Karl Hanke was interested in architecture, and was a friend of Hitler's favourite architect, Albert Speer, and it was he who had discovered the house on the Bogensee. Whenever Magda had practical difficulties with her various houses, Hanke was at her side. He was of petty-bourgeois origins and was shy and reticent with Magda, and yet his presence did her good, acting as a distraction and allowing her to forget Goebbels' indifference for a while. On Hanke's initiative, having been very unathletic up until now, she began to take riding lessons. As always when Magda took a new interest, she did so with a suitable level of ambition, and soon became a very good rider, so that she could go out riding with Hanke.[3]

By now Goebbels's had managed not only to Aryanise all the theatres and the recording industry, but, on behalf of the Propaganda Ministry, to buy up the UFA, the film company with its studios in Babelsberg. As a result, his Ministry was responsible for the theatre, the press and all radio broadcasts, and from now on no film could be made without Goebbels' approval of script and casting. In this way, he could also ensure that Lida's earlier films were constantly being repeated, and that he was present at the shoots.

Goebbels understood very well that of all the media film was the best-adapted to propaganda purposes, and that its aesthetic held a special appeal for the masses. It has already been pointed out that enthusiasm for National Socialism was not primarily rational. According to Hilmar Hoffmann, it was unleashed by 'the songs, the seas of flags, marches, the cult of the body, the fire symbolism and the like,'[4] and actually had some religious traits. Saul Friedländer explains this phenomenon in his book *Kitsch und Tod*:

> The broad mass of people consists neither of professors nor of diplomats. The small amount of abstract knowledge that they possess directs their feelings more towards the world of the emotion . . . But at the same time their emotional attitude conditions their extraordinary stability. Faith is harder to shake off than knowledge, love is less subject to alteration than affection, hatred is more enduring than

dislike, and the most powerful revolutions in the world have always been driven less by the possession by the masses of some scientific knowledge than by their being roused to fanaticism, and sometimes even by hysteria.'[5]

As Goebbels correctly recognised, film was an even more effective vehicle for propaganda than radio. In film, the differences between reality and advertising blur, and a new, manipulated reality is born. Connections between unrelated phenomena can be suggested by refined editing; the passive viewer is drawn into the world of the director.

Despite the fact that Goebbels was in love with Baarova, he still maintained his sexual relationship with Magda; in the autumn of 1937 she became pregnant again. Dr Stoeckel now urged her to withdraw to Schwanenwerder, and to put her social obligations in abeyance for the time being. Magda took his advice. Out in Schwanenwerder she discovered that her neighbour's land was being annexed to the Goebbels property. It belonged to the Jewish director of the Goldschmidt-Rothschild Bank, Samuel Goldschmidt, who was now being forced by the Mayor of Berlin, in a process of Aryanisation, to sell the land cheaply to the city of Berlin. Once the purchase had gone through, however, Goebbels was revealed to be the true buyer, acquiring the land along with the house.

The fence between the two plots was torn down and the Jugendstil building completely redesigned as a 'fortress', as Goebbels was to call his refuge. Magda oversaw the work, perhaps hoping in this way to regain some of his attention and awaken fresh interest in their domestic life together. The old stables became a private cinema, because Goebbels no longer seemed able to get through the day without seeing a number of films. He lived alone in his 'fortress', and even Magda had to phone him up before she was allowed to enter his 'hideaway'. She put up with everything, even the fact that he would disappear with female house guests to his 'fortress' or the adjacent annexe, under the

threadbare pretext that he was playing records for his guests
there.

Goebbels' life now became significantly more comfortable,
since he could lead a family life and a bachelor's existence on one
and the same plot of land. His diaries give the image of a happy
family. There he is always the tender paterfamilias, delighted to
see his family, to play with the children and sleep late either in
Lanke or in the annexe. We learn that Magda's health has
improved, that she is sweet and kind, and in many diary entries –
as though this was a special event – 'talked to Magda.'[6] Often
these conversations took place on the telephone. The various res-
idences enabled Joseph and Magda to avoid one another, and to
avoid getting under one another's feet. For her birthday, however,
Magda came to Berlin with the children. 'We are all very happy. I
gave her a beautiful new car. What a joy! The Führer had written
Magda a touching letter. And masses of flowers. I am so grateful to
Magda.'[7] Nothing points to the double life that Goebbels was
leading at this time, when, for example he notes on 19 December:
'. . . Otherwise, talked with Magda . . . Sunday, day off. Married for
six years. Magda is very happy I gave her a wonderful piece of jewellery. We are all so happy. The children play around our feet. I sit
in my new apartment in the annex. Outside, thick snow.'[8]

According to Goebbels, it could not be lovelier, and yet it was
known in Berlin that the idyll was false. And Magda? We don't
know whether she believed at the time that Goebbels had
changed for the better. Time and again she clung to excuses that
she had invented for him, and which made it possible for her to
protect him, even on occasions that a woman of her upbringing
and social position would not normally tolerate. When, for example, they both attended theatre premières or went to the opera,
Goebbels travelled ahead in his car, and Magda had to come
inconspicuously along behind in a second vehicle. 'At the theatre,
she didn't usually sit next to him in the box. However upset that
must have made her, Magda did not complain. She tried to
explain his behaviour to herself and others by saying that he alone

was exposed to the public eye, while she was fortunate enough to be able to disappear into her private life.'⁹

In fact Magda no longer really had a private life. Her role in public was too exposed. Because of Goebbels' constant affairs, her behaviour throughout this permanent marital crisis was closely observed both by other senior Nazis and by the general public.

At this time the Nazi leadership was affected by a scandal that caused great consternation to Hitler and Goebbels. The Reich War Minister, General Werner von Blomberg, had remarried, this time to a young woman whose origins were highly ambiguous. According to one version of her background, she had been a shorthand typist in the Ministry, and according to the other, the version that was gaining credence, she had been a prostitute in Friedrichstrasse. Then, when pornographic pictures of the young lady began to circulate, Hitler became furious, and von Blomberg was forced to resign. The second bombshell concerned the army's Commander-in-Chief, Werner von Fritsch, who was accused – wrongly, as it turned out – of infringement of paragraph 175, or homosexuality. The two men who had founded the Wehrmacht had fallen into disfavour, and had to be replaced. Hitler appointed himself Commander-in-Chief of the armed forces, thus becoming War Minister at a stroke.

Mutual espionage among the NS leadership was a major factor within the system. But even ordinary families were victims of this spying. Parents who refused to go along with the system and bring up their children accordingly, could expect their children to be taken away. Cases such as this did arouse public attention, as, for example, a pacifist Christian couple in Silesia refused to indoctrinate their children with the official ideology. The court decided that German parents were only legally authorised to bring up their children in a way corresponding to the expectations of nation and state. In the case of the Silesian family the court ruled that the children brought up by their parents to be enemies of the regime must be placed under the guardianship of the state.

When it was a matter of issues relating to the family or the role of women, Magda could become quite vociferous. That was her area, and as a wife and mother she not only felt strong within Nazi society, she actually was strong, because of her large family. On one occasion when Hitler was putting forward his ideas about the 'Lebensborn' Association, Magda reacted with horror. According to Hitler's idea, 'Lebensborn' was to care for and bring up the illegitimate children of SS men or of 'racially valuable' women for free, with the support of the state. 'What particularly interested Hitler about this was the fact that these children had no parents. Their parents did not care for them, and they were taken from their mothers shortly after their birth.'[10] Hitler saw these children as the property of the state, because they had not formed a bond with their parents. The Nazi Reich was to take the place of those parents, and the children would feel obliged solely to the state – always prepared to serve and to die for it. Magda was not afraid to voice her criticism. 'No state, not even the best, can replace a child's parents!'[11] Magda's commitment was surprising, and this was one of the few occasions when she adopted an independent stance. Of course her own role as a mother reinforced her confidence in this case; but 'home' had a special status for her as the site of the family, and of course it was also this desire for an idyllic family life that kept her in her marriage to Joseph Goebbels.

Ordinary people were significantly better off than they had been – not only in comparison with earlier years, but in comparison with the rest of Europe. In return, the German population was willing to put up with the dictatorial regime; otherwise, the years from the Nazi seizure of power in 1933 to the end of 1937 were relatively peaceful.[12] There was no place in the dictatorship for trade unions or strikes. Germany was not only intellectually isolated, but separated from economic developments in other countries, and this made things easier for Hitler. The Nazi government's international political successes also counted for a great deal in the eyes of the masses. The regions that Germany had been forced to relinquish at Versailles had been taken back, and the Allies had not intervened. Hitler had restored the country's faith in itself, and from a country with an army of one hundred thousand men Germany had risen to become the strongest military and airborne power in Europe, a development that counted for a great deal in the eyes of the populace. The anti-Semitic excesses, on the other hand, were often seen as 'ephemeral', and even Jewish citizens did not consider them really threatening. Nonetheless, life in the Nazi dictatorship had changed fundamentally for every individual, and become a collective form of existence.

For the great majority of Germans, who were neither racially nor politically persecuted, collective life was chiefly lived in communities outside the family, and most people had to participate in this. Schoolchildren belonged to the *Jungvolk*, adolescents to the Hitler Youth, adult males took rifle training in the SA or the SS, and women occupied themselves in the National Socialist Women's Organisation. But all this did not make people unhappy. The occupations, 'the hiking, marching and camping, the singing and partying, the arts and crafts, the gymnastics and shooting' doubtless brought 'feelings of security, camaraderie and happiness, which flourish in such societies.'[13] Word had filtered down that concentration camps existed, but for most people it was not terribly difficult to ignore such information.

In March 1938 the plans of the Nazis became clearer. The Wehrmacht invaded Austria. At first the Nazis were going to allow Chancellor Schuschnigg to hold a referendum to decide whether or not Austria was to join the German Reich, but when the German troops had already invaded, Hitler broke his word and forbade the vote. It was too late. The journalist William Shirer had just settled in Vienna:

Before I knew it I was being swept along in a shouting, hysterical Nazi mob, past the Ring, past the Opera, up the Kärntnerstrasse to the offices of the German 'Tourist' Bureau, which, with its immense flower-draped portrait of Hitler, has been a Nazi shrine for months. The faces! I had seen these before at Nuremberg – the fanatical eyes, the gaping mouths, the hysteria. And now they were shouting like Holy Rollers: 'Sieg Heil! Sieg Heil! Sieg Heil! Heil Hitler! Heil Hitler! Heil Hitler! Hang Schuschnigg! Hang Schuschnigg! Hang Schuschnigg! Ein Volk, ein Reich, ein Führer!' And the police! They were looking on, grinning.[14]

The procedure, which had been planned for a long time, was in fact very simple: the Austrian Nazis provoked disturbances, asked for help, the German Nazis invaded. The *Anschluss* was complete, and almost two hundred thousand more Jews were handed over to the Nazis. Saul Friedländer comments: 'The persecution in Austria, and particularly in Vienna, exceeded anything elsewhere in the Reich. The public humiliation was more crass and sadistic, the expropriation better organised, the compulsory emigration faster.'[15]

The anti-Semitic attacks in Austria had already begun before the Wehrmacht crossed the border, and soon money, jewels, cars, furniture and even apartments and businesses were being torn from the hands of their horrified Jewish owners.

'On 4 June, eighty-two-year-old Sigmund Freud was allowed to leave Vienna, the city that had been his home since the age of four. His apartment had been searched twice by the Gestapo, and his daughter Anna had been questioned. The Nazi authorities confiscated some of his possessions and charged him *Reichfluchtsteuer*, the tax to be paid for fleeing the Reich, and he signed a declaration saying that he had not been mistreated.'[16]

In May 1938, two weeks before the aged and ailing Freud went into his London exile Magda's fifth child was born. Once again it was a little girl: Hedda. Goebbels was accompanying Hitler on a state visit to Italy, and did not see his fourth daughter until two weeks later.

After the birth Magda was well, but once again she and Goebbels were rowing more and more. Magda could and would not perceive the signs of a severe marital crisis between herself and Goebbels, so threatening were the consequences. So for the time being she fled to the sanatorium in Dresden to take a cure. But matters came to a head. Goebbels was not only having difficulties with Magda, but also with Lida, who had been telling her colleagues that Herr Minister planned to marry her once his divorce came through. At this point, however, Herr Minister had no intention of altering the status quo, and so – because of his tensions with both women – he often suffered from sleeplessness and other psychosomatic complaints as summer approached.

As he did so often when he had personal problems to deal with, Goebbels projected his rage and frustration on his old enemy, the Jews. So while the situation deteriorated for Vienna's Jews, attacks and reprisals continued to mount against the Jews of Berlin as well. Bella Fromm, who was about to leave the country but was still waiting for her papers, drove through Berlin with her friend Mia, who was a member of the diplomatic corps. Mia took photographs as a way of collecting proof.

28 June 1938. A new wave of Jew-baiting. Scenes of ferocity and misery are carved into my mind . . . The renowned old linen house of Gruenfeld was the first place we saw surrounded by a howling mob of SA men. Mia took a picture of them 'working' on an old gentleman who had insisted on entering the shop. We proceeded, finding the same thing going on everywhere. Varying only in violence and ignominy. The entire Kurfürstendamm was plastered with scrawls and cartoons. 'Jew' was smeared all over the doors, there were revolting and bloodthirsty pictures of Jews beheaded, hanged, tortured and maimed, accompanied by obscene inscriptions. Windows were smashed, and loot from the miserable little shops was strewn over the pavement and floating in the gutter.[17]

Just a week later a good friend asked Bella Fromm, at an American Embassy garden party, whether she had recently visited the North of Berlin. 'There's something going on. The concentration camps are being enlarged. Better get out, Bella. We're all with you. Here you can't help much any more. Nobody can.'[18]

Chapter 30

The weather had not really been warm that summer. Magda rode beside Hanke through the dark, damp wood. They said nothing, Magda was lost in her thoughts. She had only returned from Bayreuth a few weeks previously, and had not been sleeping well, because she was having endless debates with Goebbels almost every day. She levelled accusations at him, justified accusations as she knew, because the clues about his constant affairs with other women were piling up. But he managed to wriggle out of it every time, and Magda was unable to pin him down.

For a moment Magda slackened the reins, her horse set off at a gallop and she flew back and forth in the saddle. But immediately Hanke was at her side, calling, 'Rein him in'. Then he grasped the reins. Magda's horse calmed down and slowed to a light trot. Hanke looked over at her. She could feel his admiration. When he suggested they rest for a moment, Magda was happy to dismount. He spread his jacket on the ground, and they let their horses graze a little way away in a clearing. The summer sky was grey and only peeped through the foliage of the trees that curved away, heavy and dark green, above them. Hanke took a flat silver flask from his pocket, and offered Magda a sip. The fine brandy loosened

Magda's tongue. In a few words she explained to Goebbels' closest collaborator that she felt betrayed and mistreated by her husband, and that if she complained he threatened to take the children away. Hanke, both touched and flattered by her candour, took her hand in embarrassment: 'You can always depend on me, my dear, whenever you need help I will be there for you.'

The fine weather finally arrived in August. As though to make up for lost time, the heat was sweltering, discharging itself in violent storms. Anticipating one magnificent summer day, Goebbels invited a few close friends on a boat trip, and Magda invited them to tea afterwards.

Magda was standing motionless on the top deck of Goebbels' motor yacht *Baldur*. The Havelsee shimmered in front of her, and Berliners who had fled the city picnicked on the opposite shore. Fluffy clouds dotted a blue sky. The boat ploughed through the tranquil water, and the spray burst gently around her in a myriad tiny droplets. But Magda seemed not to notice them. For days she had felt almost paralysed. Her every movement was difficult, apparently automatic, puppetlike. Her friend Ello, who was standing beside her, looked at her with concern, and then her eyes followed Magda's gaze, which was held in thrall by the scene that was taking place on the lower deck. There, in his white linen suit, Goebbels lay stretched out on his deck chair, his face turned towards the sun. Although he liked to have a tan, because of his feeble little body he did not undress in public even in the greatest heat. And he wasn't enjoying the sun on his own. Relaxing next to him was Lida, wearing only a short white two-piece bathing suit. Magda remained motionless, but could do nothing to stop the tears running down her cheeks. Magda seldom allowed her feelings such free expression. At Ello's urging, Magda opened her heart to her friend and told her what had happened some days previously, and what she had been carrying around with her all this time. Ello later told Meissner: Goebbels had announced that he was coming to tea in Schwanenwerder, and that he was bringing Lida Baarova. This was in itself not so unusual, as she had already visited the house several times. Magda unsuspectingly agreed. Goebbels was showing his charming side, and brought flowers for Magda, and even Baarova was very pleasant. As they were sitting down cosily for tea, Goebbels suddenly turned to Magda:

"'I have something serious to discuss with you . . . Frau Baarova and I love one another."

'Lida immediately confirmed this with great resolution: "Yes, we love one another!"'

In spite of all their earlier crises, this revelation came like a bolt from the blue. Goebbels went on, "'Of course you are the mother of my children, you are my wife, my own. But after so many years you will understand that I need a girlfriend . . . a steady and serious girlfriend."'[1]

Magda was so shocked that she could not reply. Goebbels took her silence for agreement. Magda rose to her feet to be alone. Goebbels also stood up, and took her in his arms: 'I knew I could rely on you, my dearest Magda,' he cried. 'You are and remain my dear old thing.'[2] Immediately after this the couple took their leave, and drove back to Berlin together. The 'dear old thing', who had just turned thirty-six, and given birth to her sixth child three months previously, stayed behind, profoundly hurt and insecure.

On that lovely summer day, taking Magda's agreement for granted, Goebbels had invited Baarova on to his boat with the other guests. Ello could hardly believe her ears when she heard Magda's account. Unlike Magda she had long known about the affair, but she could not understand how Magda could continue to forgive Goebbels: 'I don't know, in the end Joseph is not a normal man . . . at least he isn't a normal human being. One must tell oneself that, and I am forever telling it to myself. A solid bond with Baarova, whom he obviously really loves, what he calls a second wife, might keep him out of countless other adventures . . . out of adventures that might cost him his reputation and his position. I will try to persevere, to understand him. Perhaps with magnanimity I'll be able to keep Joseph. One day his affair with Baarova will be a thing of the past as well. If I leave him now . . .

I will have lost my husband forever. But this way I am keeping Joseph for the future. In our old age he will be all mine.'[3]

But it was not so easy to feel slighted by Goebbels and Baarova, and then to act the role of the generous party. When the weather threatened to turn, and they had to make for the shore as fast as possible, Magda and the young actress were left alone in the cabin for a moment. Magda made a remark at which Lida Baarova pulled a wounded face. Later, in the house, when Magda tried to start a trivial conversation, she was insultingly interrupted first by her husband and then by Baarova. This was so striking that even third parties were unable to ignore the insult. Magda rose to her feet and took her leave. She told Ello, who came after her, that she could no longer bear the situation, and that she wanted a divorce. Once the guests had gone, Goebbels came irritably into her room to accuse her of insulting Frau Baarova. By now Magda had regained sufficient composure to tell him calmly that she wanted to divorce him. Goebbels refused to take her seriously, told her she was hysterical and left the house.

Of course Magda knew that divorce from Goebbels could not be a purely private matter, and she was aware that unambiguous proof was required if he was to be identified as the guilty party. His Ministry colleagues, his drivers and personal adjutants, all of whom, of course, knew all about his private life, would continue to stand by their boss, because he was the one who gave them their work and their daily bread. And they knew that Goebbels was unpredictable when furious and vengeful, and was even capable of violence. That was a risk that no one wanted to take too lightly.

A few days after events in Schwanenwerder, Goebbels' city palace was the site of a private screening of the French film *J'accuse*, about the Dreyfus affair. Meissner describes the situation: 'The Minister was in the front row as usual, with Lida Baarova next to him. Magda had pointedly sat down in the back row. The moment the auditorium was darkened, permanent secretary Hanke sat down next to her.

'When the light went on during a break, Goebbels thought it

necessary to free his fingers from Lida Baarova's. Everyone could see it, and everyone did. So did Magda. She looked at those inter-linked hands as though she could not take her eyes off them.

'Hanke understood what she was thinking. So he said in his broken French: "Moi aussi – J'accuse!"'[4]

The next day Hanke met Magda and Ello. When Magda described her problems to him, he took a piece of paper from his pocket, a list of all the 'ladies' with whom Joseph Goebbels had had affairs, or was still having affairs, because Hanke had the com-plete trust of the Minister, and even had the keys to his post-box, which meant that all Goebbels' letters, official and private, passed through his hands. He had precise knowledge of all of his boss's amorous adventures, and he, the respectable son of a Silesian train-driver, the convinced Nazi, was repelled by the double game that Goebbels was playing with Magda. Magda and Ello had their breath taken away. Hanke quoted so many names – about forty, it is said – that the whole business bordered on the grotesque. For all her rage, Magda could still not believe that her husband had gone behind her back like that. Hanke seriously explained that he was even prepared to repeat this list to a judge, under oath. Magda, who had now resolved to put an end to the farce that her marriage had become, asked Hanke to arrange for her to have a private meeting with Hitler. Through some unexplained coincidence, Goebbels learned of Magda's intention to talk to Hitler on his own, and tried – since he could imagine what such a conversation would be about, and knew that Magda still had a cordial relation-ship with Hitler – to forbid any such discussion. He rushed to Schwanenwerder, had it out with Magda and, as Meissner relates, forbade her to visit Hitler and insisted that she abandon any idea of divorce. 'The Führer will never tolerate his Propaganda Minister having a divorce!' Magda reacted very promptly: 'The Führer is supposed to be in charge of Germany, not my marriage! If he doesn't want the divorce – why should that concern me? After all, this comes under the jurisdiction of the regional court.'[5]

A few days later Goebbels tried another ploy. This time his

intention was to effect a reconciliation with Magda. He arrived in Schwanenwerder with a huge bouquet of flowers and a contrite expression. He promised Magda never to see Baarova again and to turn over a new leaf, to become a new man. He showed his gentler side, and although Magda did not say much in response, she was privately more inclined to believe him than to insist on her own point of view. What she could not know, however, was that immediately after this visit to her, Goebbels was going straight back to Lida Baarova.

Some days later, when Hanke turned up to see Magda, he had fresh proof that the relationship was by no means over. He even brought the photocopy of a letter showing that Goebbels really had promised marriage to Baarova, in which she wrote: 'Is it still true that I may wait for you, as you have promised me?'[6]

Of course Magda and Ello discussed what might have prompted Hanke to side so strongly with Magda, since it amounted to a betrayal of his boss. Of course he was attracted by the rather older Magda, the most elegant and interesting woman within the Nazi elite. He himself was a respectable and rather conservative man, and for years he had seen Goebbels cold-bloodedly betraying this blameless woman. Ello Quandt thought him a romantic, nostalgic for the notion of honour of bygone days, and prepared to risk everything to rescue a 'real lady'. A 'knight without fear or blame', and hence not governed by selfish motives and hopes, which is to say that he hoped he would be able to win Magda for himself. Because of his superior's blind trust in him, Hanke had all the proof he needed of Goebbels' infidelity, and sound reasons for Magda being granted a divorce. The collapse of this model marriage, however, whose image had been impeccably maintained for the outside world, was not merely a private matter, but might also have political consequences among the Nazi elite, among which Goebbels was not in any case terribly popular. Hanke held not only the legal and political key to the affair, but he also had a psychological key at his disposal: without him Magda would not have taken the step of questioning the future of her marriage. He gave her the security of not standing alone. With a knight in shining armour at her side, the awful sense of being unimportant to Goebbels suddenly didn't seem quite so threatening.

Throughout all those years, ever since Goebbels had begun to take an interest in other women, Magda had played the victim's role. She lived in the constant hope that Goebbels would change, if not immediately then at least in old age. The many rows she had with him testify that she herself could hardly do anything on her own account, so dependent was she on him, always reacting to his provocations. But the marriage worked in terms of the Nazi collective. A child every year meant that her status as a mother was secure, that she was seen as a complete woman. Even Goebbels seems to have been able to accept Magda more readily as the mother of his children than as a woman in her own right. As we have seen, he had constant arguments with Magda the marriage-partner, and in the end she was the one who always gave in. Magda never really stood up to him, instead fleeing for the sanatorium complaining that her heart was in pain.

Magda's role as a wife and mother, as well as her behaviour, must of course be seen in the context of the social situation of women in those days. In her emotional and social dependence she was by no means an exception. Nonetheless it is astonishing that a woman of her intelligence should have consented to have her life determined by others to such an extent. In August 1938 her pain had become so intense that an explosion was inevitable. But the suffering was of a purely private nature. They systematic persecution of the Jews and other innocent people does not seem to have touched her at all. But if she had questioned the ideology of National Socialism, if she had perceived the barbarism going on around her, she would probably have lost the ground beneath her feet, and then Hanke would not have stood by her, nor Hitler behind her. All links to a more humane past had been sundered. So it was easier to linger in the company of the powerful and close one's heart and mind to difficult questions, if those questions were posed at all.

Magda was not repelled by her husband's politics. His diary repeatedly bears witness to what Hannah Arendt called the 'banality of evil': he could be a loving father and yet at the same time a criminal, who had without the slightest scruple persecuted and destroyed people who had done nothing to him. We find ample evidence for that in his diary.

Magda still found it very difficult to separate from Goebbels, and for the time being she was instead inclined to effect a reconciliation with him rather than break up the relationship. He made an effort, arranging for her to have piano lessons with the pianist Michael Raucheisen, and once again she believed his promises, even if Hanke was able to give her tangible proof of his lies. Only something that she experienced herself could convince her that Goebbels was playing her for a fool. She went with friends to a performance of the *Kabarett der Komiker*. When she entered her box, she saw that Goebbels was sitting with Lida Baarova in the next box along. The whole audience seemed to be waiting for her reaction. She immediately left the theatre, feeling that she had the audience's sympathy. The next day she invited Goebbels to Schwanenwerder for a serious talk.[7]

Goebbels defended himself by saying that he had to shield Lida Baarova against the malice of her colleagues, and that the relationship must continue in its present, harmless form. Magda announced that in that case she would insist on a divorce. Voices were raised, and Goebbels observed that if he had to choose between his love of his wife and his duty as a gentleman to his former girlfriend he had no option but to shoot himself. Magda reacted frostily, suggesting that that might be the best thing for the family and for Germany. At this Goebbels put his revolver in his coat pocket with the safety catch off, and took his leave with a melodramatic 'Goodbye – for ever.' Hardly had the door closed behind him than Magda lost her composure and began to weep uncontrollably.[8]

Once she had calmed down, she phoned to find out what had happened to Goebbels, and learned that he had cheerfully spent the rest of the evening with a female guest, and not, this time, Lida Baarova.

A few days later they had another confrontation. Once again Goebbels denied having had contact with Lida. Magda, who had been given all the necessary proof by Hanke, told him straight out that she did not believe him. To stress the veracity of his statement, Goebbels decided to swear on the life of their children, and went to the chest of drawers, where photographs of the children stood in silver frames. He laid his right hand on the photograph of his oldest daughter, Helga, and swore on his children's lives that he had not had a relationship with Lida Baarova for a long time. Magda was horrified and ran sobbing from the house. At three o'clock in the morning, still in turmoil, she turned up at Ello's house, where she fainted. Having regained consciousness, she told Ello in her despair that it would probably be for the best if she took her own life and those of her children.[9]

Magda felt deeply hurt by Goebbels. Her self-esteem had taken such knocks that for a moment the idea of simply throwing her life away seemed almost desirable. The fact that she might have been capable of taking her children into death with her suggests that she saw her children as her property, as an extension of herself.

We might still wonder whether there were other factors involved in Magda's thoughts of suicide: the desire to avenge herself on Goebbels, and hatred born of spurned love, the rage that she had always kept bottled up, and which was now coming to a head. She felt that she herself counted for nothing where Goebbels was concerned. But if she took his beloved children with her, that would be the worst punishment imaginable.

Some time after the emotional outpouring in which she had sobbed out her rage and despair, she became somewhat calmer and finally said to Ello: 'Can you grasp that, can you understand a person lying so terribly? Why would he do it? I want a divorce. He's a devil, whom I took to be my god.'[10]

Chapter 31

By now Hanke had assembled enough proof, and found a number of ladies from the film world willing to testify against Goebbels: they were the ones who had found his advances unwelcome, and who had suffered professional setbacks as a result. But of course Magda knew that she had to speak to Hitler – who was the highest legal authority in the Nazi state – and win him over to her point of view. Hanke played the intermediary, preparing Hitler for Magda's visit with a series of preliminary hints. A few days later Magda had an hour's opportunity to tell her idol of her anxieties and desires. Hitler, who had known something of his propaganda minister's affairs, was nonetheless horrified that Goebbels had used his political position to put pressure on various women, and had neglected his political duties in favour of the pleasures of the flesh. He would, he assured Magda, consider the matter, and recommended that she remain patient in the meantime. The next day he called Goebbels into his office. Goebbels managed to play down the accusations against him, and to portray Magda as an over-sensitive, hysterical woman 'whose nerves were strained by having given birth so many times.'[1]

Consequently Goebbels was able to tell Magda triumphantly that Hitler would not permit the divorce, and they would have to learn to get on with each other again. But Magda was resolved to take the action further, and of course her 'knight', permanent secretary Hanke, continued to stand by her side.

He was determined to put Magda's case personally before Hitler and place all the proof before him. And indeed his calm and clear manner made more of an impression on Hitler than Magda's more emotional account. It was easy for Hanke to convince Hitler that Goebbels himself was betraying the ideals that he preached in the name of National Socialism, and that he had even lied to Hitler. This was an insult to Hitler's vanity, and Goebbels fell into disfavour.

Since Goebbels was not greatly liked within the Nazi elite, the news of his expulsion from Hitler's inner circle circulated very quickly. The loss of his ministerial post was expected daily. He himself was supposed to have applied for an ambassadorial post in Tokyo at about this time. But Hitler knew that he would need Goebbels, if war really was just around the corner – but no one apart from Hitler himself was more skilled at distorting the truth and manipulating the masses.

So a divorce was out of the question. Because of the impression that would be made in public, Hitler was not willing to allow the idyllic family image to be destroyed. Once again Hitler called Magda in for a discussion. He demanded that she stand by her husband, at least at political events. 'And then she could set any condition she wished, but they had to avoid a scandal that would provide too much matter for agitation for Germany's enemies (he meant the enemies of National Socialism).'[2]

Magda bowed to Hitler's 'paternal authority', and a kind of cease-fire ensued, but Magda's first condition was that Goebbels should give up his relationship with Baarova once and for all. So over the next four weeks the couple appeared in public together for Admiral Horthy's state visit and a performance of *Lohengrin* at the Opera. Goebbels, who complained in his diary that his heart was breaking, kept his side of the agreement that Hitler had imposed. He called Hilde Körber, Lida's best friend, and asked her to comfort Lida. He hoped in vain for understanding from Magda, but she was unyielding.

'A hard day yesterday. In the evening a long discussion with Magda, which is just one long humiliation as far as I am concerned. I will never forget that about her. She is so hard and cruel . . . I have no one to help me. And nor do I want anyone. One should drink one's pain to the dregs. At the moment I am going through the worst time of my life . . . In the afternoon out to the Bogensee. The wind is howling and the rain is falling. My heart is sore unto death . . .'[3] The next day he tried to speak to Magda once again, but she remained 'hard and cruel',[4] so he drove to his mother's for consolation. Meanwhile, along with Hanke and Ello, Magda decided which conditions she would try to impose in her next discussion with Hitler.

While their private battles raged, the whole of Europe was filled with a real fear of war. For some time Hitler had been putting out feelers towards Czechoslovakia. Prepared by Goebbels' propaganda, on 12 September Hitler demanded the right of self-determination for the three million Germans in the Sudetenland. At this the Czech government announced a state of emergency.

On 15 and 22 September the British Prime Minister, Neville Chamberlain, travelled to Germany to offer Hitler concessions at the cost of Czechoslovakia. Klemperer writes: 'The Third Reich will win again – whether by bluff or by force . . . Chamberlain flies to Hitler for the second time tomorrow. England and France remain calm, in Dresden the Sudeten German "Freikorps" is almost ready to invade. And the populace here is convinced that the Czechs alone are to blame and that Hitler loves peace.'[5]

On 29 and 30 September the four great powers met in Munich. The result was that Czechoslovakia ceded the Sudetenland to Germany, and a non-aggression pact was signed between Germany and Britain. The Czech government gave in for fear of a bloodbath. Chamberlain was celebrated as the man who had achieved 'peace in our time'.

On 3 October, Hitler, as 'liberator of the Sudeten', was celebrated in the border town of Eger, which was handed over to Czechoslovakia in 1919.

On the same day the unsuspecting Goebbels asked his permanent secretary Hanke to put in a word for him with Magda. Magda was very upset and angry. She was also not afraid to lay Goebbels bare. A letter was sent to her private secretary, in which the local office of Zehlendorf writes 'that the basic tax for 8–10 Inselstrasse has risen from RM 274.75 a month to 596.43 (retrospective from 1 April 1938).'

The secretariat replied:

'Frau Goebbels is unable to pay, along with the monthly increase of RM 321.68, the six-month arrears for April-September 1938 totalling RM 1930.08, and asks you to contact her husband. Heil Hitler!'[6]

It is rather curious that Goebbels continued to trust his permanent secretary. In mid-October he learned from his chief of police, Count Helldorf, that Hanke had been taking Magda's side for some time. While he was still coping with his shock and surprise, he reflected on how he could get as quickly as possible to Hitler, who was staying in Berchtesgaden. But Magda had got to him first. While she was drinking tea with Hitler, she was able to persuade him to fulfil her every wish: first, that Lida Baarova had to leave Germany, and had no further work commitments. The next was that no one who had helped Magda, such as Hanke and Ello, should come to any harm because of this. By the time Goebbels was called in to see Hitler the following day, the die had already been cast. He explained that he was ready to step down, to divorce Magda and marry Baarova, but Hitler would have none of it. He needed Goebbels. So both Magda and her husband bowed to Hitler's will. Magda remained very cool. In her contract she undertook to remain Frau Goebbels for an initial year as far as the public are concerned. After a year has passed she would be free to divorce Goebbels . . . During the year's wait she could and would continue to live in Schwanenwerder. Only with her agreement could her nominal husband visit his children there. If, after the course of that year, Magda did demand a final separation, Goebbels would be divorced as the guilty party, Magda would receive custody of her children and a considerable pension, and would be given the property at Schwanenwerder.

The cleanly prepared contract was signed by Hitler, Goebbels and Magda. After the signature, Hitler said to the icily silent husband: '"If one has such wonderful children as you do, doctor, and as you do, Frau Magda, one cannot part. The best thing is for you to live a fully ascetic life for a year. You, doctor, like a monk, and you, dear Frau Magda, like a nun." 'My Führer,' Magda replied without the hint of a smile, 'I've been living like a nun for years.'[7]

Later, at tea, at which Albert Speer was also present, Magda and Joseph's two daughters, Helga and Hilde, came along. They were happy to see their father again, having missed him. Hitler immediately demanded that the reconciliation of the Goebbels family be captured in tender photographs, so pictures of the 'happy' family appeared in the next day's papers.

But the final farewell did not run quite so smoothly where Lida was concerned. When the news of her impending expulsion was brought to her by Hitler's personal adjutant, she had a fit of rage that later turned into cardiac spasms. She demanded to see Goebbels, but he did not come. At first she found refuge with her friend Hilde Körber, but the Gestapo stood guard at the entries and exits to her villa. She saw and heard nothing of Goebbels, and he didn't even dare to write to say goodbye.

Hitler, who in Wagener's view had been to some degree responsible for the Goebbels marriage in the first place, had in turn intervened because the failure of this marriage did not accord with his plan. It was the only time that he had, as head of state, shown any such interest in a relationship, and if he was not guided primarily by human concerns, it was clear that Magda enjoyed his particular sympathy among the ladies of the Nazi leadership, and continued to play a special role. Hitler had granted her everything she wanted, and only with that security behind her could Magda risk her initiative.

Over the weeks that followed Goebbels reached the end of his tether, and as always when he felt insecure, he tried to regain Hitler's favour through measures involving anti-Semitic violence, which inevitably won the Führer's agreement.

In 1933 almost one hundred thousand foreign Jews were living in Germany, more than half of them with Polish citizenship. After all possible discriminatory measures had been applied against the Polish Jews, towards the end of October 1938 – after the *Anschluss* of Austria and the definition of the Sudetenland as a Reichsgau, an administrative district of the Reich – all male Polish Jews still living in Germany were compulsorily driven over the border into Poland. It was obvious that women and children without male protection would have to follow them. But the Poles didn't want the expelled Jews, so they spent days wandering back and forth between the two fronts, in the pouring rain and without food or lodging. Most of them ended up in a Polish concentration camp near Zbasyn. The Grynszpans, a family from Hanover, were among the Jews who were transported to the border on 27 October. Herschel, their seventeen-year-old son, was not with them, because he was in Paris at the time. He did not know exactly what was happening at the Polish border, but he could imagine. On 7 November he left his uncle a message that his heart bled when he thought of the tragedy of the Jews, and he wanted to register a protest that the whole world would hear. Grynszpan bought himself a pistol and went to the German embassy, where, on 7 November 1938, he fired at the First Secretary, Ernst von Rath, fatally wounding him.[8]

Since early summer 1938, Germany and the newly annexed Austria had been preparing for a pogrom. On 9 June the synagogue in Munich was set on fire, and in August the synagogue in Nuremberg burned down.

After the attack on Ambassador von Rath, on 8 November, the Nazi press was in uproar. The *Völkische Beobachter* warned that the

Paris attack would have severe consequences for the Jews.
Heydrich issued detailed instructions to Party members to use the
press and public agitation to create a climate whereby the SA, the
SS, the SD and all other Nazi organisations would rise up in a display of 'spontaneous popular anger' to retaliate for Rath's murder.
This meant that Jews were effectively fair game for humiliations
and mistreatment. Jewish property of any kind could be damaged,
destroyed or set on fire as the crowd saw fit, and no one would be
punished. The only restriction imposed was that there was to be
no plundering. Of course German lives and property would not be
endangered by these measures.[9]

Throughout Germany, in the night from 9 to 10 November,
synagogues burned, red flames towered into the dark night sky, and
the fire service would only extinguish fires when they threatened
adjacent buildings. Glass shattered and smashed in the windows of
shops and private homes. The next day the press announced that
the Jews themselves had to pay for the damage, and that the insur-
ance companies would not pay a penny. For the next few days
Hitler ordered as many Jews to be arrested as could be accommo-
dated in prison, and affluent, healthy young men were to be
selected for deportation to the concentration camps. The entire
action was planned to injure and humiliate the Jewish population,
and the pogrom and the initiatives following on from it have quite
correctly been described as a 'ritual of humiliation'.[10]

In his diary Goebbels writes very little about the events
described here. Two days later, on 11 November, it was Magda's
birthday. He drove out to Schwanenwerder, but Magda remained
cool.

In accordance with the terms of the contract, Goebbels was
living in the palace behind Wilhelmstrasse at this time. Whenever
he wanted to visit the children, he would telephone beforehand,
and if Magda happened to be at home as well, they would talk
about this and that, to maintain the façade in front of the children. But Magda had decided to enjoy life a little more. She went
out, with Ello, with Hanke, to the Artists' Club, she went dancing,

she went to the theatre, she went to the races. She had firmly decided to divorce Goebbels, as revealed in a letter from her father, with whom she had resumed closer contact since her marital crisis. She had clearly told her father about the gravity of the situation, and had spoken openly about her own concerns. This is Ritschel's hand-written answer of 3 December 1938:

'In consequence of recent events I agree more than ever with the decision you have informed me about. Be good and brave, my child.

'Your father has now become bigger and more independent as well, and both here and abroad you will always find in him a secure and financially sufficient resting-place for yourself and your children . . .'[11]

The rabble-rousing anti-Jewish propaganda continued after 'Kristallnacht', and the restrictions on the daily life of the Jews became more and more grave – their driving licences were withdrawn, for example. Fragmentary and terrifying news from Buchenwald concentration camp filtered through, and it seems clear that the Jews could no longer live in Germany. Of course the consulates issuing exit visas were besieged by thousands of people. And the chances of individuals emigrating legally were falling daily, particularly in view of the fact that they had to show that they had a small amount of starting capital for their exile.

Magda was affected by the course of events in her own way. She was always extremely thrifty, but she had had work done in the most elegant fashion houses. Now she was particularly gloomy about the fact that Salon Kohnen was closing down. She told Hans-Otto Meissner's mother: 'What a nuisance that Kohnen is closing . . . we all know that when the Jews go, so will the elegance from Berlin.'[12] Once again Magda's remark demonstrates the extent of her capacity for empathy and imagination.

When Magda had health problems again, she took her usual cure in Dresden, and in December 1938 Goebbels also became very ill. He had such severe stomach problems that the famous surgeon Professor Sauerbruch was fetched from Dresden one evening, and wanted to send him to the Charité Hospital for an operation. He did not go. Instead he made a gradual recovery, and the Goebbels had a frosty Christmas together, or rather side by side. 'Christmas Eve. The family is celebrating over there. Then they're all coming to my place. It is enough to make you cry.'[13]

For Victor Klemperer, fired from his professorship, and who saw almost no possibility of getting hold of an exit visa, the year ended in profound resignation: 'Recently I have been doing everything humanly possible to get out of here . . . But that any of it will do any good at all is more than doubtful.'[14]

Chapter 32

The press ball was held on 29 January 1939. Magda allowed herself to be persuaded to appear in public with Goebbels. There was a tension between them, however, and the evening passed in silence.

A few days later Goebbels complained about a 'frosty lunch amongst my loved ones. The sweet children . . . And today just such another cruel week is beginning.'[1]

His domestic difficulties did not prevent Goebbels from attacking the last bastion of free speech in Germany, in the form of a Berlin theatre. The 'Kabarett der Komiker' was closed down by fresh legislation. 'The political joke will be eradicated, root and branch,'[2] he swore in his diary. Goebbels' reaction to any kind of political criticism, even in joke form, demonstrates the great insecurity of the National Socialists, and shows how vulnerable and fragile was their sense of their own power.

Magda was becoming less and less self-conscious with Hanke in public. Gossip spread, and Hanke himself hoped that, once the year's wait had passed, Hitler had given his agreement and the divorce from Goebbels had come through, he would be able to marry Magda. She had had the same thought from time to time, and told Ello: 'I have grown desperately unhappy with Joseph the genius, perhaps I might find peaceful happiness with a solid bourgeois like Hanke.'[3] But at the same time she found Hanke too simple, not sufficiently charismatic or cultured. Hanke was necessary and welcome in his capacity as saviour and knight in shining armour, but his chances as a future husband dwindled each time Goebbels paid her a little attention.

In March 1939 Magda decided to take a trip through Sicily and Southern Italy. She travelled with a small party grouped around Albert Speer. Speer, who was a friend of Hanke, knew of the background to the Goebbels affair. In his memoirs Speer wrote[4]:

Hanke and I, were entirely on the woman's side, but Hanke complicated the marital crisis by falling in love with his minister's much older wife. In order to extract her from potential embarrassment, I invited her to travel south with us. Hanke wanted to come after her, and bombarded her with love-letters on the journey; but she strictly refused. On this journey, Frau Goebbels was a charming and balanced woman.

On the way back we stopped for a few days in Rome. The fascist government discovered our illustrious travelling companion, and the Italian Propaganda Minister invited us all to the opera; but none of us could come up with an especially plausible reason for the second lady of the Reich[5] travelling abroad on her own, so we set off homewards as quickly as possible.

While we had been moving dreamily through the ancient Greek past, Hitler occupied the Czech lands and incorporated them into the Reich. We found a gloomy atmosphere in Germany. We were all highly apprehensive about what the future held in store.[6]

Hitler reneged on his word to the western powers that the

Sudetenland would be his final demand. On 15 and 16 March 1939 German troops marched into Czechoslovakia.

The German Nazis in the Memel region of the Baltic were on the rampage, and on 22 March Germany forced the Lithuanian government to relinquish the zone, incorporating it within Eastern Prussia.

Despite the euphoria prompted by the extension of the 'Greater German Reich', the German population continued to feel that there was a danger of war in the air. Civilians were ordered into harvest duty and labour service. Food rationing was a further clue to war preparations. In particular there was a shortage of coffee, to which even the Goebbels family fell victim. Oskar Ritschel had managed to find a Germanophile business partner in Haarlem, near Amsterdam. This man, by the name of Heringa, as Ritschel's letter to Auguste – c/o Frau Magda Goebbels – was willing to export coffee to the family. He asked Magda to send Herr Heringa a short message 'to keep this source actively flowing'.[7]

In Magda's letter of reply to her father, dated 17 June 1939, she explained that it would unfortunately not be possible for her to thank Herr Heringa in person, 'as this letter would be addressed to a foreigner, and the contents would refer to the coffee shortage prevailing here in Germany . . . I cannot run the risk that something in writing from me . . . could be assessed to our disadvantage . . . If you think it correct, I include my most recent photograph of myself with Helga for Herr Heringa . . .' She went on to tell her father that the 'so-called fortress' had been sold, and that she was in the process of buying a more beautiful and comfortable property, although it would need to be completely renovated. 'I am looking forward to this work, which will do something to distract me from the more or less difficult thoughts that my imperfect fate still causes me.' She planned to travel to Gastein with the children from the end of June until the end of July, and there 'to undertake a strict, consistent and thorough health cure, which I ardently hope will do much to lift my spirits.'[8] She was no longer speaking of divorce.

Goebbels turned up all of a sudden while she was taking her cure in Gastein. The children were happy to see him. The year's waiting period was drawing to a close, and he had probably noticed that Magda was not quite so dismissive of him as she had been a few months before. Goebbels, who by now knew of Hanke's 'betrayal', but who continued to work with him and acted outwardly as though nothing had happened, suddenly suspected that Hanke was attempting to have an intimate relationship with Magda. But Goebbels was resolute that things should not go that far. He suggested trips together with Magda, they travelled to the Salzburg festival, and once again he showed her his charming side. When he asked her how she imagined their future together, and Magda hesitantly mentioned the idea of living with Hanke – telling him that he had even shown her the house he had bought in the Grunewald – Goebbels stepped up his efforts. He took her in his arms and told her that Hanke was not the man for her – and once again Magda was inclined to believe him.[9]

The idea of her loss of power and prestige as Hanke's wife might have played a part in this, because Magda was very well aware that to go from being a minister's wife to the wife of a permanent secretary would involve a drop in social status. But she had not yet fully made her mind up. Goebbels invited her to come with him to Bayreuth, where she would also see Hitler again. She agreed. But on the way there she almost fainted with inner tension. She could still not decide between the two men, and yet she knew instinctively that she would go back to Goebbels. Perhaps, though, she also knew that if she did so she would be taking the route to self-destruction. Hanke, who was in Berlin, was unsettled by this turn of events. He tried to mobilise his friend Albert Speer to support him.

At the start of the Bayreuth Festival, Hanke came to my house in desperation. Joseph and Magda Goebbels had had a reconciliation, he told me, and they had gone together to Bayreuth. I thought that was the most sensible thing where

Hanke was concerned as well. But one cannot console a desperate lover with congratulations. So I promised him to find out what had happened while I was in Bayreuth, and immediately set off.

Goebbels and his wife arrived in Bayreuth the same day as I did, and had, like Hitler, set up in the extension of Wahnfried [the Wagner house at Bayreuth]. Frau Goebbels seemed very downcast, and she spoke to me quite openly: 'My husband's threats were terrible. I was just beginning to recover in Gastein when he simply turned up at the hotel. He talked at me for three days; in the end I couldn't take it any more. He blackmailed me with our children; he would have them taken away from me, he said. What could I do? We had only had an outward reconciliation. Albert, it's terrible! I had to promise him that I would never again meet Karl privately. I am so unhappy, but I have no choice.'10

The opera that evening was *Tristan and Isolde*. Joseph and Magda sat in the big central box with Hitler and Winifred Wagner. Richard Wagner's emotionally charged music worked its spell: Speer reports that Magda, who was sitting to his right, wept quietly in the darkness throughout the whole performance, not stopping when the lights came on. 'During the interval she sat racked with incessant sobs in the corner of one of the drawing rooms, while Hitler and Goebbels showed themselves to the audience through the window, and attempted to ignore the embarrassing display.'11

The next morning, when Hitler learned the cause of the tearful evening and the background to the reconciliation of the couple, he was happy with the turn that events had taken, but in Speer's presence he called Goebbels in and 'told him rather crisply that it would be better if his wife left Bayreuth the same day. Without giving him the opportunity to reply, without even shaking his hand, he left the Minister and turned to me: "Goebbels is a cynic where women are concerned."'12 Goebbels demanded that

Magda telephone Hanke and explain the situation to him, and when Hanke lost his composure and could barely speak for sobbing, Magda did not even attempt to explain the reasons for her attitude.

However she did impose new conditions on a further cohabitation with Goebbels: Hanke must be moved away, he could no longer be responsible for the interests of his Minister. Hitler promoted him to the position of Gauleiter in Silesia, the province he came from, and from now on he lived in the castle in Breslau (present-day Wrocław). In addition, Magda made a list of people who were no longer to come to the Goebbels house, including all the ladies that Hanke had enumerated as particular girlfriends of Goebbels. Goebbels had to promise Hitler personally, in response to Magda's wish, that Lida Baarova would not be allowed to return to Germany. And, on the legal basis of the year's wait, Magda received a guarantee from Hitler that she could divorce Goebbels whenever she wished. In agreeing to this, Hitler was making a massive intervention into the private life of his minister and his minister's wife. It appeared to be very important to him that the public image of this relationship – a working marriage, a beautiful woman corresponding to the ideal of the Nazi aesthetic, the healthy, pretty children – should remain unimpaired. And in order to preserve this model family, in terms of Nazi propaganda, Hitler allowed himself to come under pressure from Magda, one might even say that he allowed himself to be blackmailed.

At the end of August the 'reconciliation contract' was signed between Magda and Goebbels, with Hitler as guarantor. Despite favourable conditions, and despite the support that her father had agreed to give her, Magda was unable to break free from Goebbels. Her position as the first or, next to Emmy Göring, the second lady in the Reich, was secure, as was her closeness to Hitler. She had achieved everything she wanted from him, and with his support she had even been able to humiliate Goebbels in revenge for the many injuries he had done to her. She retained her position as the exemplary wife and mother for the Reich, and in return the Reich gave her its support.

A few days later, on the morning of 1 September 1939, Magda called her mother and urged her to attend the Reichstag session as a spectator, saying that it would be a historical event.[13] An unsuspecting Auguste duly went along to the Kroll Opera. She too had sensed the rising political excitement, but she was still unprepared when Hitler dramatically announced, 'Last night, for the first time, Poland fired on our own territory with regular soldiers. Since 5.45 we have been returning fire, and we have paid them back bomb for bomb.'

After Hitler's announcement Magda's mother was shaken by a violent weeping fit. After all, she had already been through one world war, and her memories of it were still painfully vivid. Auguste describes the situation: Behind her, 'one of those fanatical Women's Organisation types snapped "control yourself", but immediately clammed up when the others standing around her whispered to her: "Psst, that's Frau Goebbels' mother!" In a feeling of fear and despondency that I could not explain at the time . . . I was unable to share Magda's enthusiasm in any way. From the very start Magda's unshakeable faith in Adolf Hitler's mission had been puzzling to me.'[14]

What was portrayed to the German people as a defensive war was really an offensive campaign: the beginning of the Second World War.

Chapter 33

The third of September was a beautiful day in Berlin, a mild and balmy Indian summer day, a day made for driving to the surrounding lakes to swim, or stopping in a wayside pub after a walk through the countryside. Until now no one had paid much attention to the war on the Eastern Front, and the official communiqués expressed the opinion that the Polish campaign would be a long one. Admittedly there had been food cards for some time, petrol was being rationed and there were blackouts at night, but no Polish plane had ever appeared in the sky over Berlin. Britain and France had set Germany an ultimatum for that day, 3 September, but so far they had always given in, and on this occasion too the radio assured its listeners that everything would be fine. As on earlier occasions Germany gave no signs of yielding, and once again ignored the date fixed for the ultimatum.

But this time it was different: Britain and France were not satisfied with warning Hitler and threatening him with possible sanctions. This time they reacted by declaring war on the German Reich.

No one in the Nazi government was prepared for that, nor had they really been expecting it. Speer wrote in retrospect that Hitler himself had probably not quite realised that he had unleashed a World War, and that this was characteristic of his generally unrealistic way of operating and thinking.[1]

The people understood what was about to happen to them very much better than the Nazi leadership, and reacted rather nervously, not as they had done in 1914. This time there was no enthusiasm, no flower-bedecked regiments, no hysteria. 'The streets stayed empty. No crowds appeared in the Wilhelmsplatz calling for Hitler.'[2] William Shirer noted that there was not even any noticeable 'hatred' of the British or the French, despite Hitler's repeated declarations that the British war-mongers and Jewish capitalists had caused this war.[3]

Among the Nazi leadership, Goebbels and Göring in particular were opposed to a war at this point. Goebbels warned that the risk was too great, and canvassed in Hitler's immediate circle for a peaceful solution.

Magda, on the other hand 'entered the war with a practically fanatical love of the fatherland.'[4] She was prepared for all kinds of personal deprivations, and decided to train as a Red Cross nurse. At the specific request of Magda and Goebbels, Magda's son Harald, by now eighteen years old, was not given preferential treatment, but was instead dispatched to the Polish campaign. But when he came home on leave in October 1939 – Magda had just been released from the clinic, suffering once again from heart problems – she was very relieved to see him in good health. In the war, Harald had become a young man, and, having experienced the hardship and cruelties of war at the front, he had his own opinion about what was happening, an opinion which deviated from the official version, and which he must have expressed to Goebbels and Magda, since Goebbels noted that Harald 'worried him'.[5] He brought home a girlfriend with whom Magda was not overly 'impressed'.[6] Otherwise the war made little impact on the Goebbels household. The ministerial palace, which had just been rebuilt for the third time in five years – by now it had attained princely dimensions, with a total of forty rooms – had been completed during the year's wait. In the first week of December, after their initial euphoria, the family decided to spend most of their time living in Schwanenwerder. The house in Berlin was too large, and at this point – because of the war – the party season had come to a standstill. The expensive new building project on the Bogensee, which was still being directed by Hanke, had also been completed, and was causing Goebbels temporary financial difficulties. But all in all life was going nicely for the erstwhile scourge of the bourgeoisie, and if he was dubious about a war, at least part of the reason was that such a course of action might threaten his own comfortable lifestyle.

The Polish resistance was quickly defeated by the superior German forces, and Warsaw fell at the end of September.

For the German population, the war meant greater deprivations than they had been expecting. Each person was allowed one pound of meat, five pounds of bread, three quarters of a pound of fat, three quarters of a pound of sugar, a pound of coffee substitute, and only a single piece of shaving soap for the next three months. Material for suits or coats was rationed, since Germany did not have its own cotton or wool, and shoe-leather was also in short supply. The fact that Frau Goebbels – at least outwardly – was not exempt from these regulations is revealed in an exchange of letters between her private secretary and the ration-card issuing officer on 9 January 1940: 'In issuing clothes cards for Frau Goebbels you must have made an error,' her secretary wrote. 'You have docked 16 points from Frau Goebbels for three pairs of stockings. First of all, Frau Goebbels had already bought these stockings in September, and secondly she needs them for her work as a nurse in the hospital. Accordingly, they should not be included in the calculation. I request your prompt reply.'[7]

Wilhelm Breitsprecher, Master Court Shoe Manufacturer to His Majesty the former Kaiser, dispatched a reply to Frau Reich Minister: '. . . I return to your kind note of 21 February 1940.

'I regret to say that the ration cards have not yet been received, so that I am unable to begin the work on your shoes. So I would be grateful if I could receive the cards in the near future.

'According to the current regulations, shoes may once again be made from crocodile leather, so that I can fulfil your order for shoes according to your wishes once I have received the ration cards.'[8]

On 29 September the German Foreign Minister Ribbentrop returned from Moscow. In his pocket he had the German–Soviet non-aggression pact, sealing the fate of Poland. In a secret addendum to their agreement, the Soviet Union and Germany had divided Poland between them, and from now on the country did not even exist on the map. The treaty between Germany and Russia would, the Germans hoped, support their peace offensive. The western powers did not react to the treaty as Germany and Russia had intended, however, instead seeing it as their legitimation to enter directly into the war.

Once the October clashes were over, and the persecution of the Polish Jews was beginning, Poland's leadership class was wiped out on Hitler's orders. As usual, only verbal orders were given, and these were not strictly followed, for example: 'Heydrich is talking about an extraordinarily radical special order from the Führer [the order to liquidate, which applied to wide sections of the Polish leadership; the victims numbered in their thousands], and the governor general of Poland, Frank, quotes a verbal warning from Hitler, from 30 May 1940: 'What we have now established to be the Polish intelligentsia is to be liquidated, its successors should be identified and, within a suitable space of time, eliminated also.'[9]

A month later the people's hope of peace collapsed once and for all, when Ribbentrop announced on a visit to Danzig that the war must now be fought to the bitter end.

As a consequence of this, Goebbels once again had a real task to perform. Even if he himself had not wanted the war, his own importance was bolstered by the fact that he had to prepare the German people psychologically for war. His propaganda was designed to make the deprivations and hardships of the war easier to bear, to address each individual's willingness to sacrifice himself, and to use his lies to create an image of the enemy so powerful that the people would be more willing to fight.

During this phase, in which Goebbels' aggression was discharged outwardly, and everything contemptible could be projected on to the enemy – along with the Jews the British, and Churchill in particular, were the targets of his attacks – life with Magda was relatively calm. The war gave them both the opportunity to project all their negative emotions upon others, as they had done in the early days of their marriage. The process allowed them to grow together again for a while.

Each evening Magda and Goebbels chatted with each other, swapped reminiscences and spent Magda's birthday on 11 November 1939 alone in Lanke. When Goebbels returned from a trip to Poland, during which he had visited the ghettos in Warsaw and Łodz, where the Jewish population lived crammed together in the most terrible conditions, his anti-Semitism was reinforced to such an extent that he decided to produce one of the most terrible anti-Jewish films, *The Eternal Jew*. Magda was fully informed about all of this, and shared his attitude.

On one occasion the marital harmony of this period was threatened by the reappearance of Lida Baarova. Baarova now lived in Prague, which had been occupied by the Germans since March 1939, and had – according to Meissner – made herself 'useful' by entertaining the Reich troops, and was trying to return to Berlin. Hitler, who had promised to Magda that Lida Baarova would never again set foot on German soil, had Hanke's successor, Secretary of State Werner Naumann, discreetly inquire of Magda whether, under the changed circumstances, she had any objections to the return of the actress. Magda stated categorically that she did. Lida Baarova then wrote a personal letter to Magda, which Magda read to her sister-in-law, Ello:

'Can you be so harsh, my dear lady, when you yourself are happy once again? My only crime was to have loved a man who happened to belong to another woman. I have paid terribly for that.

But I love Germany more than anything, and have not deserved to suffer so terribly. Now the question of whether or not I can come back to Germany is in your hands. So I beg you, have mercy and allow me to come back.'[10]

Magda was not to be moved, even refusing to reply to Baarova, and Goebbels learned nothing of these events.

By now Hitler had celebrated some triumphs in the west. The German Wehrmacht attacked Holland, and Holland capitulated. The Germans crossed the Belgian-French border, and on 14 June 1940 marched into Paris. Millions of refugees fled the city for the south. The German writers who had sought political asylum in France after 1933 were also forced to leave – the fortunate ones to the south, while the others were imprisoned in French intern-ment camps as 'undesirable aliens'. With his propaganda, Goebbels suggested that they were Nazi spies that he had managed to smuggle in, and this made their situation all the more difficult. But worst off were those those who had been tracked down by the Gestapo; they were promptly deported to German concentration camps.

Magda was pregnant again. Her father fell seriously ill and she was unable to travel because of her condition, but she tried to give him as much long-distance attention as she could. She wrote to the hospital and regularly phoned the doctors who were treating him, and every Sunday she sent him flowers. Ritschel, who had at first distanced himself from National Socialism, now wrote an extraordinarily anti-Semitic letter: '7 July 1940 . . . My illness is very gradually advancing towards recovery . . . But what comforts me in my suffering is the events that the Führer has bestowed upon the German people with his incomparable achievement. During these weeks, then, we must face against the arch-enemy, England, so that peace will finally come. Of course this is basically not a war against England and France, but a war between Jewry and Teutonism, that is the quintessence of this mighty conflict.'[11]

Ritschel's letter came as a surprise. His statement contrasted with everything that we have heard from or about him hitherto.

He was initially opposed to Magda's commitment to National Socialism, and against her marriage to Goebbels. Ritschel was an entrepreneur, a businessman, and, as we know, he had connections with Belgium and Holland; he was a man accustomed to thinking in larger dimensions. But in some letters – including those he wrote to Magda – he reveals his links with business partners who admired the Nazi regime. So even before this letter he had relaxed his originally critical stance, and come to terms with, perhaps even exploited, the fact of Magda's marriage to Goebbels. In his letter he now unmasked himself as a devotee of the Nazi regime – either because the propaganda had had its effect, and influenced his thoughts to such an extent that he was now convinced about what he was writing, because he assumed that Goebbels might read his letters, or only in order to emulate Magda. We have no real clue to what it might have been that really provoked his massive anti-Semitic reaction. Perhaps he was only showing us the reaction that was typical of many 'average citizens', who were not necessarily convinced by the Nazi regime in the beginning, but who, over the first war years, impressed by Hitler's victories, became a victim of propaganda.

In his letters Ritschel conveyed his greetings to the children, particularly Harald, and included small gifts of money. When his condition improved after his operation, he devoted himself to his will, and had his property in Remagen put in Magda's name.

For the birthdays of Auguste, Goebbels, Magda and Harald, he promised to send one thousand Reichsmarks – a very generous amount for the times – along with a request that Magda should seek out something nice for everyone involved. Then he wished her very best wishes for her coming birth.

On 29 October 1940, Goebbels' birthday, Magda's baby was born. The parents celebrated a 'double birthday' and called Heide the 'child of reconciliation'.

Ritschel's condition was deteriorating, and he was operated on once again. He had lost forty pounds of body-weight, and Magda was very concerned about him. In January 1941 she travelled to

Duisburg. The old man was happy to see his daughter again – and later gave her back her travelling expenses. Magda thanked him for the enjoyable stay that he had paid for in the Duisburg hotel. Time and again he wrote to his 'dear grandchildren', including little presents or chocolate, and in every letter he sent greetings to 'Mother Auguste'.

In early April he died in the hospital in Duisburg, and Magda received the various letters of condolence which reveal that he was a popular and respected businessman.

Although Ritschel had hardly devoted any personal attention to Magda when she was a child, he had always given her and Auguste a certain financial security, and in the final years of his life he assured Magda of his support if she were to divorce Goebbels. His death was a real loss to her.

The calm period of reconciliation, in which Goebbels was almost a model husband, came to an end within a few months. Magda's deteriorating health required that she take a new cure in Dresden in late January 1941. Göring invited the children to his villa on the Obersalzberg to recover from their poor diet and disturbed nights in Berlin. So Goebbels was left on his own, quickly finding consolation with the young Ursula Quandt, recently divorced from Herbert Quandt, Magda's former stepson. She now spent a lot of time in the house. Goebbels constantly praised her company in his diary,[12] saying how refreshing, uncomplicated and agreeable it was to be with her, and when Magda took another cure for her heart problems in Feburary, he drove to the Bogensee with Ursula.

Magda made her next disappointing discovery one night some months later, when she surprised Goebbels' pretty young secretary climbing through the window from the garden into her boss's study.

Magda became very worked up, and, according to Ello, the next day she suffered a weeping fit followed by a nervous collapse. 'I've had enough now,' she told her sister-in-law. 'I can't go through all that from the beginning again. I'm going to get divorced now, and I don't care what kind of a scandal there is.'[13]

Ello tried to calm down the desperate woman, and phoned Goebbels to inform him that Magda had firmly resolved to see Hitler the following day to apply for a divorce. Goebbels, who naturally had no desire for any kind of fresh scandal, immediately drove to Magda, assuring her that he missed her, and she was the only one who understood him, and then they walked arm in arm around the lake. Magda calmed down temporarily, but she complained to Ello: 'The sly old fox has been buttering me up again. But it's going to be of no use to him! Tomorrow morning I'm definitely going to the Führer. I swear I'm going to do it this time.'[14]

The next morning, 22 June 1941, the German Wehrmacht began 'Operation Barbarossa', the offensive against the Soviet Union.

The bond of friendship between Hitler and Stalin, viewed with suspicion at home and abroad, had ceased to exist. For the sake of that allegiance, Goebbels had held fire until now, but now he was finally able to unleash all his ammunition against Bolshevism, something he had practised before the war, and immediately began to dispatch his verbal attacks against Russia. In this role he had become completely indispensable to Hitler. Goebbels knew very well that Hitler no longer had any reservations about him, so he no longer bothered to conceal his affairs. As a result, Magda's situation became more painful than ever before. Even if she managed to frighten off one of the young ladies who now came to her house quite openly, the next one would come tripping in, and she told Ello with resignation:

I've spoken openly to Jupp [Joseph]. He was fairly sensible, and promised me that in future he wouldn't have any girlfriends who I didn't like or who were cheeky to me. Now he's got one who has behaved very well so far, and I've come to terms with it . . . Look at me . . . I'm getting old. I often feel exhausted and can't do anything about it. These girls are twenty years younger than I am and haven't given birth to seven children. There are only two possibilities for me: if we win the war, Joseph's stock will be so high that I, an ageing, worn-out woman, will be surplus to requirements. If we lose the war, my life's over anyway. I can still shoulder the burdens of this war with him. Then everything will be over . . . there is no way out for me.[15]

Magda was profoundly depressed and embittered, and at the same time astonishingly clear-sighted. But she remained so dependent on Goebbels that she could only see herself and the further course of her life in relation to him. She could clearly see no possibility of escape from that inner prison, not even through the children, but instead tried to defend herself against Goebbels' continued infidelity with his own weapon, cynicism. On one occasion – supposedly on Goebbels' orders – she had one young lady come to a particular crossroads at night, from which she was to be collected by Herr Minister's car. Herr Minister was at home at the time, completely unaware, and when Magda told him of her trick he was unmoved. There were many such 'jokes', but it was not really Magda's style to find satisfaction in this way. Unlike Goebbels, she felt the difficulty of her position more clearly as the war progressed. She could not understand that someone who bore as much responsibility as her husband could be so unscrupulous in his private life. One day she said to Ello, 'Joseph is actually the greatest rogue that has ever betrayed the German people.'[16]

Her remark shows that she was aware of Goebbels' lies – at this point clearly in reference to his propaganda – but she still accepted the war itself as something 'ordered' by Hitler, something 'inevitable'. She did not dare harbour doubts about the ideology of the Nazi regime. Had she done so she would have been 'lost' – not because she had anything to fear but because she would have fallen into the abyss, she would have had no safety-net, no one would have been there to catch her, and Magda always needed someone to carry her.

Not only did the Russian campaign create a completely new situation, but the expulsion of the Jews gave the Nazi leadership new problems and led to radical proposals.

The situation of the Polish Jews in the ghettos of Warsaw and Łodz had further deteriorated since 1940. People were living in unspeakable misery: crammed together into the tiniest space, without hygiene or provision for the sick, starving, frightened of the brutality of their guards, and in complete uncertainty.

On 30 January 1939 Hitler expressed himself very clearly on the subject. In case of war he announced – as he had predicted in his book *Mein Kampf* – the 'annihilation of the Jewish race in Europe'.[17] The further the war actually advanced, the more clearly did the annihilation of the Jews become a visible goal.

In October 1941 the mass-deportation of the Jews eastwards began in Berlin. Each day one Jewish family after the other was dragged from its apartment or its hiding place, and brought to the ruins of the synagogue in Lietzenburger Strasse. From there they were all individually registered, driven to the station and, among indescribable conditions, loaded by the thousand into cattle-trucks. The trains travelled first to Poland, to the Łodz ghetto, and then to the concentration camps in Minsk or Wilna. Later still the concentration camps dotted the whole of the east. Auschwitz became a metaphor for inhumanity and endless suffering for millions of people from the whole of Europe.

In the attack on the Soviet Union and the invasion of the Russian hinterland there were mass-shootings of Russian Jews by SS *Einsatzgruppen*, or task forces, which meant that anti-Jewish policy was stepped up at the front. The historian Ian Kershaw writes that the *Einsatzgruppen* were involved in the murder of over two million Russians overall. And for the first time the Wehrmacht and the police battalions were also responsible for the massacres in Russia. On 30 March 1941 Hitler delivered a speech to high-ranking officers, in which he commanded them to commit murder: 'We must step back from the viewpoint of soldierly comradeship. The Communist is not a comrade before, and he is not a comrade afterwards. This is a war of annihilation . . . We are not waging war to preserve the enemy . . . Harshness in the east is mildness for the future . . . '[18]. It was not only Russian Jews who were shot, however, but also Red Army prisoners, in their hundreds of thousands. The rest ended up in the – at this time – small concentration camp of Auschwitz, which was enlarged to accommodate the rest of the Soviet prisoners of war. They were also to be the first victims in the gas chambers.

In autumn 1941 the transports of deportees rolled eastwards out of the Reich and out of Western Europe – clearly on Hitler's orders and with the approval of Goebbels' propaganda. The deportations led to logistical problems. Where were so many people to be put?

In order to remove them as inconspicuously as possible, they had come up with a new idea: the Reich Commissar for the Baltic was granted permission to liquidate 'Jews incapable of work' – including those deported from Germany – with carbon monoxide gas. This action was to be perofrmed in 'gas vans'. At this point not only the SS leadership knew what was happening in the East, so did the Foreign Office and the Minister for the Occupied Eastern Zones. All the measures seemed to have only one goal: the annihilation of the Jews. The notorious Wannsee Conference was held on 20 January 1942. Its purpose 'was to regulate and coordinate an extermination policy already underway.'[19]

For those Jews who were temporarily in the Reich, daily life was becoming harder and harder. Since September 1941 – from the age of five – they had been obliged to wear the yellow star, and request permission from the police the moment they wished to leave their immediate surroundings. One further measure required them to add the Jewish forenames Sarah or Israel to their German forenames in their identity cards and in all correspondence.

It was around this time that an episode occurred which I have learned from private sources: during her time in the boarding-school in Holzhausen Magda had befriended a young Jewish girl, a promising pianist. She married a Christian and moved to Katowice. The daughter from this marriage was given more of a Catholic than a Jewish upbringing. But because of the 1935 racial laws the girl's mother was concerned about her daughter's future, and decided to send her to France. When the Germans occupied

France, a half-Jewish foreigner who had fled Germany seemed to be more at risk than she would have been in the Reich, where this girl had a certain amount of protection from her 'Aryan' father. So her parents set about bringing their daughter back to Germany. This was not an uncomplicated matter and the girl's mother remembered her erstwhile friend from boarding-school, Magda, now Frau Goebbels. She wrote to Magda asking her for help.

Magda received a lot of post, and during the war much of it consisted of begging letters. As the files show, she studied all her letters before authorising the sending of a radio or a small amount of money. For this post she employed a secretariat run by Frau Freybe, also a former friend from Holzhausen. We do not know for certain, but we may assume that Magda saw the request from her Jewish friend, because it is unlikely that Frau Freybe would have held back this one letter. But the reply to the unfortunate woman was not only in the negative, she was even punished for not having added 'Sarah' to her forename as the regulations required. She had to report to the police in Katowice and was sent to Auschwitz. For the first few months her husband was allowed to meet her at the gate of the camp, bringing her manuscripts that she had asked for, because she had to play the piano for the SS. After a short time she died in the camp. Her daughter managed to return to Germany, where, thanks to the protection of her 'Aryan' father, she survived, and emigrated to the USA after the war.[20]

We might wonder why Magda did not help her. The possibility exists, however unlikely it may be, that she never received the letter. But Magda's refusal to become involved is also open to another interpretation. To support her former schoolfriend Magda would have had to confront her past. As we have already seen in the cases of Friedländer, Arlosoroff and Lisa, since committing herself to the Nazi regime she no longer wanted to have anything to do with her past. Otherwise she would have had to engage with that past, and wonder why it should be necessary to ask protection for an innocent young girl at a politically exposed point. It would have been within Goebbels' power to grant that protection. But

Magda was embittered, and had suffered so much as a result of her own muddled situation that she was clearly unable or unwilling to get involved in other people's problems.

The fact that she passed the matter out of her own area of responsibility, effectively handing her former friend over to the police, testifies to a considerable coldness of heart. After all, Magda must surely have known that this was a matter of life and death for her former fellow-pupil.

It was well known in Nazi circles that Magda – unlike Emmy Göring – had little influence on her husband. But Auguste writes of individual cases in which Magda did intervene with Goebbels. One such occasion took place in January 1942, when Goebbels'· former personal press secretary, Wolf von Schirrmeister, had come on leave to Berlin from the Russian front, and was staying in the Goebbels house with his wife. The mood of the soldiers on the Eastern Front was already extremely tense. Hitler had granted Goebbels, who had learned of this, the necessary permission for exemplary executions of rumour-mongers. Frau von Schirrmeister knew nothing of any of this, and chipped in with a story of a rela-tion, an officer on the northern section of the Eastern Front, who had told her that 'the Russians were on the edge of Riga, and that within a very few days they would be flooding into Eastern Prussia.' At first Goebbels did not respond, and merely said in passing, 'What you have just told me is of great importance. Please tell me the officer's name, and I guarantee: he will have been shot within twenty-four hours.'[21] Frau von Schirrmeister refused, and when one of Goebbels' adjutants called the couple to learn the officer's name, Herr von Schirrmeister asked that Goebbels be told that the couple would rather take their own lives than betray their relative. For days they heard nothing more from Goebbels, but then it turned out that Magda had intervened.[22] In such a case as this, in which she was not personally involved, it was obviously easier for Magda to act as a human being.

After the early onset of winter in November 1941 the German troops needed to take Moscow if they were to survive the cold weather. But they were very badly equipped, and therefore already inferior to the Russian army, which was used to temperatures of minus twenty-five degrees and colder. A feeling of rage and desperation did not help, finally leading to the first German defeats. Sebastian Haffner suggests that from this point onwards the General Staff of the Wehrmacht clearly knew that victory was impossible. But on 11 December 1941 Hitler went on to declare war on America.

Chapter 34

By now the rest of the world knew that the Hitler regime had to be toppled at all costs. The British Royal Air Force intensified its nightly bombing raids, primarily on military and industrial targets; but of course civilians, women, children and old people were hit in the cities. Out of revenge, Hitler bombed historical English cities such as Exeter, Bath and Coventry. Coventry was almost razed to the ground. In November 1942 the Royal Air Force began to carpet-bomb whole areas of Germany to break morale on the ground. The British secret service already knew of the massacres of German, Russian and Polish Jews. And there was also news that further plans were afoot for the destruction of the rest of the Jews. Even today it is hard to explain why the Allies did not intervene at that point.

Goebbels, who was busy spreading, lies, hatred and rallying calls, looked into the future with growing concern. He was well aware that the war could no longer be won, and within the family he was open in his criticism. Magda too was incautious: 'During Hitler's speech on 9 November 1942 in the Bürgerbräukeller in Munich, to which she was listening with a group of friends, she suddenly leapt to her feet and switched off the radio. "My God, what terrible nonsense he's talking today!'"[1] Magda's spontaneous outburst shows that at this point she no longer had unreserved faith in Hitler, but her criticism was limited to this kind of off-hand remark, and she did not really engage with the subject.

On 19 November 1942 the Soviet counter-offensive began. After only three days Red Army troops managed to encircle the German sixth army at Stalingrad. The Germans had no hope of breaking through their forces. The Russian winter, which had meant death for Napoleon's army, had the German army by the throat. Hitler ordered a news blackout, since there was no need to disturb anyone's Christmas celebrations, and Goebbels spread false reports to the effect that everything was going well. Hitler forbade capitulation, but on 31 January 1943 General Paulus defied Hitler's orders. Under his leadership forces to the south of Stalingrad capitulated, and on 2 February 1943 those to the north did likewise. Ninety thousand German soldiers entered Russian prisoner-of-war camps.

Snow covered the endless Russian wastes like a winding-sheet.

Magda's depressions increased as the war progressed. When the sixth army was still desperately fighting for survival, in December 1942 and January 1943, Magda went back into hospital with serious heart problems. Gallstones made matters worse. She was only forty-two, but her anxieties, worries and disappointments, as well as her repressed aggression against Joseph, her frustration, took their toll on her health. Ello was still her only confidante. Her other problems included worries about Harald, who was fighting in Crete and was later brought into action in Africa as a parachutist under General Rommel. The General had once been among Magda's personal friends – now she hoped that he would help to protect Harald.

Magda was largely shielded from the worst of the everyday hardships that war entails. Of course she knew what the citizens in Berlin and the other German cities were going through, but the deprivations did not touch her directly to any great extent. The Goebbels ostentatiously demonstrated their 'solidarity' by asking dinner guests to deposit their food cards on a silver tray held by a white-gloved butler. Like other senior Nazis they were unable to imagine what the war really meant for ordinary people; each of the Goebbels houses was equipped with a highly luxurious air-raid cellar, which it would be more accurate to call a second underground apartment. As soon as the air raid siren began to sound, one took a lift forty feet down into a comfortable flat, whose walls were panelled with wood or stretched with material, white carpets and expensive paintings adding to the cosy atmosphere. 'There was a bath with both cold and hot running water, as well as an electric kitchen with refrigerator, a well-stocked wine cellar and an air conditioner . . .'[2]

The top layer of the Nazi government was worlds away from the millions of people who were tormented by not getting enough sleep at night, by their anxiety about their loved ones in the field, about those who were fighting, those who were missing. Those who still had houses lived in nightly fear of their roofs collapsing in flames, terrified that they would share the fate of those who had already been bombed out.

Magda knew of Goebbels' propaganda lies, and also about what was happening in the east. In reference to the Nazi bid to annihilate the Jews, Goebbels wrote in his diary on 27 March 1942 'of a process that will not look too conspicuous,' and later: 'a fairly barbaric and rather indescribable process is being applied, and not much remains of the Jews themselves . . . here too the Führer is the untiring pioneer and spokesman for a radical solution.'[3] Goebbels had always felt a great need to keep Magda informed, and even now, during this difficult time, he continued to discuss the events of the day with her. What he told her shocked Magda so much that she did not even dare to confide to Ello about individual cases. All she said was, 'It's terrible all the things he's telling me now. I simply can't bear it any more . . . You can't imagine the awful things he's tormenting me with, and I have no one I can pour my heart out to. I'm not supposed to talk to anyone. But I have to speak to somebody . . . only to you. You know, he's clinging to me now. He unloads everything on to me because it's getting too much for him.'[4]

Once again Magda fell ill, and the right-hand side of her face was paralysed. It turned out that this was a case of trigeminal neuralgia. At the end of 1943 she had an operation, but the results were not aesthetically satisfactory, and her features were left rather distorted. She was also suffering terrible pains, but Goebbels forbade the doctors to give her morphine. She went to recover in the Dresden sanatorium as usual, and stayed there until August.

At the end of July 1943 the Allies launched the terrible inferno of a fire-storm in their bombing raids on Hamburg, and a little later Berlin became the target of an unparalleled bombing raid. Goebbels had all women with children evacuated to the country, and his own family now moved to the country house on a long-term basis. Goebbels' mother and daughter, as well as Magda's mother, had seen their homes go up in flames in November, when almost the whole of the western part of the capital and the government district were set on fire. Auguste recalled that the whole of Berlin resembled a flickering torch, and the flames raged through the centre of the city.[5]

In contrast, Magda's children led an almost idyllic life in Lanke. In the morning they would take their pony and trap to school, and in the afternoon they enjoyed themselves at home in the big park, where they had animals to play with and were able to forget the terrible things happening in the rest of the world. Here they were surrounded by farming land, local people duly ate better than city-dwellers, and the children were not constantly faced with the puzzling miseries of the beleaguered capital. When Goebbels took the time to drive out to Lanke, he did not betray anything about the mood of the war. He played with the children as he had before, read them fairy-stories and kept their idyll untroubled by everything that was happening in the world outside – things that were happening partly as a result of his own actions.

Magda's psychological and physical condition was giving more and more cause for concern. She had always smoked and drunk a great deal, significantly more than Goebbels. As Auguste remembered, her need for alcohol rose to an extraordinary degree as the war progressed, and this in turn made her various illnesses and depression even worse. The only ones to benefit from the presence of strong liquor were the adjutants who were also staying at the house, and who apparently had to numb themselves with alcohol.[6]

During this time Auguste, who had also been living in Lanke since the bombing of her house, did not act as a mainstay for her daughter, but, perhaps out of fear of the approaching catastrophe, made her life even more difficult by expecting her to help, and to 'change things'. When Magda was unable to calm her down, she threatened '"to walk into the lake". Sometimes she dashed hysterically – even at dead of night, when everyone was asleep – into Magda's room to inform her loveless daughter that she wished them to fish her mortal remains, please, from the cold water the following morning.'[7]

Magda's salivary glands were giving her trouble again. Along with the depression, she now had to live with constant pains as well. During one dinner with Hitler, his personal doctor, Dr Morell, who was keeping Hitler alive with rather dubious injections, established that a new operation was urgently necessary for Magda. This time, at Hitler's suggestion, she went to Breslau, and was operated on by the specialist there.

In Breslau Magda saw Hanke again. He had returned from the Polish campaign covered in medals, he was the Gauleiter for Silesia, and was about to marry the aristocratic daughter of a Silesian property-owner. When Goebbels came to visit Magda in the clinic, all previous disagreements were buried. Hanke gave a splendid dinner for his former superior and his wife in the city castle of Breslau. Forgotten were the romantic outings on horseback along the Havel, the plots against his boss with his boss's lovely wife. He could see that Magda was bound to Goebbels for better or for worse. And Hanke himself had come closer to his dream of a feudal life.

After the operation in Breslau, Magda recovered in the 'White

Hart' sanatorium in Dresden. Hans-Otto Meissner's mother met Magda there, and she spoke of a 'severely ill Magda: she had deep shadows under her eyes, and wrinkles around the corners of her mouth. She was careworn, and much thinner than before.' Meissner's mother thought it was 'less of a physical sickness' that was tormenting Magda, and 'more of a mental breakdown'.[8] That, then, was the impression of a society lady, who had known Magda for many years, and who confirmed her statement that Magda's sufferings were primarily psychological in nature.

On 20 July 1944 Magda was still in Dresden. When Ello, who was also there to take a cure, walked into Magda's room, she noticed that her friend looked grey and in decline, and that she was weeping. Magda responded to her questions by gesturing to her to be quiet, and pointed at her little radio, which stood on her bedside table: there had been an attempt on Hitler's life, and immediately afterwards Goebbels announced that 'the Führer was uninjured, and the revolt of some criminal officers had been crushed'.[9]

Hitler was in his headquarters, the Wolf's Lair in East Prussia, for a discussion of the worsening situation on the Russian Front, when a violent explosion shook the conference room, killing three officers – but Hitler himself escaped with a few minor scratches. After the initial confusion, tracking down the conspirators was a simple matter. They were executed in the cruellest way, by being hanged on meat-hooks. Hitler told the German people that 'Providence' had saved him because his task was not yet completed.

The day after the attack Hitler appointed the 'loyal' Goebbels Reich Commissar for the total war effort. He was granting Goebbels the comprehensive powers for which he had been striving for a long time, and which made it possible for him to proclaim 'total war'.

The aristocratic conspiracy against Hitler aroused in Goebbels fresh feelings of hatred for a class of society that had always been a thorn in his side, but which had until now remained fairly immune to his fanaticism. At a dinner with famous artists he gave free rein to that hatred: 'When we have removed the last half-Jew, we must set about getting rid of the aristocracy . . . even without their titles these people are the same. They remain discontented, foreign bodies in the state . . . they only ever intermarry, and thus deepen their degeneration. Like the Jews, the nobility have international connections, and they never cease to form a caste of their own. They must be expunged entirely . . . leaving nothing, men, women and children must be eliminated.'[10]

It would appear that Magda was living in a world of her own. In 1944 she had fallen in love once again, this time with Hanke's successor as permanent secretary, Dr Werner Naumann. In this case it was more of a Platonic infatuation, because Naumann was ten years younger than she was, and happily married with four children. He too, like Hanke before him, was keeping a close eye on his boss, and waiting for an opportunity to topple him, because although he admired Goebbels' talent for propaganda he despised the cynicism with which he spread his lies. Naumann could also see how his boss was lying to Magda and betraying her, and watched her suffering both psychologically and physically. He felt sorry for her, and told her of his feelings of friendship for her. In his capacity as permanent secretary he spent a great deal of time in the Goebbels household. These gatherings were purely social, but Magda only needed to be treated with warmth to feel an intensity of emotion. Of course it was a pointless relationship – Magda knew that from the start – but she couldn't bear anything else, either. According to Ello, she wrote romantic poems which she sent him anonymously. She behaved like a young girl who sees her longings projected on to an unattainable ideal. When Goebbels learned of the matter he called Naumann in and took him to task. Naumann immediately severed all contact with Magda.

In the winter of 1944–45, already under the shadow of the coming end, Magda and Goebbels became closer to one another once again. Goebbels used Magda as a support. He was able to spend hours sitting with her in the air raid cellar and holding her hand, and if he had to stay in the city at the ministry, Magda would travel from Lanke to see him. Even the low-flying aircraft and bombs could not keep her away; the feeling of being needed outweighed any fear she might have had.

Just before Christmas 1944 Hitler made his final visit to the Goebbels house. As Auguste describes him, Hitler was by now a wreck: 'Slowly, his shoulders bent markedly forwards, his arms hanging limply along his body, he crept rather than walked up the stairs. When he took off his coat he groaned as though at death's door. His voice was shrill and cracked, his laughter false – this was the man who held Germany's fate in his hands.'[11]

Christmas 1944 was spent in quiet resignation. By November Magda had learned that Harald was in a British prisoner-of-war camp in Italy. It was known in the Goebbels household that the war could now not be won. Goebbels was disappointed that the Ardennes offensive, of which Hitler had already promised great things in mid-December, had been a failure. But there was a Christmas tree in Lanke, and Magda played Father Christmas and handed out little presents to the children. 'Late in the evening – the children were already asleep – Magda put out the candles on the Christmas tree. "Next year there will definitely be peace," she said to her secretary. Her secretary felt a chill run down her spine. An obscure premonition told her that Magda was convinced that she would not survive the next Christmas.'[12]

Despite the mood of resignation, Magda was still able to cling to a scrap of everyday life. On 10 January 1945, for example, her secretary asked permission for a pair of tailor-made shoes for Frau Goebbels, since she had received leather for uppers and soles as a gift from abroad.[13] In reply to their invoice of 16 January 1945 Frau Freybe informed Salon Berthe that the 220 Reichsmarks for the green velvet hat, the black turban and the brown hat with the mink trim was being transferred. 'Frau Goebbels is very pleased with these hats. As regards the brown velours hat,' Frau Freybe wrote, 'I must leave the amount open. When times are a little more peaceful, Frau Goebbels would like this hat altered slightly.'[14]

In the east, the Soviet Army was advancing steadily. In mid-January the Russian troops took Budapest, where they soon revealed themselves to be the new oppressors. On 23 January 1945 the Russians discovered Auschwitz. When their tanks rolled through the gates they found only five thousand living prisoners, along with piles of corpses. The few survivors were also close to death, so clearly ravaged by hunger and illness that the SS had left them behind to die rather than forcing them westwards on the death march that the other unfortunates still had to endure.

The discovery of Auschwitz by the Russians provoked indescribable horror and rage among the western Allies. Although they had known of the extermination camps in the east for years, what met their eyes was worse than they could ever have imagined.

On 13 February the Allies flew one of their worst bombing raids of the entire war on Dresden. The city on the Elbe had been compared with Florence, and had been spared until now. Dresden was one of the most beautiful German cities, rich in rococo and baroque architecture, and its museums housed Dutch and Flemish masters. Apart from the six hundred thousand or so people who lived in Dresden in peace time, in wartime almost twice as many people fled there, most of them from the east, because Dresden was considered relatively safe. But that city, too, was left in rubble and ashes. During the night from 13 to 14 February, and on the next day, the bombs fell. All that remained was rubble, smoke and mountains of corpses. An estimated 130,000 people lost their lives that night, and a further 400,000 were injured.

Victor Klemperer, who lived in a 'Jewish house' in Dresden, and who had been sufficiently protected by his 'Aryan' wife that while he had been forced to work in a factory he had not been deported, during the past weeks had expected that he too would be taken away. The terrible bombing raid and the resulting confusion made it possible for him to flee with his wife. And in this way he was able to survive the war.

At the time of the bombing Magda's friend Ello Quandt was in a sanatorium just outside Dresden, in the Elb hills. The sanatorium was not hit by the bombs, but she was able to see the terrible sea of flames sweeping through the city. The fire had risen to a storm that raged between the ruins. It was in the sanatorium, about three weeks after the bombing raid, that Ello had her last encounter with Magda. Ello told Meissner how Magda came to Dresden in a cigarette company's delivery van to see her friend one last time. On the way she had to take cover with the driver a few times, when low-flying bombers had fired at the van. In Ello's room Magda threw herself exhausted on the bed. But before she went to sleep she reassured her friend, who was looking into the future with fear and concern, telling her: 'The new weapons will save us . . . it will only be a matter of days! All of a sudden the page will turn. Victory will come at once!'

Ello might have had her doubts about this, but she assumed that Magda must know best. Magda was so exhausted that she slept all afternoon. When Ello looked in on her later, she found Magda pale and careworn, her hair loose. She asked Ello to sit down next to her: 'I have to tell you something. I lied to you this afternoon, I told you about the miracle weapons that will be coming soon . . . it's all nonsense, just some fraudulent rubbish that Joseph has cooked up. We have nothing left, Ello . . . total defeat is barely a matter of weeks away. – We're all going to die, Ello . . . but by our own hands, not by the force of others!'

Ello was horrified, she refused to believe that there was no way out.

Magda explained her pessimistic views: 'In the longer or shorter term the whole of Europe will fall to Bolshevism. We were the last bulwark against the red deluge. As regards ourselves, we who were at the summit of the Third Reich, we must take the consequences. We have made unimaginable demands on the German people, we have treated other peoples harshly and relentlessly. The victors will take thorough revenge for that . . . and we cannot appear cowardly. Everyone else has the right to go on living, but we do not . . . We have failed.'

When Ello objected that Magda was not guilty of anything at all, she replied:

> I was there, I believed in Hitler and I believed in Joseph Goebbels for long enough. I am part of the Third Reich that is now being destroyed. You don't understand my situation . . . what am I to do? If I stay alive, I will be arrested immediately and interrogated about Joseph. If I were to tell the truth, I would have to portray him as he was . . . I would have to describe what went on behind the scenes. Then any respectable person would turn from me in revulsion. Everyone would think that, since my husband was dead or in prison, I was now most terribly traducing the father of my six children. As far as the outside world is concerned I have lived by his side amidst brilliance and luxury, I have enjoyed all his power. As his wife I have stayed with him until the bitter end. No one would believe me if I said I had stopped really loving him, and . . . perhaps I still do love him, against my reason, in the face of all my experiences with him. Regardless of what is behind me, Joseph is my husband, and I owe him loyalty, real loyalty . . . , and comradeship beyond death. For that reason I could never say anything against him. After all this, after his plunge into the abyss, I could not do that!

But Magda also assured her friend that she would never be able to defend him and the things he had done, 'justify him to his friends, stand up for him out of genuine conviction . . . I can't do that either. That would go against my conscience.'

When Ello asked what would become of the children, Magda replied: 'We'll take them with us, because they are too beautiful and good for the world that's coming,' and she added that posterity would avenge the father's crimes upon the children.

Ello violently disagreed. She could not imagine that anyone would want to take their revenge upon the children. In her reply,

Magda revealed how much she had known and how much she had repressed about the atrocities of Hitler and his regime, and how she herself was not without responsibility for them.

> Don't forget, Ello, what happened! You remember . . . I
> told you, once when I was very upset . . . how the Führer,
> in the Café Anast in Munich, when he saw the little
> Jewish boy, said he'd like to crush him on the floor like a
> bug. Don't you remember? I couldn't believe it, I thought it
> was just provocative talk. But then, much later, he really
> did it. So many unspeakably cruel things happened, under
> a system that I too represented. So much thirst for revenge
> has collected in the world . . . I can do nothing else, I have
> to take the children with me, I have to do this! Only my
> Harald will remain. He is not Goebbels' son, and
> fortunately he's in an English prison . . .

She went on to tell Ello that the death of her children had already been prepared for, and comforted herself: '. . . I believe in rebirth. They won't die, none of us die . . . we just go through an apparently dark portal into the next life.'[15]

The following day Magda drove back to the bombed city of Berlin in the cigarette company delivery van.

Ello, who told Meissner about this final meeting with her friend seven years later, also mentioned that Quandt had offered to save the children. He would put a house at their disposal in Switzerland and see that they were properly housed and educated, and probably even doing the same for Magda. Ello said she remembered him talking about giving them all an allowance. At this point it would still have been possible for Goebbels to bring the children to safety in a neutral foreign country.

In her conversation with Ello, Magda quite clearly showed what was moving her: her faith in National Socialism had proved to be a false belief, her ideals had been used to construct a regime of inhumanity and barbarism. With the catastrophe on the horizon, the idea of the revenge of the victors uppermost in her mind, she became aware of the crimes of the regime, and she could now see them with the eyes of those who would judge them. That insight created an insoluble conflict for Magda. Intellectually, she could see through National Socialism and everything that had been done in its name. She now understood Goebbels' and Hitler's character, but she refused to take this understanding to its conclusion, and free herself from the old ideals and relationships. She said: 'We have failed', meaning that the Third Reich, of which she had been a part, had failed. If the Third Reich had been victorious, we may presume that she would not have called it into question, in spite of all its atrocities. But even the collapse of the regime and her own disappointment changed nothing about the fact that she still felt connected to the Reich. She belonged to that world, she was the very image of it, and the idea of living in another world seemed impossible to her.

She fled that conflict for an attitude of idealism, for self-sacrifice. Goebbels had always promulgated a kind of death-cult, linking up with a German tradition that begins in the *Nibelungenlied*, and continues into the First and Second World Wars. The song of the 'good comrade' (meaning death) was a favourite among German soldiers and the German people, as was the song of the 'dawn' that lights the singer's way to 'early death'. For Germans, death has always held a strange fascination – as, perhaps, it had for Magda.

She tried to put forward sensible reasons for her decision to take her children with her into death, speaking of her fear that they might otherwise be tortured and despised. Ello clearly replied that there were possibilities that the children might be rescued, and that such innocent children would never be taken to task for the crimes of their parents. But Magda was not to be moved. As she could not solve her own conflicts, she decided to say goodbye to life. In deciding to take her children with her, she was planning an extended suicide. The children seemed to belong to her in a symbiotic relationship, just as she belonged to the Reich. She did not want to grant them independent life. As though those children were her personal possessions, she herself decided that they were 'too good and too beautiful for the world that is coming'. They had no right to a future life, independent of hers, in another world.

Magda saw herself as part of the fallen Reich that had collapsed; the children, too, were part of that Reich, and had to perish with it.

Unlike Goebbels' children, Harald was allowed to live, because he was the product of another relationship. A future for him – independent of National Socialism – was imaginable in a future world, and Magda clung to that fact almost joyfully.

The other explanation for taking the children to their deaths, the theory of Magda's Buddhist ideas, according to which she wanted to sacrifice the children, since they would not really be leaving life behind but would instead be reborn, is more than questionable. Rather it would appear, that Magda used this notion as a source of consolation. The nanny who had looked after the children before they died told Meissner that Magda had inclinations towards Buddhism, but did not seem to be deeply influenced by it.

Chapter 35

In March 1945 the Russians had reached the River Oder. To the west, the Americans had already crossed the Rhine, and in a few weeks the western and eastern Allied troops would meet in central Germany. By this time the great mass of Germans had had enough of fighting, and wanted an end to the bombing, the war, the senseless death and destruction. Most people wished for the approach of the western Allies as a kind of salvation. The people hung tablecloths and bed-linen from their windows, and begged those German officers who were still issuing orders to abandon their resistance and protect the cities and villages against further destruction. The population in the east, however, was worried about the approaching Russians, and was in flight. For weeks streams of refugees had been flooding westwards from the eastern regions. Thousands came, most of them women with children and old people because the men were still away fighting at the front. They also drifted past the Bogensee in Lanke, endless columns with carts that kept collapsing, anxious people driven onwards by fear. Every now and again tales of atrocities were told about the Russians, and the Goebbels children got wind of some of this. For that reason Goebbels had ordered that the household be transferred to Schwanenwerder, and the country house in Lanke was left to itself. While he was spreading his propaganda and lies over the radio, the lie of the werewolf and the miracle weapons,[1] boys and girls of fourteen and fifteen were manning anti-aircraft guns and attacking Russian tanks with their bare hands.

Hitler's hatred was by now quite openly directed against his own people. On 27 November 1941 he announced, 'If the German people is no longer strong enough, no longer sufficiently willing to sacrifice itself, to shed its blood for its own sake, it should perish and be destroyed by another, stronger power. I will shed no tears for the German people.'[2] Hitler wanted the Germans to die a 'people's death', and his order of 19 March 1945 includes the paragraph: 'All military installations for communication, news, industry and supplies, as well as any material assets within the Reich, which the enemy might somehow be able to use for the continuation of their struggle, either immediately or at some point in the future, must be destroyed.'[3] It was Speer, ordnance minister at this point, who protested, and to whom Hitler explained in a steely tone: 'If the war is lost, the people too will be lost. There is no need to consider the bases that the German people needs for its most primitive survival. On the contrary, it is better to destroy these things ourselves. Because the people has shown itself to be the weaker, and the future belongs entirely to the stronger people of the east. All that remains after this struggle is the inferior, because the good have fallen.'[4] Magda had taken on board some of the cynicism with which Hitler spoke of the 'inferior' who were left behind after the struggle, as when she told Ello that her children were too good for the world that would come after them. But we may assume that this observation was merely a protective mechanism to make the failure and collapse of the Nazi regime seem more attractive, since Magda – as we have already seen – had clear-sightedly recognised the inhumanity of which the regime had been guilty.

The Schwanenwerder peninsula seems to have been spared the nightly bombing raids. It was spring, and as they did every year, the first crocuses and daffodils were sprouting from the wintry earth. The children were still playing in the garden, and there was no school. All that could be heard in the distance was a curious rumble of thunder. It was not a coming storm, but the Russian front, which was coming closer to the capital each day. At the age of thirteen Helga, the eldest, understood very well that disaster was coming for them all. She asked her mother if the war was lost, and where the parents would go with their children. We do not know what Magda replied. She explained the terrible noise that was echoing across from Berlin to the peaceful garden, the smoke over the capital, by saying that 'the Führer was triumphing over his enemies'.[5]

The rumour that Magda and Goebbels planned to take their children with them to their deaths shocked everyone, even the most fanatical devotees of the regime. When Albert Speer came to hear of it, he wanted to do everything he could to prevent such a thing, and drove to Schwanenwerder to talk to Magda. But he could do nothing to change her terrible conviction. Shaken, Speer sent his secretary, Annemarie Kempf, out the next day to try and persuade Magda, because he thought a woman might be able to persuade her to change her mind. Speer had worked out a plan according to which Magda could leave Berlin with her children along the waterways. A houseboat with a crew and enough supplies for several weeks was put at her disposal. It was waiting by their own jetty in Schwanenwerder, ready to bring her and her children to safety. The captain had orders to travel only at night, and to bring them via a tributary to the Elbe, where they would be safe from the Russians.

Annemarie Kempf reports that Magda stood up to her as well. 'One knew she would; one knew how close she was to Hitler. Many people thought she had always been in love with him, although Speer didn't. He had got to know her very well during her passionate love affair with Hanke; he was her confidant then . . .'[6]

On 19 April Berlin was encircled by Russian troops on three

sides. Magda, who was in the bunker of the ministerial palace with Goebbels, called Schwanenwerder and gave instructions that the children were to come to the city with their nanny. While the nanny hurried to pack a few belongings together – each child was allowed to bring a favourite toy – grandmother Auguste was in utter despair. She wept and cried: 'I want to see my daughter one more time!'[7] Then she pressed her grandchildren to her, sensing that this would be the last time she saw them.

On Hitler's birthday, 20 April, the children made little presents for him as they did every year. On 21 April the situation in the city had become so much worse that Goebbels moved his family out of the bunker in the ministerial palace to the bunker beneath the Reich Chancellery. The 'old bunker', in which Magda now occupied three rooms with her family, was connected by a passageway to Hitler's bunker, the 'Führer bunker'. This formed part of a massive subterranean labyrinth that operated completely independently of the outside world. It had its own supplies of electricity, water and fresh air, it had sick bays, machine-rooms, garages for about eighty vehicles, armouries and broadcasting equipment.[8]

Speer was one of the last visitors to the bunker. He had unofficially resisted Hitler's order to turn Germany into a desert. Nonetheless – in a way inexplicable even to himself – he went one last time to bid Hitler farewell. When he saw Goebbels there, Goebbels told him that Magda and he had decided 'to end their lives in this historic place.' Speer takes up the story: 'He was in complete control of his emotions; one could not have known that he had finished with life.'[9] Speer also wanted to say goodbye to Magda. An SS doctor told him 'that Frau Goebbels was in bed, that she was very weak and suffering from heart attacks.' Speer asked to be received by her.

> I would have liked to speak to her alone, but Goebbels was already waiting in a lobby, and led me into the little bunker room where she lay in a simple bed. She was pale,

and only spoke about the most unimportant things, although one could tell that she was suffering from the idea of the inevitably approaching hour of the violent death of her children. Goebbels remained steadfast at my side; that meant that the conversation was restricted to her condition. Only towards the end did she give a hint of what was really moving her: 'I am so happy that at least Harald is alive.' Even I was self-conscious and could barely speak – but what was one to say in such a situation? We bade one another a silent and self-conscious farewell. Her husband had not even allowed us a few minutes to say goodbye.[10]

In her 1995 biography of Albert Speer, based chiefly on conversations with him, Gitta Sereny mentions how annoyed Speer was that Goebbels had given him no opportunity to exchange a private word with Magda in the bunker: 'It was he, that monster,' he told Sereny, 'who, for the sake of appearing heroic to posterity, had forced upon her this appalling decision [to kill their children]. And then he wouldn't even allow her a few minutes alone with me. Disgusting.'[11]

On 25 April – by now Berlin was completely surrounded, and there was fighting in all the streets – Hitler gave the order that all dispensable staff were to leave Berlin. It was still possible to reach the west in one of the last planes from Tempelhof Airport.

Hitler offered to have Magda Goebbels ferried away from Berlin with her children while it was still possible. Magda rejected the opportunity. Although Hitler agitatedly repeated his desire to save the mother and her six children, she would not give in.[12] Hitler's chauffeur, Erich Kempka, also attempted to persuade her. He still had three tanks at his disposal, and in these he believed he could bring the children safely to the airport. Seats would be held for them for another hour. Magda was alone with him when he suggested this possibility, and he later said that she seemed to heave a sigh of relief, apparently prepared to accept his offer. This was probably the only time that Magda showed the natural reaction of a mother, wanting to bring her children to safety. She could only make such a gesture to this simple man, a chauffeur, to whom she had nothing ideological to prove. When Goebbels joined them, she froze once more. He listened to the rest, and declared that his wife was free to bring herself and the children to safety, but he himself would stay and commit suicide with the Führer. Magda's attitude changed immediately, and she assured him that she and the children would stay.[13] So, on 25 April, the final aeroplane left Gatow airport at dawn – without Magda and without her six children.

Over the days that followed the Reich Chancellery and even the bunker shook beneath the Soviet grenades. The children were frightened, unable to understand why they couldn't leave, and Helga repeatedly asked whether they were all going to die. The only diversion for the children came in their daily visits to Hitler. His dog Blondie had just given birth, and the children enjoyed playing with the puppies, a welcome distraction from the general tension which they too must have been feeling. They walked in single file through the underground labyrinth. It must have broken the heart of anyone who saw them, wondering why on earth these innocent children should be sacrificed. We can only imagine how frightened the children must have been, but according to the accounts of survivors Helga is believed to have suffered terribly. She was aware that they had all been consigned to death, and she repeatedly begged to be allowed to leave the bunker, saying she didn't want to die.[14]

On 28 April Hitler called in his remaining colleagues to tell them that he wanted to kill himself. He appointed a new Reich government, and Goebbels was made Reich Chancellor. A triumph – however short-lived – for Goebbels, who had, by the end of his life, stood by Hitler for longer than any of his colleagues.

On the evening of that day Hitler celebrated his marriage to Eva Braun, his secret companion for so many years. Goebbels was their witness. The ceremony was followed by a small reception with sparkling white wine, but no one could bring themselves to congratulate the couple. 'Instead they talked about the various ways of committing suicide. The predominant view was that cyanide was the safest means of taking one's life. Almost everyone was equipped with cyanide.'[15]

On the morning of 30 April Hitler said goodbye to the faithful who remained. When he shook Magda's hand, Meissner reports, 'he gave her a long look, and his chalk-white, wrinkled face twitched faintly. All of a sudden, to the complete surprise of everyone present, he snatched the gold party insignia from his grey army coat. He fastened the little round thing, as quickly as he possibly could with shaking fingers, to the lapel of Magda's tailored jacket. Magda, always controlled, always outwardly cool, burst into tears . . .'[16] The gold party insignia was the highest honour that a woman ever received in the Third Reich.

Throughout the whole of that day they all waited for Hitler to take his life. Only his bodyguards had access to Hitler's rooms. One of them, Otto Günsche, was right outside Hitler's door. He later said they had been the longest ten minutes of his life, when all of a sudden Magda had walked along the corridor and hammered on the door with her fists. Günsche, who did not want to seem too impudent where Magda was concerned, knocked on Hitler's door and opened it to ask Hitler's instructions. Just as the door opened Magda dashed past him into the room. Seconds later she was outside again, sobbing in despair.[17]

That evening the time had come. Behind a closed door, Hitler shot himself in the mouth, after biting on a cyanide capsule. Eva Braun poisoned herself at the same time.

On 1 May at nine o'clock in the evening, some of the workers who had stayed in the bunker decided to risk escape. Goebbels said he was no longer interested in life, and told his adjutant Schwägermann that he and his wife wanted to take their lives. He asked him to burn the corpses. He said nothing about the children.

We do not know exactly how the tragedy of the children was played out, or if it happened in the way that Magda had planned.

An eye-witness, Rochus Misch, who operated the telephones in the bunker, later described to Gitta Sereny what had remained ineradicably in his memory from that day:

> It was only just after 5 p.m. when Frau Goebbels walked past me followed by the children. They were all wearing white nightgowns. She took them next door; an orderly arrived carrying a tray with six cups and a jug of chocolate. Later somebody said it was laced with sleeping pills. I saw her hug some, stroke others as they drank it. I don't think they knew about their Uncle Adolf's death; they laughed and chatted as always. A little later they passed me on their way upstairs, Heidi [Heide] last, her mother holding her hand. ['Heidi' and he had been special friends.]
>
> Heidi turned around. I waved to her, she waved back with one hand, and then, suddenly, letting go of her mother's hand, she turned all the way around and, bursting into that happy clear laugh of hers, she scraped one forefinger along the other and chanted that little rhyme she always sang when she saw me: 'Misch, Misch, du bist ein Fisch, [Misch, Misch, you're a fish]' Her mother put her arm around her and pulled her gently up the steps, but she went on chanting it. I can still hear it now.[18]

As Misch recalled, Magda came back a little later and went to her own room. After a while she followed the doctor, Dr Stumpfegger, upstairs. The next time she came downstairs she was crying, and she sat down at the big table and played Solitaire. Goebbels joined her, but Misch has no memory of them talking to one another.

The preparations for the burning of the corpses had already been made when Magda, on her husband's arm, climbed the steps to the garden. Goebbels realised that they were going upstairs themselves so that no one would have to carry them up there later on. Then he shot himself. Magda bit a cyanide capsule. They both died immediately.

The next day the Russians forced their way into the bunker. They found the six lovely children in their white nightgowns, the girls with white bows in their hair, as though asleep in their beds.

Only Harald, Magda's son from her marriage to Quandt, survived. On 28 April, three days before her death, Magda wrote him a letter, which she gave to the aviator Hanna Reitsch. Almost miraculously, after taking several detours the letter finally reached Harald in his English prison.

Written in the Führerbunker, 28 April 45
My beloved son!
We have now spent six days here in the Führerbunker, Papa, your six little brothers and sisters and I, to give our National Socialist life its only possible, honourable conclusion. I don't know if you will receive this letter. Perhaps there is a human soul who will make it possible for me to send you my final greetings. You should know that I have stayed with Papa against his will, and that last Sunday the Führer wanted to help me to get out of here. You know your mother – we have the same blood, and I did not even have to think. Our magnificent idea is finished – and with it everything beautiful, admirable, noble and good that I have known in my life. The world that will come after the Führer and National Socialism is not worth living in, and for that reason I have brought the children here as well. They are too good for the life that will come when we have gone, and a merciful God will understand me if I give them their release myself. You will go on living, and I have only one request to make of you: never forget that you are a German, never do anything dishonourable, and ensure that through your life our deaths will not have been in vain.

The children are wonderful. Without any outside help, they help themselves in these more than primitive conditions. Whether they sleep on the floor, whether they can wash themselves, whether they have anything to eat and so on – with never a word of complaint or tears. The impact of the missiles is shaking the bunker. The bigger ones protect the littler ones, and their presence here is a blessing, not least because they can extract the occasional smile from the Führer.

Yesterday evening the Führer removed his gold Party insignia and pinned it on me. I am proud and happy. May God grant that I have the strength to do the final, hardest thing. We have only one goal left: loyalty to the Führer unto death, and that we may end our lives with him, is a blessing from fate that we would never have dared to expect.

Harald, my dear boy – for your journey I give you the best thing that life has taught me: be true! True to yourself, true to other people and true to your country. In every way! (New page)

It is hard to start a new page. Who knows whether I will be able to fill it. But I would like to give you so much love, so much strength, and to relieve you of all grief at our loss. Be proud of us and try to have proud and happy memories of us. Everyone must die one day, and is it not finer to live honourably and courageously for a short time than to live long under pitiful conditions?

The letter must go . . . Hanna Reitsch is taking it with her. She's setting off again! I embrace you with deepest, most cordial maternal love!

My beloved son
Live for Germany!
Your mother[19]

When Magda was writing this letter she was standing at the edge of the abyss. Before her was death, nothingness, and for that reason she had to cling once more to the old ideals. She fell back on her refusal to compromise, the unconditional obedience that National Socialism demanded of its devotees. She invoked the false emotionalism of 'German honour'.

National Socialism used the idealistic tendencies of the German people to pervert them in the most shameful way. Its ideals were cruel, barbaric and anti-life. But even in the face of death, Magda could and would not admit that. Knowing the conversation she had had with Ello, one might even have been able to imagine a different final letter to her son.

But she preferred to leave Harald with the impression of a rigorous and demanding ideal requiring unconditional devotion, rather than a sense of collapse. By making this categorical demand upon herself she was taking refuge in an attitude that made dying easier – even before the eyes of her own son – because all that would otherwise have remained was the void.

Epilogue

Magda was the only wife among the Nazi leadership to go to her death with her husband and children after the collapse of the Third Reich. Emmy Göring, for example, survived the end of the war with her daughter, and went on living unmolested in the Federal Republic. We might wonder: why did Magda Goebbels, of all people, have to die such an awful death? There is no clear answer. Her character is not easily accessible. However much one deals with her and her life she remains in the dark, marked by a terrible fate, but strangely alien.

Perhaps this has something to do with the fact that as a biographer – without consciously wanting to do so – one erects an invisible barrier between oneself and one's subject. Perhaps she is so thoroughly wrapped up in that era, with its indescribable acts of cruelty, that one wants to avoid identifying with her in any way.

But our detachment from Magda must also have something to do with the fact that she was unable, to the bitter end, to find herself, and it is no coincidence that we see her primarily through the eyes of other people: her mother and the various men who did more to define her life than she did herself.

Magda was attracted by men with charisma and power. These

men had achieved everything that struck her as worth striving for. In her place, they had attained the goals she longed for: significance, influence, responsibility, dominance. In identifying with them, she also shared in what they represented.

As a young girl, Magda was fascinated by Victor Arlosoroff, in his personality which, even at an early age, combined high intelligence, rhetorical brilliance and passion, tenacity and love of his fellow man.

When Quandt appeared and wooed her, she was highly impressed. In his authority and solidarity he represented the father figure that she had never really known. By marrying him she was granted access to a higher level of society of which she had had a foretaste through Ritschel. She had felt drawn to this world, as we can tell by her wish to be educated at an elegant finishing-school. Otherwise, she was enticed by the idea of life at the side of a rich man, who promised her travel and luxury, at a point when she was surrounded in Berlin by poverty and misery. Quandt was a representative of early capitalism. With a steady gaze he correctly recognised the signs of the coming age, and knew how to exploit both the First World War and inflation and industrialisation, to negotiate his way through the politics and economics of the day to construct his empire.

Magda was not happy with him and divorced him.

When Arlosoroff turned up again, he fascinated Magda once more. But the relationship did not last, and they lost sight of one another.

Disgusted with the boredom and emptiness of her life, Magda tried to find a new source of security. When she allowed herself to be persuaded to visit an NSDAP gathering, where she heard a speech by Goebbels, it was as though he had cast a spell over her. Once again it was someone whose 'will to power' swept her off her feet – more than ever before – although she admitted to her mother that it was not the content of the speech that fascinated her so much as the charisma of the speaker. Only later did she also turn her attention to the ideology of National Socialism. When

Hitler, as well as Goebbels, took an interest in her, suggesting that as Goebbels' wife she might rise to be the first lady of the Reich, the more questionable aspects of the party's programme counted less than ever. This time it was more a matter of the opportunities it opened up for her. She would not listen to the doubts of her nearest relatives or her own internal questions, because these would have shattered her apparent security.

In her early years Magda was a beautiful woman, although not a woman with a particularly erotic aura or great vitality, not an actress or a singer, who could have commanded attention with her particular talent. Rather one would be inclined to wonder what it was that made her so attractive that so very different men, all of them crucial representatives of political or economic power in the twentieth century, all paid her such lavish attention.

One clue to Magda's success must have lain in her ability to adapt with extraordinary ease to any situation. She was not really attached to any of the various milieus in which she grew up, neither to the Catholic, nor the Jewish, nor the Protestant. She was not fixed to anything, everything seemed possible. In social terms, too, she was not really bound to anything. Where she herself was concerned that meant a great inner insecurity, a state of mind that was also bound up with the ambition and desire to become something 'better' than – for example – her mother had been. Thanks to her good school education and her intelligence she was able to compensate for that lack of inner security with skilled and polished manners, so that she appeared entirely secure to the outside eye – while her inner insecurity remained, and Magda spent her whole life seeking admiration from others. She exerted her power over her various admirers by virtue of the fact that she was not socially easy to pin down, she was unusual, perhaps even enigmatic and mysterious. In addition to this there was her faint French accent, which she had retained from childhood, a serenity and sweetness in her early years and the ability to listen to others. It is as though Magda had adapted her identity according to the image that other people, particularly the men she was interested in, made of her. These men all had strong egos, and in turn used her as a screen on which to project their own ideas and fantasies (Quandt, Hitler, Goebbels).

For her part, Magda expected these men to show her the way and give her an opportunity to shape her life, and the one most radically able to do that was Goebbels.

We might, of course, ask how it was possible for Magda, who had grown up in a loving Jewish milieu, to have become a convinced National Socialist. As far as we know, no traumatic experience led to that. The explanation may lie in the fact that Magda did not take her bearings primarily from any system of values, but was more concerned to achieve membership of a layer of society, and thus to achieve power and prestige. In becoming part of the National Socialist movement – which its devotees perceived as enormously dynamic – and in a particularly exposed position, she was able to share in the experiences that the movement offered, and repress her own negative sense of herself by over-emphasising a general, 'German' quality. Goebbels had raised her out of the common run, and she allowed herself to be swept along by his character and his fanaticism.

It was Magda's downfall that she could never break away from that kind of behaviour, since she was never aware of it. So she remained in a state of emotional dependence both upon Goebbels and upon the ideology that she had absorbed. Despite her talents and her attractive appearance, her sense of self-worth was so fragile that it depended primarily on confirmation and affection from others. Consequently she suffered all through her life from a lack of genuine warmth, and people she could depend on. But she did not generate many impulses herself, she never really assumed responsibility for her own life, instead always hoping and waiting for her partner to make her happy. If that didn't work, she felt impotent and lost.

Since she had no real self-confidence, her situation became all the more difficult the more she feared her outward attractiveness was waning. Then, when the conflicts became too great and threatened to overwhelm her, she took refuge in various illnesses. Her heart, her gall bladder, the paralysis of one side of her face revealed that her sufferings also involved an inwardly directed, suppressed aggression. In this way Magda remained trapped, not only in her relationship with Goebbels, but within herself. With the collapse of the ideal of the National Socialist movement, which had carried her for so long, her only escape lay in death.

Notes

Chapter 1

1 By 1952 Auguste Friedländer had resumed her maiden name, Auguste Behrend, and it was under this name that she wrote the memoirs of her daughter Magda, in the *Schwäbische Illustrierte*. She had been impoverished after the war, and lived in a furnished room in Berlin. These personal reminiscences are an interesting source for the biography of her daughter, but at the same time they contradict established sources. For the expulsion of the Friedländer family from Belgium see: Auguste Behrend, Meine Tochter Magda Goebbels. In: *Schwäbische Illustrierte*, Stuttgart, 1 March 1952 (subsequently referred to as: Behrend, Schwäb.).

2 Richard Friedlander was born in Berlin on 15 February 1881. He died in Buchenwald on 18 February 1929.

3 Behrend, Schwäb., 1 March 1952.

4 Ibid.

5 Ibid.

6 Ibid.

7 Ibid. 'When Magda was born on 11.11.1901 I was just 22 years old. We lived in Bülowstrasse in Berlin, and it was there that Magda

was born. My husband was working as an engineer in Belgium, so I had to decide on my daughter's name myself. I called her: Johanna Maria Magdalena.'

8 See Birth Certificate No. 101/1901, Berlin-Kreuzberg, Standesamt Nr. 4, Institut für Zeitgeschichte (IfZ Akte F82).

9 Behrend, Schwäb., 1 March 1952: 'It was agreed that I should send Magda to Cologne on the train on her own. Her father would collect her there. I had handed her over to the ticket collector, and hung a large sign around her neck, so that everyone could see which little monkey was going from where to where. So that she didn't starve on the way I had packed fruit, porridge and a bottle of milk. What can I tell you? It didn't suit Magda to drink milk even on such a long journey. To get rid of the milk without much ado, she therefore simply threw the bottle out of the window between stations. The little frog was five years old at the time! Magda only told me that much later.'

10 Ibid.

11 Ibid.

12 Ibid.

13 Ibid.

14 Ibid.

15 In Vilvoorde convent an old nun remembered Magda Friedländer even in the 1970s. In: Jacques de Launay: *Hitler en Flandres*. Brussels, Ed. Byblos 1975, p. 12: 'Maria Magdalena est, dès la rentrée de 1906, inscrite au pensionnat des Ursulines de Vilvoorde, sous le nom de son beau-père Magda Friedländer. Je me souviens très bien de Magda Friedländer,' nous dit l'une des deux religieuses de 85 ans qui furent ses professeurs à Vilvoorde. 'C'était une jeune fille très active et intelligente.' [Since the beginning of the schoolyear in 1906, Maria Magdalena had been enrolled at the Ursuline Boarding School in Vilvoorde, under the surname of her stepfather: Magda Friedländer. I remember Magda Friedländer very well,' we were told by one of the two 85-year-old nuns who had taught her in Vilvoorde. 'She was a very active and intelligent girl.'

16 Behrend, Schwäb., 1 March 1952.

Chapter 2

1 Karl König, *Sechs Kriegspredigten*. Jena 1915, p. 6.
2 Klaus Vondung, *Die Apokalypse in Deutschland*. Munich 1988, p. 191ff.
3 Ibid.
4 Carl Busse (Ed.), *Deutsche Kriegslieder 1914/16*, new and enlarged edition. Bielefeld and Leipzig 1916, p. vi.
5 Ibid.
6 Vondung, op. cit., p. 194.
7 Ibid., p. 197.
8 Max von Schenkendorf, *Gedichte*. Stuttgart and Tübingen 1815, p. 6.
9 Vondung, op. cit., p. 201.
10 Karl König, Neue Kriegspredigten. Jena 1914, p. 15.
11 *Deutsche Reden in schwerer Zeit*, Vol. 1, p. 292 ff. Walther Buder, *In Gottes Heerdienst. Fünfzehn Feldpredigten 1917/19*. Eggert Windegg, *Der Deutsche Krieg in Dichtungen*, p. 144.
12 From Lisa Arlosoroff's notebooks. In: *Chaim Arlosoroff. Zum zweiten Todestag*. Hechaluz. Berlin, June 1935, p. 23ff.
13 Ibid.
14 Ibid.
15 Behrend, Schwäb., 1 March 1952.
16 Ibid. Auguste Behrend: 'Magda later told me – she was already married to Dr Goebbels – that a gypsy had laid out the cards during an unscheduled stop on the journey, and had predicted her future by reading her palm. That is not true.'
17 Ibid.

Chapter 3

1 Behrend, Schwäb., 1 March 1952. Here Auguste Behrend mentions Lisa Arlosorow (sic) . . . 'Magda and Lisa were one heart and one soul.' . . . 'for this friendship proves that Magda had no antipathy against her fellow human beings of the Jewish faith. Neither then nor later on, when she was married to Dr Goebbels . . . I clearly remember how Magda, in 1943 – after a well-known director and screenwriter had intervened with her – helped Hans Moser's Jewish wife return from Hungary to join her husband in Vienna . . . She also got on very well with my second husband,

Friedländer, who was also of the Jewish faith.'
2 Ibid. The three-and-a-half-room apartment was in Wilmersdorf,in Lietzenburgerstrasse, on the corner with Pfalzburger Strasse.
3 Ibid.
4 In: *Chaim Arlosoroff*, op. cit., p. 25.
5 *Jüdische Lebenswelten*. Berlin 1992.
6 *Jüdische Korrespondenzen*, August 1997.
7 *Chaim Arlosoroff. Zum zweiten Todestag*. Berlin 1935. p. 25ff.
8 Ibid.

Chapter 4

1 A personal document in the possession of his sister Lisa. A photocopy of this document is in a private collection in Israel.
2 Eretz Israel, 'the land of Israel', means the biblical Canaan as occupied by the Israeli tribes. In our context E.I. refers to Palestine before the foundation of the state of Israel.
3 Behrend, Schwäb., 1 March 1952: 'For months her father Ritschel had been wheedling with Magda to visit him once more after such a long separation. My husband was opposed to the idea. He thought we shouldn't send Magda on such a long journey on her own. By now she was already a little teenager, who didn't know what she wanted, but perhaps for that very reason wanted what she didn't know. For that reason I sent a telegram to Godesberg: Papa won't allow it. Shortly afterwards we thought about the subject again – I took Magda to the station at short notice, then went to the post office and sent a telegram: 'Papa has allowed it. stop. Magda is coming.' Magda set off. I had given her food for the journey as I had when she travelled to see Father Ritschel to go to Belgium with him. And five marks for unexpected expenditure. What can I say? Magda had simply thrown away her five marks in the buffet car! When she arrived in Cologne her father was not on the platform to collect her because he had so far received only the first and not the second telegram. Magda was standing in Cologne without a penny. She knew from before which hotel Father Ritschel usually stayed at. She quickly made up her mind and went there, and to her annoyance learned that no Ritschel had taken a room there. She did not think for long, but spoke to a chambermaid, gave her a ring as a deposit and borrowed two marks to

telegraph home for money. I immediately sent her 20 marks, which arrived with Magda at about the same time as Magda's grandmother from Godesberg, a widowed Ritschel and remarried Schmidt.'

4 From Bella Fromm's diary: *Blood and Banquets. A Berlin Social Diary*, London 1943.

'May 13, 1933. Doing a serial about German hostesses for B.Z. Couldn't leave out a profile of Magda Goebbels, naturally. (. . .) All such material must be checked with Goebbels' office, so I sent a copy there. Got it back with rather interesting additions, and a letter from the secretary to the wife of the Propaganda Minister that I thought rather amusing. It read:

"Dear Frau Fromm,

"Frau Reichsminister Goebbels has received your friendly communication with the enclosed proof of your article and wishes to express her thanks. Frau Reichsminister does not desire the fact to be made public that she is interested in Buddhism. Furthermore Frau Reichsminister enjoys playing chess but chess is not one of her hobbies, so Frau Reichsminister asks you to remove the last sentence."'

5 Jürgen Kuczynski, *Geschichte des Alltags des deutschen Volkes*. Berlin (Ost) 1982.

6 Sebastian Haffner, *Der Verrat*. Munich 1993.

7 Ibid. p. 40.

8 Ibid. p. 76.

9 Klaus Vondung op. cit.

Chapter 5

1 Sebastian Haffner, *Der Verrat*. Munich 1993.

2 The general descriptions of the state of civil war and the rabble-rousing propaganda against the Jewish population are taken from the correspondence between Gershom Scholem and his mother: *Betty Scholem – Gershom Scholem. Mutter und Sohn im Briefwechsel. 1917–1946*. Munich 1989.

3 Sebastian Haffner writes on the murders of Rosa Luxemburg and Karl Liebknecht, op. cit., p. 139ff.:
'Since the turn of the century Rosa Luxemburg had been a political figure of the first rank in Germany – an outsider in three ways,

as a woman, a Jew and a foreigner. And of course as a bogey of the middle-classes, and even as a bogey of the Social Democrats, so radical were her views . . . Reluctantly admired for a great variety of talents bordering on genius. The other important leader of the Spartacists, Karl Liebknecht, had written a book against militarism, which led to him being imprisoned for one and a half years. Since 1912 he had then sat as a member of parliament in the Reichstag. On 1 May 1916 he began an address at a Mayday demonstration on Potsdamer Platz in Berlin with the words: 'Down with war! Down with the government!' He got no further than that. Policemen overpowered him and led him away, and for the next two-and-a-half years he disappeared into prison again. When Liebknecht came out of jail on 23 October 1918, he was, for the whole of Germany, the incarnation of anti-war protest and the incarnation of revolution. Rosa Luxemburg did not come out of jail until 9 November 1918, and although they both rejected the violence of a German Bolshevik revolution, because they believed that the revolution should grow democratically and naturally out of the consciousness of the proletarian masses, they were hated by the new government because they saw through and analysed the hypocrisy of the government. Hatred of the two Spartacist leaders was apparent in posters that appeared on hoardings throughout Berlin: 'Workers, Citizens! The fatherland is close to collapse. Save it! It is threatened not from without but from within: by the Spartacist group. Kill its leaders! Then you will have peace, work and bread! The front-line soldiers.'

4 Ibid.
5 'Magen David' is Hebrew for the Star of David, a symbol of membership of the Jewish people. According to verbal statements by Curt Riess and Max Flesch, Magda is supposed to have worn it.
6 Haffner, op. cit.
7 Behrend, Schwäb., 1 March 1952.
8 Ibid. 'Magda heaped accusations upon me and grumbled: Mama, you should really have dealt with all this six months ago.'
9 Ibid.
10 Ibid.
11 Gerda Luft, *Chronik eines Lebens für Israel.* Stuttgart 1983, p. 52ff.
12 Behrend, Schwäb., 1 March 1952.

Chapter 6

1 Hans-Otto Meissner, *Magda Goebbels. Ein Lebensbild*. Munich 1978. p. 24.
2 Ibid. p. 25ff.
3 Ibid.
4 Ibid.
5 Ibid.
6 Behrend, Schwäb., second instalment, 8 March 1952.
7 Ibid.
8 Ibid.
9 Ibid.
10 Ibid.
11 Ibid.
12 Meissner, op. cit., p. 29.
13 Ibid. p. 29. There is also the corresponding document in the Standesamt Kreuzberg, see Chapter 1.
14 Behrend, Schwäb., 1 March 1952.
15 Behrend, Schwäb., 8 March 1952.
16 Ibid.
17 Erich Ebermayer/Hans Roos. *Gefährtin des Teufels. Leben und Tod der Magda Goebbels*. Hamburg 1952. p. 21. 'Father Friedländer later, shortly before his death, called this name-change the loveliest present of his life.'
18 On the basis of various statements we may assume that Friedländer really was so fond of his stepdaughter that he was happy to give her his name.
20 Behrend, Schwäb., 8 March 1952

Chapter 7

1 Behrend, Schwäb., 15 March 1952.
2 Ibid.
3 Ibid.
4 Ibid.
5 Ibid.
6 Gerda Luft: *Chronik eines Lebens für Israel*, Stuttgart 1983 p. 54ff.
7 Ibid.
8 Ibid.

9 Ibid.

10 Behrend, Schwäb., 15 March 1952.

11 Ibid.

12 Kurt Pritzkoleit, *Günther Quandt. Die Macht des grossen Unbekannten*. Düsseldorf 1953.

13 Meissner, op. cit., p. 36.

14 Behrend, Schwäb., 22 March 1952 and Meissner op. cit., p. 35: 'Magda had her problems with him in concerts and theatres . . . When the newly-weds attended a revue [. . .] in the Admiral Palace, a little scene ensued, provoking merriment, although not on the part of Magda.

A group of pretty girls had been dancing on the stage, dressed only in a single little muff. At the end of the dance, each one pulled from the muff a complete evening dress, and threw it on. These were not light little evening dresses, but proper ones, with a whole gallery of buttons down the back. The buttons had to be fastened. And so the young girls, dazzling to look at, left the stage, spread themselves out in the auditorium and asked any willing gentlemen to do up their buttons. A most agreeable liberty, and a task which the gentlemen in question were all too willing to perform. – Not so Herr Director Quandt, however, who had sunk into a deep sleep after a hard day at work. As the lighting engineers had been instructed to follow the girls with floodlights as they walked through the auditorium, the bright beam of light suddenly caught the sleeping Quandt and wrested him out of the surrounding darkness. Only slowly did the waking man work out what was happening, while the still unbuttoned girl danced nervously up and down in front of him, pleading with him to do up her dress. Of course the audience at the Admiral Palace found this terrifically amusing.'

15 Behrend, Schwäb., 15 March 1952, and Meissner, op. cit., p. 42ff.

16 Behrend, Schwäb., 15 March 1952.

Chapter 8

1 Aliyah refers to the wave of Jewish emigration.
2 *Chaim Arlosoroff: Leben und Werk. Ausgewählte Schriften, Reden, Tagebücher und Briefe.* Berlin 1936, p. 29ff.
3 Ibid.
4 Ibid., p. 31ff.
5 Ibid., p. 264.
6 Hagen Schulze, *Weimar. Deutschland 1917–1933.* Berlin 1982. p. 238ff.
7 Ibid.
8 Ibid. p. 264.
9 Ibid.

Chapter 9

1 Curt Riess, *Joseph Goebbels*, Zürich 1949. Curt Riess was a fellow-pupil of Arlosoroff at the Werner Siemens Realgymnasium in Berlin. He emigrated to America, and came back to Berlin with the Allied Forces for the liberation of Germany. His biography of Goebbels is based on the reports of many eye-witnesses whose memories were still fresh shortly after Germany's collapse.
2 Ibid.
3 Quote from Joseph Goebbels, *Michael.*
4 Riess, op. cit.
5 Viktor Reimann, *Dr. Joseph Goebbels.* Vienna, Munich, Zürich 1971.
6 Riess, op. cit.
7 Helmuth Heiber, *Joseph Goebbels.* Munich 1965.
8 Ibid.
9 Curt Riess is quoting from: Joseph Goebbels, *Michael.*
10 Ibid.
11 Heiber, op. cit.
12 Riess, op. cit., p. 10. In 1922 Goebbels' doctorate was passed by a colleague of Professor Gundolf, Professor von Waldberg, on the subject of: Wilhelm von Schütz. A contribution to the history of the drama of the Romantic School. (Professor von Waldberg, to whom Goebbels wrote an enthusiastic letter of thanks, was a half-Jew.) Later Goebbels understood that his intense preoccupation with Romanticism had been a flight from himself. Upon becoming

Propaganda Minister he not only removed his doctorate from Heidelberg Library, but also had its subject changed in official bibliographies. He changed the title of his dissertation to: 'The intellectual and political currents in Early Romanticism.' In this way his literary studies were given the late addition of a political undertone.

13 Riess, op. cit, p. 10.
14 Guido Knopp, *Hitlers Helfer*, Munich 1996, p. 32.
15 Knopp, op. cit., p. 32.
16 The abbreviation for the Nationalsozialistiche Deutsche Arbeiterpartei, the National Socialist Party.
17 Heiber, op. cit.

Chapter 10

1 Hagen Schulze, op. cit., p. 37.
2 Behrend, Schwäb., 29 March 1952, fifth instalment.
3 Eleonore Quandt, who was almost the same age as her sister-in-law, was according to Hans-Otto Meissner Magda's best friend, with whom she remained in an intimate relationship until her death. Ello entrusted Meissner with most of her reminiscences of Magda, and granted him the authority to write Magda's biography on the basis of those memories.
4 Meissner, op. cit., p. 43ff.
5 Behrend, Schwäb., 29 March 1952.
6 Yishuv: The Hebrew word for a 'settlement' refers to the Jewish population of Palestine before the foundation of the state of Israel in 1948.
7 Letters from Arlosoroff in: *Arlosoroff, Life and Work.*
8 Behrend, Schwäb., 29 March 1952.
9 Gerda Luft, *Chronik eines Lebens für Israel.* Stuttgart 1983, p. 74. Therese Flesch remembers Lisa telling her that Magda had come to the station in tears to say goodbye, and regretted that she could not go with them to Palestine.
11 Luft, op. cit., p. 73.
12 Ibid., p. 74.
13 Ibid. Mussa is the Arab word for Moses, and Moses is one of the prophets of Islam. For the Moslems, Moses' grave lies north of Jericho, and in the spring many people visit it in a great procession.

On the mountain, from which Jerusalem can be seen, they begin the celebrations with singing, the playing of oriental instruments and the dancing of the men. It was a great honour for Arlosoroff to be invited to this festival.

14 Luft, op. cit., p. 103.
15 Dérogy et Carmel, op. cit.
16 Ibid.
17 Luft, op. cit., p. 95ff.
18 Meissner, op. cit., p. 49.

Chapter 11

1 Behrend, Schwäb., 22 March 1952, fourth instalment.
2 Ibid.
3 Ibid.
4 Ibid.
5 Meissner, op. cit., p. 66.
6 Ibid., p. 65. See also: Volker Elis Pilgrim, '*Du kannst mich ruhig Frau Hitler nennen*', Hamburg 1994. P. 55ff.

'Her [Magda's] social paralysis finds particular expression in an event that would have required her to sidestep conventional rules if she were to wrest control of it. Her stepson Hellmuth Quandt . . . had fallen in love with Magda, indeed for him being an adult meant being in love with his stepmother. As he reached the age of twenty, the young man's feelings for Magda became more clearly apparent . . . Magda's relationship with her husband, Günther Quandt, had been over for some time. She too loved Hellmuth, indeed it was she who made his emotions explode, but this time she should have *acted*, the breach of social convention should have come from *her*: by leaving her husband, by daring to love her stepson Hellmuth!'

Chapter 12

1 Meissner, op. cit., p. 62.
2 Ibid.
3 Ibid., p. 66.
4 Ibid., p. 62.
5 Behrend, Schwäb., 29 March 1952, fifth instalment.

6 Ibid.
7 Meissner, op. cit., p. 63.
8 Ibid., p. 70.
9 Behrend, Schwäb., 29 March 1952.
10 Pilgrim, op. cit.
11 Meissner, op. cit, p. 71.
12 Ibid., p. 73ff.
13 Ibid.
14 Meissner, op. cit., p. 74. Meissner is quoting from Günther Quandt's account of his own life, written solely for friends and relations. Edited by his sons, Herbert and Harald Quandt. Mensch und Arbeit Verlag, Munich 1961.

Chapter 13

1 Hagen Schulze, op. cit., p. 125ff.
2 Ibid., p. 126.
3 Ibid., p. 128.
4 Friedrich Georg Jünger, *DerAufmarsch des Nationalismus*. Leipzig 1926, p. 21, quoted in Kurt Sontheimer, *Antidemokratisches Denken in der Weimarer Republik*. Munich 1978, p. 57.
5 Ibid.
6 Knopp, op. cit., p. 34ff.
7 Ibid., p. 29.
8 Meissner, op. cit., p. 58.
9 Ibid., p. 59.
10 Knopp, op. cit., p. 37ff.
11 Ibid., p. 37.
12 Ibid. p. 38.
13 Viktor Reimann, *Dr Joseph Goebbels*. Vienna 1971, p. 126.
14 Knopp, op. cit., p. 42.

Chapter 14

1 Meissner, op. cit., p. 85.
2 Ibid.
3 Henriette von Schirach, *Frauen um Hitler*. Munich 1983, p. 174.
4 Pilgrim, op. cit., p. 28.
5 Meissner, op. cit., p. 87.

6   Ibid., p. 99.

7   Ibid. p. 88.

8   Behrend, Schwäb., 29 March 1952, fifth instalment.

9   Ibid.

10 George Steiner, *In Bluebeard's Castle. The Great Ennui.* p. 18, London 1971.

11 Explanations of the 'Nordic Ring' will be found in: *Meyers Lexikon*, Vol. 8 (1940).

12 Behrend, Schwäb., 29 March 1952, fifth instalment.

13 Knopp, op. cit., p. 39.

14 Behrend, Schwäb., op. cit.

15 Reimann, op. cit., p. 138.

16 Behrend, Schwäb., 5 April 1952, sixth instalment: 'After his first speech she was rhapsodic and aflame. According to her own words she had stopped listening to the words after the first few sentences, hearing only the manner of their delivery. She felt that this man was addressing her as a woman, rather than as a devotee of the "Party", which she as yet barely knew. She had to meet this man, who could make one boiling hot and icy cold from one second to the next.'

17 Meissner, op. cit., p. 91.

18 Ibid., p. 92.

19 *Die Tagebücher von Joseph Goebbels. Sämtliche Fragmente.* Ed. Elke Fröhlich. Munich, New York, London, Paris 1987. (Henceforward TB JG).

20 Meissner, op. cit., p. 93.

Chapter 15

1   Behrend, Schwäb., 5 April 1952, sixth instalment.

2   TB JG, 7 November, 1930.

3   Meissner, op. cit., p. 94.

4   Heiber, op. cit., p. 89ff.

5   Saul Friedländer, *Das Dritte Reich und die Juden.* Munich 1998.

6   Meissner, op. cit., p. 100.

7   TB JG, 14 November 1930.

8   Ibid.

9   Meissner, op. cit., p. 100.

10 Ibid.

11 Ibid.
12 TB JG, 15 February 1931.
13 Bella Fromm, op. cit., p. 31.
14 Ibid., p. 34.
15 TB JG, 21 February 1931.
16 Ibid., 23 February 1931.
17 Ibid., 26 February 1931.
18 Ibid., 14 March 1931.
19 Ibid., 15 March 1931.
20 Ibid., 21 March 1931.
21 Heiber, op. cit., p. 91.
22 TB JG, 12 April 1931.

Chapter 16

1 Meissner, op. cit., p. 101.
2 TB JG, 14 April 1931.
3 Ibid., 17 April 1931.
4 Ibid., 18 April 1931.
5 Ibid., 19 April 1931.
6 Ibid., 20 April 1931.
7 Ibid., 25 April 1931.
8 Ibid., 29 April 1931.
9 Ibid., 10 May 1931.
10 Ibid., 23–31 May 1931.
11 TB JG, 13 June 1931.
12 Ibid., 26 July 1931.
13 Ibid., 17 July 1931.
14 Ibid., 24 July 1931.
15 Ibid.
16 Ibid., 17 July 1931.
17 Ibid., 31 July 1931.
18 Ibid., 15 August 1931.
19 Ibid., 16 August 1931.
20 Ibid., 18 August 1931.

Chapter 17

1 Ron Rosenbaum, *Explaining Hitler*. London 1998.
2 *Aufzeichnungen Wageners über Magda Quandt*, Institut für Zeitgeschichte, Munich, ED/60/25, 1539–1547 (henceforth: Wagener).
3 Wagener, op. cit.
4 Ibid.
5 Ibid.
6 Ibid.
7 Behrend, Schwäb.
8 Wagener, op. cit.
9 Ibid.
10 Ibid.
11 Hilmar Hoffmann, '*Und die Fahne führt uns in die Ewigkeit*'. Frankfurt am Main 1988, p. 72.
12 Hedda Kalshoven, *Ich denk so viel an Euch. Ein deutsch-holländischer Briefwechsel 1920–1949*. Munich 1995. The book records the correspondence of a well-to-do bourgeois family. The daughter marries and goes to live in Holland, and sings at benefits for Jewish refugees, while her parents in Braunschweig become enthusiastic followers of Hitler. Their descriptions of daily life give an idea of how Hitler spoke to the emotions –short-circuiting any form of criticism – of the conservative bourgeois population. p. 124.
13 Ibid., p. 122.
14 Wagener, op. cit.
15 Ibid.
16 Ibid.
17 Alexander Mitscherlich: *Die Unfähigkeit zu trauern*. Munich 1967, 1977. p. 76.
18 Joseph Goebbels, 'Wenn Hitler spricht'. 19.1.1928. In: *Der Angriff. Aufsätze aus der Kampfzeit*, Munich 1935, p. 217ff.

Chapter 18

1 Behrend, Schwäb., 5 April 1952, sixth instalment.
2 Meissner, op. cit., p. 107.
3 Ibid., p. 119.
4 Behrend, Schwäb., sixth instalment.
5 Ibid.

6 Meissner, op. cit., p. 101ff.
7 Ibid.
8 Behrend, Schwäb., op. cit.
9 Ibid.
10 Heiber, op. cit., p. 95.
11 Meissner, op. cit., p. 116.
12 Bella Fromm, op. cit., p. 43.
13 Ibid., pp. 43–44.
14 Hagen Schulze, op. cit., p. 359.
15 Ibid.
16 Ibid.
17 Reimann, op. cit., p. 155.
18 Ibid., p. 160.

Chapter 19

1 TB JG, 10 October 1932.
2 Bella Fromm, op. cit., p. 68.
3 Ibid., p. 62.
4 Ibid., p. 64.
5 Ibid., p. 81.
6 TB JG, 9 December 1932.
7 Behrend, Schwäb., 12 April 1952, seventh instalment
8 TB JG, 16 December 1932.
9 Ibid., 23 December 1932.
10 Ibid., 24 December 1932.
11 Ibid., 30 December 1932.
12 Ibid., 1 January 1932.
13 Ibid., 2 January 1933.
14 Ibid., 3 January 1933.
15 Reimann, op. cit., p. 174.
16 Heiber, op. cit., p. 105.
17 Bella Fromm, op. cit., p.71.
18 Horst Möller: *Europa zwischen den Kriegen. Grundriss der Geschichte*, Vol. 21. Munich 1998.
19 TB JG, 30 January 1933.
20 Sontheimer, op. cit., p. 241.

Chapter 20

1 TB JG, 2 February 1933.
2 Ibid.
3 Ibid.
4 Ibid., 11 February 1933.
5 Ibid., 13 February 1933.
6 Scholem, op. cit., p. 278.
7 TB JG, 5 March 1933.

Chapter 21

1 Friedländer, p. 29.
2 Ibid.
3 TB JG, 26 March 1933.
4 Friedländer., p. 21.
5 Ibid., p. 24.
6 Victor Klemperer, *I Shall Bear Witness*, Translated by Martin Chalmers, London 1998 (henceforth TB JG Klemperer). 30 March 1933.
7 Klemperer, op. cit. and German ed., 31 March 1933.
8 Heiber, op. cit., p. 121.
9 Meissner, op. cit., p. 135.
10 Ibid.
11 TB JG, 17 April.
12 Meissner, op. cit., p. 135.
13 Scholem, op. cit., p. 289.

Chapter 22

1 Quoted from: Lisa Steinberg, in conversation with Max Flesch.
2 TB JG, 10 May 1933.
3 Friedländer, op. cit., p. 70.
4 TB JG, 10 May 1933
5 Meissner is quoting Quandt, op. cit., p. 148.
6 TB JG, 7 May.
7 Yehuda Bauer, *Jews for Sale?* Yale University Press 1994. p. 10. The Ha'avarah Agreement was concerned with granting German Jews the possibility of using their capital to buy industrial products in Germany, such as cement mixers or pipes, which could be used

for the construction of Palestine. This idea was, as Bauer describes, 'picked up by the leaders of the Jewish Agency, especially by the head of its political department, the young Labour leader Chaim Arlosoroff. Arlosoroff knew Germany very well and in fact had been a close friend of Magda Quandt, the woman who became Joseph Goebbels' wife. In a series of intensive contacts an agreement was worked out . . . it was signed in August.'

8 There is a photocopy of this in the possession of the author.
9 This conversation was related to Dr Max Flesch.
10 Bella Fromm, op. cit., p. 105ff.
11 TB JG, 4 June 1933.
12 Ibid., 6 June 1933.
13 Max Flesch saw this letter to Lisa, but it disappeared after her death along with other papers.

Chapter 23

1 Haviv Kanaan, 'Goebbels gave the order' (A new version of the Arlosoroff murder) in: Ha'aretz, supplement of 13 June 1975. Tel Aviv.
2 On Richard Kunze in Meyers Lexikon Vol. 7, Leipzig 1939: 'Richard Kunze, nationalist politician. Primary and then secondary school teacher (until 1909), and city councillor in Berlin Schöneberg, had, since the November Revolt, been fighting the Weimar system and Jewry, whose relentless opponent he was; . . . 1921–4, Berlin city councillor, then joined the NSDAP. Member of the Reichstag 1924 and after 1933.'
3 Kanaan's article is backed up by the files of the Political Archive of the Foreign Office, dealing with the 'Palestinian Gold'. These reveal that between February 1933 and January 1934 the General Consulate in Jerusalem reported to the Foreign Office seven times on the subject of the treasure. All those named by Kanaan are mentioned in these reports.
4 Baron Otto von Bolschwing, NSDAP and SS file in the Berlin Document Center, NSDAP No. 984212; SS No. 353603. From these documents it emerges that O.v.Bolschwing had written anti-Semitic tracts during the thirties, which helped Eichmann and the SS to formulate the 'practical' and 'modern' measures which became the cornerstone of the Nazi persecution of the Jews.

In 1932, at the age of 23, O.v.Bolschwing had become a member of the NSDAP, and was almost immediately employed as an inform-ant of the SD (the SS security service, or Sicherheitsdienst). He very quickly developed into one of the senior agents in the NS secret service in the Middle East, and won the trust of Eichmann, who wanted to 'profit' from Bolschwing's knowledge of Zionism. In 1936 and 1937 they collaborated on the first comprehensive pro-gramme for the systematic plundering of European Jews.

The important role he played in a pogrom in the Jewish quarter of Bucharest in 1941 is documented.

Chapter 24

1 In: *Jüdische Rundschau*, 20 June 1933.
2 Ibid., 27 June 1933.
3 Meissner, op. cit., p. 139.
4 Behrend, Schwäb., 26 April 1952.
5 Ibid.
6 Ibid., 12 April.
7 Ibid.
8 Meissner, op. cit., p. 164.
9 Ibid., p. 165.
10 Ibid.
11 Ibid.
12 Ibid., p. 166.
13 Ibid.
14 Ibid.
15 Reimann, op. cit., p. 238.
16 TG Klemperer, 11 November 1933.
17 Loc. cit.
18 Op. cit., 14 November 1933.

Chapter 25

1 TB JG, 22 January 1934.
2 Ibid., 2 April 1934.
3 Behrend, Schwäb., 26 April 1952.
4 Meissner, op. cit., p. 148.
5 William L. Shirer, *Berlin Diary. The Journal of a Foreign*

Correspondent. 1934–1941. 14 July 1934 (henceforth Shirer).
6 Friedländer, op. cit., p. 225.
7 Shirer, op. cit., 25 July 1934.
8 Klemperer, op. cit., 21 August 1934.
9 Bella Fromm, op. cit., p. 205.
10 Meissner, op. cit., p. 153ff.
11 Bella Fromm, op. cit., p. 162.

Chapter 26

1 Bella Fromm, op. cit., p. 172.
2 Shirer, op. cit., 16 March 1935.
3 TB JG, 31 August 1935.
4 Friedländer, op. cit., p. 155.
5 Ibid., p. 149.
6 Klemperer, op. cit., 11 August 1935.
7 TB JG, 15 September 1935.
8 Ibid., 23 September 1935.
9 Ibid., 3 October 1935.
10 Ibid.
11 Behrend, Schwäb., 26 April 1952.
12 TB JG, 7 October 1935.
13 Shirer, op. cit., 4 October 1935.
14 ZstA Rep 90, Go 2, Vol. 2.
15 Ibid.

Chapter 27

1 Meissner, op. cit., p. 171.
2 Ibid., p. 172.
3 Ibid., p. 179.
4 Bella Fromm, op. cit., p. 192ff.
5 Ibid., p. 189.
6 Ibid., p. 189ff.
7 Ibid., p. 190.
8 Reimann, op. cit., p. 249.
9 TB JG, 3 May–11 May 1936.
10 Ibid.
11 Ibid.

12 Ibid.
13 Ibid.
14 Friedländer, op. cit., p. 198.
15 Bella Fromm, op. cit., p. 250.
16 Meissner, op. cit. p. 184.

Chapter 28

1   Reimann, op. cit., p. 225.
2   TB JG, 14 September 1936.
3   Ibid., 15 September 1936.
4   Ibid., 18 September 1936.
5   Ibid., 19 September 1936.
6   Ibid., 13 October 1936.
7   Bella Fromm, op. cit., p. 200.
8   Meissner, op. cit., p. 167.
9   Reimann, op. cit., p. 250.
10 Meissner, op. cit., p. 213.
11 Ibid., p. 212.
12 TB JG, 2 November 1936.
13 Ibid., 3 November 1936.
14 Bella Fromm, op. cit., p. 201.
15 Ibid., p. 257.
16 TB JG, 11 November 1936.
17 Ibid., 12 December 1936.
18 Behrend, Schwäb., 26 April 1952.
19 TB JG, 29 December 1936.
20 Ibid., 4 June 1937.
21 Ibid., 17 January 1937.
22 Ibid., 7 February 1937.
23 Ibid., 6 February 1937.
24 Ibid., 20 February 1937.

Chapter 29

1   TB JG, 15 May 1937.
2   Ibid., 16 May 1937.
3   Meissner, op. cit., p. 168.
4   Hilmar Hoffmann, op. cit., p. 72.

5 Saul Friedländer, *Kitsch und Tod*. Munich 1984, p. 118.

6 TB JG, October 1937.

7 Ibid., 12 November 1937.

8 Ibid., 19 December 1937.

9 Meissner, op. cit., p. 173.

10 Ibid., p. 191.

11 Ibid.

12 Sebastian Haffner, *Anmerkungen zu Hitler*. Munich 1978, p. 42 (henceforth Haffner, Anm).

13 Ibid.

14 Shirer, 11–12 March 1938.

15 Friedländer, op. cit., p. 262ff.

16 Ibid.

17 Bella Fromm, op. cit., p. 236.

18 Ibid., p. 236.

Chapter 30

1 Meissner, op. cit., p. 214.

2 Ibid., p. 216.

3 Ibid., p. 220.

4 Ibid., p. 222

5 Ibid., p. 226.

6 Meissner, op. cit., pp. 228–232.

7 Ibid.

8 Ibid.

9 Ibid.

10 Ibid.

Chapter 31

1 Meissner, op. cit., p. 234.

2 Ibid., p. 237.

3 Ibid., 18 August 1938.

4 Ibid., 19 August 1938.

5 Klemperer, 20 September 1938.

6 ZStA Rep 90, Go 2, Vol. 3.

7 Meissner, op. cit., p. 238ff.

8 Friedländer, *Das Dritte Reich und die Juden*. Munich 1998. p. 239ff.

9 Ibid.
10 Ibid., p. 299.
11 ZStA Rep 90, Go 2, Vol. 3.
12 Meissner, op. cit., p. 243.
13 TB JG, 30 December 1938.
14 Klemperer, New Year's Eve 1938.

Chapter 32

1 TB JG, 6 February 1939.
2 Ibid., 3 February 1939.
3 Meissner, op. cit., p. 244.
4 Albert Speer, *Erinnerungen*. Berlin 1969.
5 Here Speer describes Magda as the 'second lady of the Reich', because Emmy Göring occupies the role of first lady. He assumes that Göring enjoyed greater esteem than Goebbels within the Nazi leadership, and so, for that reason, did his wife Emmy. But with her personal closeness to Hitler, Magda rivalled her for this position, and she was frequently identified as the 'first lady of the Reich'.
6 Speer, op. cit., p. 161ff.
7 ZStA Rep 90, Go 2, Vol. 3.
8 Ibid.
9 Meissner, op. cit., p. 246.
10 Speer, op. cit., p. 164ff.
11 Ibid.
12 Ibid.
13 Behrend, Schwäb., twelfth instalment.
14 Ibid.

Chapter 33

1 Speer, op. cit., p. 180.
2 Ibid.
3 Shirer, 3 September 1939.
4 Meissner, op. cit., p. 252.
5 TB JG, 2 November 1939.
6 Ibid., 29 October 1939.
7 ZSta Rep 90, Go 2, Vol. 3.

8 Ibid.
9 Haffner, Anm., p. 130.
10 Meissner, op. cit., p. 257.
11 ZSta Rep 90, Go 2, Vol. 2.
12 TB JG, 16, 17, 21, 24 February. 1941.
13 Meissner, op. cit., p. 258.
14 Ibid., p. 259.
15 Ibid., p. 261.
16 Ibid., p. 263.
17 Haffner, Anm., p. 134.
18 Ibid., p. 132.
19 Ian Kershaw, *The Nazi Dictatorship*, London 1993, p. 104.
20 The story of this pianist, who died in Auschwitz, was told me by the daughter of the professor of music who taught her in Katowice.
21 Behrend, Schwäb., thirteenth instalment.
22 Ibid.

Chapter 34

1 Meissner, op. cit., p. 268.
2 Ibid., p. 275.
3 TB JG, 27 March 1942.
4 Meissner, op. cit., p. 287.
5 Behrend, Schwäb., fourteenth instalment.
6 Ibid., thirteenth instalment.
7 Meissner, op. cit., p. 304.
8 Ibid., p. 279.
9 Ibid., p. 280.
10 Ibid., p. 286.
11 Behrend, Schwäb., fourteenth instalment.
12 Ibid.
13 ZSta Rep 90, Go2, Vol. 2.
14 Ibid.
15 Meissner, op. cit., p. 295ff.

Chapter 35

1 Goebbels used the legend of the werewolf, handed down from Old German tales, to spur young people on to resist the Allies.

2 Haffner, Anm., p. 153.
3 Ibid.
4 Ibid.
5 Meissner, op. cit., p. 307.
6 Gitta Sereny, *Albert Speer: His Battle with Truth*. London 1995, p. 508.
7 Behrend, Schwäb., fourteenth instalment.
8 Meissner, op. cit., p. 310.
9 Speer, op. cit., p. 484.
10 Ibid.
11 Sereny, op. cit., p. 531ff.
12 Meissner, op. cit., p. 314.
13 Ibid.
14 Meissner, op. cit., p. 324.
15 Ibid., p. 326.
16 Ibid., p. 329.
17 Sereny, op. cit., p. 539.
18 Ibid., p. 540ff.
19 Meissner, op. cit., p. 337ff.

Selected Bibliography

Arendt, Hannah: *Elemente und Ursprunge totaler Herrschaft*. Munich 1987 (Original edition 1955).

Arendt, Hannah: *Eichmann in Jerusalem. Ein Bericht von der Banalität des Bösen*. Munich 1986 (Original edition 1964).

Brockhaus, Gudrun: *Schauder und Idylle*. Munich 1997.

Bronnen, Barbara: *Geschichten vom Überleben. Frauentagebucher aus der NS-Zeit*. Munich 1998.

Broszat, Martin: *Der Staat Hitlers. Grundlegung und Entwicklung seiner inneren Verfassung*. Munich 1969.

Browning, Christopher: *Ganz normale Manner. Das Reserve-Polizeibatallion 101 und die 'Endlösung' in Polen*. Reinbek 1993.

Fest, Joachim: *Hitler. Eine Biographie*. Berlin 1987.

Fischer, Fritz: *Griff nach der Weltmacht*. 1994 reprint of the original edition, Düsseldorf 1967.

Friedländer, Saul: *Das Dritte Reich und die Juden*. Munich 1998.

Friedländer, Saul: *Kitsch und Tod*. Munich 1984.

Fromm, Bella: *Blood and Banquets*. New York, 1944, republished in a slightly extended form as: *Als Hitler mir die Hand küsste*. Reinbek 1994.

Goebbels, Joseph: *Michael. Ein deutsches Schicksal in Tagebuchblättern*. Munich, 1929.

Goebbels, Joseph: *Die Tagebücher von Joseph Goebbels. Samtliche Fragmente*, *hrsg. von Elke Frölich im Auftrag des Instituts für Zeitgeschichte und in Verbindung mit dem Bundesarchiv.* Munich, New York, London, Paris 1987.

Haffner, Sebastian: *Der Verrat. Deutschland 1918–1919.* Munich 1995.

Haffner, Sebastian: *Anmerkungen zu Hitler.* Frankfurt 1981.

Heiber, Helmut: *Joseph Goebbels.* Munich 1988.

Hillberg, Raul: Täter, *Opfer, Zuschauer.* Frankfurt 1996.

Hoffmann, Hilmar: *'Und die Fahne führt uns in die Ewigkeit.' Propaganda im NS-Film.* Frankfurt 1988.

Jung, Carl Gustav: *Wotan: In: Aufsätze zur Zeitgeschichte.* Zurich 1946.

Kershaw, Ian: *The Nazi Dictatorship.* London 1993.

Klemperer, Victor: *LTI.* Leipzig 1975.

Klemperer Victor: *Ich will Zeugnis ablegen bis zum letzten. Tagebücher 1933–41.* Berlin 1995; English edition: *I shall bear witness,* edited and translated by Martin Chalmers. London 1998.

Knopp, Guido: *Hitlers Helfer.* Munich 1996.

Koonz, Claudia: *Mothers in the Fatherland. Women, the Family and Nazi Politics.* London 1988.

Luft, Gerda: *Chronik eines Lebens für Israel.* Stuttgart 1983.

Mann, Thomas *Betrachtungen eines Unpolitischen.* Frankfurt 1956.

Meissner, Hans-Otto: *Magda Goebbels. Ein Lebensbild.* Munich 1978.

Mitscherlich, Alexander and Margarete: *Die Unfahigkeit zu trauern.* Munich 1977.

Mosse, George L.: *Der nationalsozialistische Alltag.* Meisenheim 1993.

Pilgrim, Volker Elis: *'Du kannst mich ruhig Frau Hitler nennen'.* Reinbek 1994.

Reimann, Viktor: *Dr. Joseph Goebbels.* Vienna, Munich, Zurich 1971.

Rosenbaum, Ron: *Die Hitler-Debatte.* Munich 1999.

Schadlich, Karlheinz; *Die Mitford Sisters.* Düsseldorf 1990.

Schirach, Henriette von: *Frauen um Hitler.* Munich 1983.

Schoeps, Julius H.: (Ed.) *Zeitgeist der Weimarer Republik.* Stuttgart 1968.

Scholem, Betty and Gershom: *Mutter und Sohn im Briefwechsel 1917–1946.* Munich 1989.

Schuddekopf, Charles: *Der alltägliche Faschismus: Frauen im Dritten Reich.* Berlin, Bonn 1982.

Schulze, Hagen: *Weimar. Deutschland 1917–1933.* Berlin 1982.

Schwarz, Gudrun: *Eine Frau an seiner Seite.* Hamburg 1997.

Sereny, Gitta: *Albert Speer. His Battle with Truth.* London 1995.

Shirer, William L.: *Berlin Diary. The Journal of a foreign correspondent*

1934–1941. USA 1941.

Sontheimer, Kurt: *Antidemokratisches Denken in der Weimarer Republik.* Munich 1978.

Speer, Albert: *Erinnerungen.* Frankurt, Berlin 1969.

Steiner, George: *In Bluebeard's Castle. Some notes towards the redefinition of culture.* Yale 1971.

Stern, J.P.: *Hitler. The Fuhrer and the People.* Great Britain 1975.

Toller, Ernst: *Eine Jugend in Deutschland.* Reinbek 1996.

Vondung, Klaus: *Die Apokalypse in Deutschland.* Munich 1988.

Index

Abyssinia (Ethiopia) 224
Adige, River 298, 306, 337
AEG 59
Alexandria 78
Aliyah 55, 57
Allenby, General Sir Edmund 196
Allies
    First World War 19, 29, 58, 81, 86
    Second World War 219, 299, 302, 307, 313
American War of Independence 10
Amman (Nazi) 218
Amsterdam 183, 279
anarchy 66
Anka (friend of Goebbels) 65
Anschluss (Austria) 214, 256, 273
anti-Semitism 22, 33–4, 46, 58–9, 67, 69, 106, 116, 119, 135, 147, 178, 179, 180, 187, 188, 190, 197, 220–21ff, 249ff, 255, 273, 287–8, 289–90
Arabs 56, 57, 75, 79ff, 93ff, 195ff
Ardennes offensive 306
Arendt, Hannah 266
Arlosoroff family 13–14, 17, 19–21, 23, 26, 30, 33, 37, 41, 43f, 48, 49, 53, 55, 74, 76–7, 79ff, 146, 190

Arlosoroff, Frau (Victor's mother) 74–5, 76–8
Arlosoroff, Dora (Victor's sister) 13, 19ff, 26, 78
Arlosoroff, Gerda (Victor's 1st wife) 45, 49–50, 58, 74–5, 77–80, 81, 82, 92
Arlosoroff, Shulamit (Victor's daughter) 50, 58, 74–5, 77, 78
Arlosorof, Sima (Victor's 2nd wife) 75, 80–8ff, 92–3, 190, 193
Arlosoroff, Victor (Chaim) xi, 20–21, 22–4, 26–7, 29, 32–8, 43, 45, 48ff, 54–9, 68, 74–5, 76–82, 91–5, 109, 112, 130, 135–6, 162, 181–99, 200, 222, 296, 325
Arlosoroff-Steinberg, Lisa (Victor's sister) xiii, 13–14, 16, 21, 24, 26, 31, 34, 35–6, 38, 46, 74, 76–7, 91, 149, 190, 192, 198–9, 296
armaments industry 25, 155, 231, 255
Athens 196
August Wilhelm, Prince ('Auwi') 111, 113, 125
Auschwitz concentration camp 294–5, 296, 307

Austria 4, 86–7, 132, 191, 214, 224, 255–6, 273
Austria-Hungary 30

Baarov, Lida 237–8, 239, 241, 244, 245–6, 249–50, 251, 257, 260–64, 266–7, 269–70, 271, 272, 282, 288–9
Babelsberg, 42, 72, 97, 237, 250
Bad Godesberg 28, 42, 45, 95
Bad Nauheim 91
Baden-Baden 239
Balfour, Arthur 56
Balfour Declaration 56
Ballhausschwur see Tennis Court Oath
Baltic 279, 295
Bamberg 119
Basle 22
Bastille 10
Bastille Day 83
Bath 299
Bayreuth 214, 258, 280–81
Beethoven, Ludwig van 21
Behrend, Auguste *see* Friedländer, Auguste
Belgium 4ff, 9, 19, 112, 289–90
Ben-Gurion, David 190
Benjamin, Walter 175
Berchtesgaden 165, 178, 271
Berengaria, S.S. 88
Berlin xiii, 5, 6, 9, 12, 14–17, 31–5 and throughout
Berliner Tageblatt 67, 68, 69
Berliner Zeitung am Mittag 122
Black Friday *see* Wall Street Crash
black market 25
Blomberg, General Werner von 212, 253
Blood Law 222
Blutfahne der Nazis (Flag of Blood) 143f
Blut *und Bodens* ideology 103
Bogensee 241, 242, 245, 249, 250, 270, 291, 313
bohemianism 101
Bolschwing, Baron von 196–7, 199
Bolshevism 35, 116, 148, 220, 231, 292, 308
book-burning 188–9

Bordighera 76
Boston 89
bourgeosie 11–12, 21, 24, 28, 29, 35, 36, 42, 52, 67, 101, 108, 110, 116, 120, 121, 201, 227, 286
Brandenberg 51
Braun, Eva 318–19
Braunschweig 141, 144
Brecht, Bertolt 101: '*Threepenny Opera*' 101
Breitsprecher, Wilhelm 286–7
Breslau 282, 303
Broch, Hermann 101
Bronnen, Arnolt 120
Brückner (Hitler's adjutant) 152
Brüning, Heinrich 124, 132–3, 155, 157
Bruges 7
Brussels 3–4, 6–7, 9, 16, 17
Buchenwald concentration camp 275
Budapest 307
Budhism 28, 53, 162, 312
Buffalo 89
Bulgaria 29, 234, 235; King of 234–5
Bürgerspiegel 161

capitalism 67, 82, 149, 285, 325
Carola (foster-daughter, Magda & Günther Quandt) 88
Catholicism 29, 46, 64, 67, 112, 295, 326
Central Union of German Citizens of the Jewish Faith 172
Chamberlain, Sir Neville 270
Chancellor, Sir John 93
chauvinism 25
Chelius, Erika 125, 223
Chevalier, Maurice 85
Chicago 90
Chopin, Frédéric 191, 203
Christianity 176, 220, 223
Churchill, Sir Winston 288
Ciano, Count 230, 239–40
Ciano, Countess, Edda 230
civil war (Germany 1918–19) 30–31, 32–3, 35
Cocteau, Jean 86

Cologne 6, 177
Commission for Economy and Finance 81
Communism 35, 66, 84, 87, 105, 106, 108,
    110, 128, 133, 144, 149, 158, 169–70,
    171–3, 243, 249
Compiègne 31
concentration camps 206, 208, 244, 255,
    273, 274, 289, 294, 295, 307
Constance, Lake 178
Cortina d'Ampezzo 76
Coventry 299
Crete 300
Czechoslovakia 270–71, 278–9

Dachau concentration camp 175, 214
Danatbank 132
Danzig 287
Dehmel, Richard 11
Denmark 242
Der Angriff 106, 119, 129, 133, 147, 159
Deutschvölkische Freiheitspartei 69
Dietrich, Sepp 212–13
Dirksen family 112, 124, 126, 152
Dirksen, Viktoria von 111, 161, 162–3
Djenin 196, 197
Dollfuss, Chancellor Engelbert 214
Dostoyevsky, Fyodor 66
Dresden 129, 168, 176, 238, 257, 270,
    275, 291, 302, 303–4; bombing of
    307–8
Dreyfus affair 262; trial (1894) 22
Duisberg 196, 291
Dusseldorf 154

East Prussia 279, 297, 304
Ebert, Friedrich 31, 32, 34
Eger 271
Egypt 91
Einstein, Albert 101, 175
Elbe, River 307, 315
Enabling Act (1933) 172–3
Engels, Friedrich 66
Enlightenment, the 102
Epp, Ritter von 152
Eretz Israel 27, 34
'Ernst' see Gerber, Fritz

Erzberger, Matthias 59
euthanasia programme 244
Exeter 275

Fascism 84, 144, 243, 249, 278
FBI 163
Fichte, Johann Gottlieb 11
Fiedler, Petra 210
film industry 237–8, 250–51, 268, 288
First World War 9, 10, 11, 13, 17–19, 24,
    25, 26, 27–31, 33 et seq, 50–51, 52,
    56–7, 64–5, 86, 100, 101, 187, 220,
    311, 325; cease-fire 29–31; German
    casualties 18–19, 29, 31
Fitzgerald, F. Scott 89
Flesch, Max xi, xiii, 198–9
Flanders 4
Flisges, Richard 65–6, 67–8
Florence 121, 307
'Foreign League of German Women'
    (Auslandsbund Deutscher Frauen
    161–2
Förster, Olly 120
France 4, 9, 10, 29, 31, 56, 84–5, 91,
    163, 219, 231, 270, 284–5, 289,
    295–6
Franco, General Francisco 243
François-Poncet, André 162–3
Frank, Governor Hans 287
Franz Ferdinand, Emperor 4
Frederick the Great 177
Freiburg 178
Freicorps 33, 35, 61, 270
Freud, Anna 256
Freud, Sigmund 101, 188, 256
Freybe, Frau 225, 226, 296, 306
Frick, Wilhelm 169
Friedländer family, 149, 296
Friedländer (formerly Ritschel, née
    Behrend) Auguste xiii, 3–8, 10,
    14–16, 17, 19–20, 27–8, 35–6, 38,
    41–2, 43, 45–6, 53, 72, 74, 84, 86, 90,
    96, 110–11, 113, 117, 122, 127,
    148–9, 151–2, 164, 178–9, 202, 210,
    222, 224, 245, 283, 290–91, 297,
    302–3, 306, 316, 324, 326

Friedländer, Richard 3–8, 10, 14, 17,
    19–20, 27–8, 36, 37, 41, 42, 46, 47,
    112, 135, 178–9, 180, 190, 222, 296
Friedländer, Saul 175–6, 214, 220,
    250–51, 256; *Kitsch und Tod* 250–51
Friedländer-Fuld (coal magnate) 240
Fritsch, C.-in-C. Werner von 253
Fröhlich, Gustav 237, 241, 244
Fromm, Bella 28, 122–4, 154, 161–3, 167,
    190–91, 215, 217, 219, 230–31, 235,
    239, 242–3, 257–8
Fürtwangler, Wilhelm 227, 238

gas chambers 295
Gastein 279–80, 281
Gatow 318
Gautier, Théophile 111
Geneva 206
Genf 194
George V, King 84
George, Stefan 66
'George-Kreis' circle 66
Gerber, Fritz ('Ernst') 94–5, 109–10, 115,
    119, 120, 121, 122, 127, 128–30,
    132–3, 134, 135, 136
Gerda *see* Arlosoroff, Gerda
German Academy of Arts 175
German Community Party 34
'German Labour Front' 174, 226
German National Party 165, 172
Ghent 7
Gleichschaltung policy 174, 178 198, 211
Goebbels family 63–4, 227–9, 234, 244–5,
    248–9, 252, 254, 267, 272, 276, 277,
    279, 290–91, 302, 305, 306, 309–10,
    311–12, 313–18, 319–23
Goebbels, Friedrich (father of Joseph) 63,
    64, 67
Goebbels, Hedda 227–8, 256
Goebbels, Heide 290, 320
Goebbels, Helga 160, 220, 227–8, 246,
    267, 272, 279, 315, 318, 320
Goebbels, Helmut 224, 228, 239
Goebbels, Hilde 209–10, 211, 227–8, 272
Goebbels, Holde 228, 246–8
Goebbels, (Paul) Joseph xi–xii, 61–70,

    103–8, 111, 112, 115–16, 117–37,
    140–43, 145–54, 155–79, 186–92,
    195–9, 200–221, 223–4, 227–30,
    232–53, 256–78, 280–82, 285, 286,
    287–93, 296–7, 299–305, 309,
    310–12, 313–20, 325–8
    Michael 67
    The Battle for Berlin 134
Goebbels, Maria Katharina (mother of
    Joseph) 63, 64, 67, 152
Goebbels, Maria Magdalena (Magda) (née
    Behrend, adoptive name Friedlander,
    also known as Ritschel, former
    married name Quandt) *passim*
    throughout
    appearance, dress, looks 19, 38, 39, 89,
        91, 94, 99, 112, 115, 122, 124, 128,
        162, 192, 204–5, 239, 264, 306,
        308, 326, 327
    Brussels to Germany 3–15
    children and 50, 73, 76, 88–9, 110, 220,
        225, 227–8, 229, 234, 249, 265,
        267, 302: plans and does kill them
        309–11, 314–15, 316–18, 319–20,
        321–2
    early years 3–10, 11–23
    education 4, 6–7, 16–17, 28–9, 35–7,
        39, 112: finishing school 36–42,
        325–6
    emotions 53, 74, 86, 128, 130, 204, 260,
        297, 305, 318
    household management, routine 48–9,
        52–3, 73, 153–4, 177, 203–5, 229,
        233, 234, 244–5, 249
    ill-health 88–9, 90–91, 110, 111,
        164–6, 169–70, 216, 238, 245–6,
        248–9, 252, 259–60, 275, 285,
        291, 300–304, 316–17: suicide
        320
    marriage to Quandt 42–6, 73–4, 76,
        81–2, 83–6, 88, 91–2 and divorce
        94–9, 100, 109, 110, 115, 117
    marriage to Goebbels 28, 110, 115, 117
        et passim, and planned divorce
        262–7, 268–75, 278, 279, 282,
        291–2

need for attention 110–11, 170, 232, 242, 243–4, 325–6, 328
pregnancies and births 154, 158–9, 209–10, 211, 218, 220, 223–4, 234, 238, 241, 243, 245, 246–7, 248, 251, 256, 261, 289–90
views on marriage 36, 41, 42–3, 46–8, 72–3, 265
Zionism and 23–4, 27, 34, 36, 37–8, 82, 112, 135, 136, 162, 190
Goethe, Johann Wolfgang von 23, 68, 177, 186
Goldschmidt, Samuel 251
Göring, Emmy 218–19, 282, 297, 324
Göring, Hermann 139–40, 157, 158–9, 169, 171, 191, 202, 218–19, 222, 235, 240–41, 291
Goslar 36, 38, 40–42
Granada 249
Granzow, Herr (G. Quandt's brother-in-law) 99, 151–2
Granzow, Frau 152
Graubünden 91
Great Britain 56, 75, 78, 84, 181, 270, 284–5, 289: see also First World War, Palestine; Second World War
Greece 239
Grete (Jewish fashion house) 226
Griebnitzsee 42
Groener, Wilhelm 157
Grönda, Heinz 196–9
Gropius, Walter 101
Gründgens, Gustaf 238
Grynszpan family 273
Grynszpan, Herschel 273
Gundolf, Friedrich 66, 68, 69
Günsche, Otto 319
Günther, Professor Hans E.K. 111

Ha'aretz 195, 198
Haarlem 279
Habsburgs 4
Haifa 54–5
Haffner, Sebastian 30–31, 298
Halle 156
Hamburg 302

Hanke, Karl 241, 249–50, 259–60, 262–7, 268–71, 274, 277–8, 280, 282, 286, 288, 303, 305, 315
Hanfstaengl, Putzi 154, 167
Hanover 273
Hapoel Hazair party 50, 78
Hartmann, Paul 238
Hartz Mountains 41
Hassidim 54–5
Hauptmann, Carl 11
Hauptmann, Gerhardt 11
Havana 90
Havel, River 232, 260, 303
Ha'vara Agreement 189
Heidaelberg 66, 178
Heiligendamm 190
Heine, Heinrich 29, 186
Helldorf, Count 271
Hemingway, Ernest 249
Heringa, Herr 279
Herzl, Theodor 22
Heydrich, Reinhard 125, 274, 287
Himmler, Heinrich 104, 175, 212, 213
Hindenburg, Oscar von 132, 157, 166–7
Hindenburg, President Paul von xiii, 126, 132–3, 156–8, 166–8, 209, 214–15
Histradut (Zionist workers' directorate) 78
Hitler, Adolf xii, xiii, 4, 62–3, 69, 103–5, 107, 108, 111, 113–15, 118, 119, 122, 123, 125–6, 127, 130, 133, 135, 138–45, 146–8, 150–54, 156–7, 158–9, 161, 163, 165, 167–8, 169–73, 174, 177–8, 179, 181, 182, 187, 190–91, 192, 201–2, 205–6, 207–8, 209, 210–16, 218–20, 222–5, 227–32, 234, 241, 243, 245, 246, 252, 253–4, 255–6, 263, 265, 268–74, 277–83, 284–5, 287, 288–90, 292–5, 297–8, 299–300, 301, 303, 304–5, 309–22 passim, 326–7; Mein Kampf 147, 294
Hitler Youth 107, 139
Hoffmann, Hilmar 143, 250
Hölderlin, Friedrich 23, 186
Holland 5, 31, 242, 289–90

Holocaust 9, 294–5, 299, *see also* anti-Semitism; Jews; Hitler, Adolf
Holzhausen 36, 295–6
homosexuality 212–14, 253
Hook of Holland 183
Hoover, President Herbert xiii, 89, 109, 132; nephew of 109–10
Horthy, Nikolaus 269
Hoyos, Countess 125
Humboldt University 26, 32

idealism 12, 27
I.G. Farben 154
inflation 52, 71–2, 81, 325
Intellectual elite 100–102, 110, 175, 289
International Brigade 248–9
Iraq *see* Mesopotamia
Israel xi, 27, 34, 194, 198
Istanbul 196
Italy 48, 76, 219, 256, 278, 306

Jaffa (pogrom) 57–8
Jaffo (suburb of Tel Aviv) 79, 195, 197
Jena University 111
Jerusalem 22, 57, 58, 79, 93, 171, 184, 200; pogrom 57; Wailing Wall 93
Jewish Agency 181, 195
Jewish homeland *see* Palestine
Jews, Jewishness 8, 19, 21–3, 27, 33–4, 36, 37–8, 56–7, 59, 69, 75, 77, 78, 80, 93–4, 101, 106, 112, 119–20, 122, 147–8, 149, 172, 175–7, 178, 180–82, 185–6, 188, 189–90, 194, 199, 200–201, 206, 220–22, 225–6, 231, 256, 257, 265, 273–4, 275, 285, 289, 293–4, 295–6, 299, 310, 326, 327: customs, holidays 8, 18; Nazi persecution 174–88ff, 190, 220–22, 256, 257–8, 273–5, 287–8, 294, 299, 301, 305
Joyce, James 85
Joyce, Nora 85
Jüdische Rundschau 185, 186, 200
Jünger, Ernst 24, 102–3: *Storms of Steel* 24
Jünger, Friedrich Georg 102–3
Jungvolk 152, 255

Kabarett der Komiker 101, 266, 277
Kafka, Franz 101
Kampfbund fur Deutsche Kultur 115
Kanaan, Haviv 195–6, 198
Katowice 295–6
K.d.d.K. (Comradeship Club for German Artists) 229–30, 274
Kempf, Annemarie 315
Kempka, Erich 317–18
Kershaw, Ian 294
Kiel 31
Kladow (Wannsee) 209–10, 213–14, 220, 232
Klemperer, Otto 175
Klemperer, Victor 176, 206–8, 215, 222, 270, 276, 307
Klepper, Jochen 220–21
Knittel, John 230; *Via Mala* 230
Knopp, Guido 103, 196, 199
Koch (Gauleiter) 196, 199
Koch, Hella 125
Koestler, Arthur 249
Köhler family 88
Kokoschka, Oskar 175–6
Königsberg 13, 34–5, 38, 45, 49, 125
Körber, Hilde 269–70, 272
Korth, Theo 196–7, 199
Kowalsky, Frau 15
Krender, Peter 303
Kristallnacht xi, 274–5
Kritzinger, Father 44
Kroll Opera 283
Krupp von Bohlen & Holbach, Gustav 154
Kunze, Richard 196

Länder (regions) 174
Lanke Castle (Bogensee) 240–42, 245, 249–50, 252, 286, 288, 291–2
Law for the Rebuilding of the Reich (1934) 211
League of German Girls (*Bund Deutsche Mädchen*) 227, 228, 240
League of Nations 56, 206, 219, 231 Plenary Group of 206
Lebanon 56

Lebensborn Association 254
Leipzig 14, 53
Lenin, Vladimir I. 66
Leopold, Prince 177
Liebermann, Max 175–6
Liebknecht, Karl 34, 59
Liliencron, Detlev von 23
Lincke, Paul 202–3
Liszt, Franz 203
Locarno Pact 231
Lodz ghettos 288, 294
London 84, 183, 192, 200, 219, 256
Lorca, Federico Garcia 240
Ludendorff, General Erich von 30
Lufban (Palestine workers' leader) 55
Luxembourg, Rosa, 34, 59

Magdeburg 41
Malraux, André 249
Manhattan 89
Mann, Thomas 116
Marx, Karl 66
Marxism 50, 66, 67, 147–8, 170, 188
Mecklenburg 99
Mediterranean 54
Meissner, Frau (Hans-Otto's mother) 179, 304
Meissner, Otto (father of Hans-Otto) xiii, 132–3, 157, 166–7
Meissner, Hans-Otto xiii, 68, 86, 94, 110, 121, 130, 132, 154, 166, 179, 204–5, 229–30, 234, 241, 260, 262–3, 275, 288, 304, 308, 310, 312, 319
Memel 279
Mesopotamia (Iraq) 56
Mexico 90
Mia (friend of Bella Fromm) 257
militarism 24–5, 51, 231, 255
Minsk 294
Misch, Rochus 320
Mistinguette 85
Mitscherlich, Alexander 146
Mizrahi group 94, 181
monarchy 51, 86, 104
Morell, Dr 303
Moscow 87, 287, 297

Mount of Olives 79
Mozart, Wolfgang Amadeus 203, 221
Munich 61–2, 69, 104–5, 125–6, 135, 165, 192, 212, 220, 245, 270, 273, 299, 310
Musil, Robert 101
Mussolini, Benito 191–2, 214, 224, 230

nationalism 61–2, 67–9, 70, 101, 103
National Socialism xi–xii, xiii, 28, 68–70, 101–4, 106, 115, 116, 123, 132, 133, 143–4, 147–50, 158, 161–2, 163, 169, 170–71, 176, 179–80, 183–7, 189, 195–9 *passim*, 206, 211–12, 213–14, 225–6, 227–8, 234–5, 240, 242–3, 250, 253–6, 263–4, 265, 268–9, 272–4, 277, 284–5, 289–90, 293, 296, 301, 310–12, 314, 321–3, 324–8
National Socialist Freedom Movement 69
National Socialist Party 103
National Socialist Women's Organisation 255
Nation, The 234
Napoleon I 300
Naumann, Werner 288, 305
Nazareth 196
Nebi Mussa festival 79
Neurath, Konstantin von 217
Neurath, Frau von 217
New York 89, 109, 123
Norden 111
Nibelungenlied 311
'Night of the Long Knives' 212
Non-Aggression Pact: Britain and Germany (1938) 270
'Nordic Ring' club 111–12, 113
Normandy 85
Noske, Gustav 34
NSDAP 69, 102–6, 107–8, 111–16, 117–21, 122–3, 124, 125–6, 130, 132–3, 143–5, 147–8, 149–50, 154–9, 160–62, 163, 166–8, 169–73, 174, 196, 211–12, 225, 227, 232, 325: policy 174, 184–9
Nuremberg 273
Nuremburg League of Culture 222

Nuremburg rally 215, 220, 222, 238
NS *Frauenschaft* (Party Women's Association) 107
NS Teachers' League 107

Obersalzberg 245, 291
October Revolution (1917, Russia) 27
Oder, River 313
Olympic Games (1936) 234–5
Orwell, George 249
Ottoman Empire 56, 196

Palestine xi, 21, 22–3, 27, 34–6, 50, 54–5, 56–8, 75–8, 80–81, 91, 93–4, 109, 177, 179–82, 186, 187, 190, 192, 195–8, 200: British Mandate in 56–7, 93–4, 197; Arabs and 56, 57, 75, 79–80, 93; immigration and 75, 78, 93–4, 160, 181, 183; Jews, Jewish homeland in 22, 56–7, 75, 78, 80, 93; White Book and 22, 181
Papen, Franz von 157–9, 160, 166–7, 169
Paris 9, 83–5, 86, 192, 219, 274, 289
Paulus, General Friedrich Wilhelm 300
Pfaueninsel 235–6, 237–8
Phalangists 249
Philadelphia 89
Piscator, Erwin 101
pogroms 13, 27, 33, 57, 176, 188, 199, 273–4, 287
Poland 27, 33, 57, 273, 283, 284–8, 294, 299, 303
Ponte, Lorenzo da 221
Potsdam 162
Prague 190, 192, 237, 288
Prang, Fritz 69
Protestantism 46, 89, 112
psychoanalysis 188

Quandt family 76
Quandt, Ello (Magda's sister-in-law) xiii, 46, 68, 73, 74, 95, 110, 120, 149, 150, 179, 203, 218, 223, 234, 240, 244, 260–64, 267, 270, 271, 274, 278, 288, 291–3, 300, 301, 304, 305, 307–10, 311, 314, 323

Quandt, Emil 51
Quandt, Günther (Magda's 1st husband) xiii, 39–53, 72, 73–4, 81–2, 83–6, 88–93, 95–9, 109–10, 112, 115, 117, 121,122, 124, 127–8, 131, 135, 136, 140, 148, 149, 150–52, 160, 162, 164, 189, 205, 210–11, 232, 310, 321, 325, 327
Quandt, Harold (son to Magda and Günther) 50, 73, 88, 96–7, 98, 99, 110, 121, 126, 139–40, 148, 153, 165, 210–11, 224, 228, 285, 290, 300, 306, 310, 317, 321–3
Quandt, Hellmuth (stepson to Magda) 46, 49, 73, 84–6, 88
Quandt, Herbert (stepson to Magda) 46, 49, 73, 88, 96, 99, 127, 291
Quandt, Ursula 291
Quandt, Werner 46

Rass 111
Rath, Ernst von 273–4
Rathenau, Walter 59–60, 61, 70, 71, 229
Raubal, Geli 138–9, 141, 169
Raucheisen, Michael 266
rearmament 174, 224, 231, 255
'Red Swastika German Women's Order' 107
Reich Association of the German Automobile Industry 202
Reich Citizenship Law 222
Reich Culture Chamber 221–2
Reich Flag Law 222
Reich Ministry of Economics 52
Reich Ministry for National Information and Propaganda 177
Reich Music Chamber 221
Reichert, Jisrael 21
Reichstag 60, 70, 115, 116, 121, 123, 133, 158, 160, 161, 169, 172, 196, 206, 213, 222, 231, 283; burning of 171–2, 174
Reichswehr 32, 33, 61, 157, 212
Reichswoll AG 51–2
Reimann, Viktor 114, 158, 166, 206, 238
Reinhardt, Max, 175
Reitsch, Hanna 321, 322

Remagen 290

Remarque, Erich Maria 119: *All Quiet on the Western Front* 119

reparations 38, 71–2, 81, 115–16, 132, 155

Reuss, Princess 111, 113

revisionism (Israel) 167, 181–2, 190, 194

revolution (Germany, 1918) 31

Rhine, River 63, 178, 313: Rhineland 28, 64, 104, 231

Ribbentrop, Joachim von 230, 235, 287

Riefenstahl, Leni 190

Riess, Curt 67–8

Riga 297

Rilke, Rainer Maria 29, 186

Ritschel, Frau (mother of Oskar) 134

Ritschel, Oskar xiii, 6, 27–8, 35–6, 39, 42, 44, 45–6, 135, 148–9, 275, 279, 289–91, 325

Röhm, Ernst 159, 211–12, 214

romanticism 29, 66

Romatzki, Hilda 225–6: fashion house 225–6

Rome 191–2, 205–6, 278

Rommel, General Erwin 230, 300

Rosenberg, Alfred 147: *Myth of the 20th Century* 115

Royal Air Force 299

Russia 4, 13–15, 25, 27, 33, 57, 66, 176, 184, 187, 231, 243: revolution 15

St Moritz 121

St Petersburg 14–15

SA (*Sturmabteilung*) 33, 105–6, 107, 111, 113, 116, 117, 119, 124, 125–6, 130, 133, 139, 143–4, 153, 157–8, 162, 169, 171, 177, 185, 211–12, 213, 231, 255, 257, 274

Saarland 219

Sachsenhausen concentration camp 179

Salon Berthe 306

Salon Kohnen 275

Salzburg Festival 280

Samuel, Herbert 79

San Remo conference 56

Sarajevo 4

Saxona 195, 197

Sauerbruch, Ernst Ferdinand 275

Schaub (Hitler's driver) 141, 152

Schaumburg, Prince 210

Schenkendorf, Max von 11

Schimmelmann (Graf) 117–18, 150, 297

Shirach, Henrietta von 109

Schirrmeister, Frau von 297

Schirrmeister, Wolf von 297

Schirer, William L. 213, 214, 219, 224, 255–6, 285

Schleicher, General Kurt von 157, 161, 167, 212

Schleicher, Frau von 212

Scholem, Gershom 171, 180

Scholem, Werner 171–2

Schönberg, Arnold 101

Schröder, Rudolf Alexander 11

Schubert, Franz 21

Schulen-Gossel, Herr 225

Schulze, Carola 88

Schulze family 53

Schulze, Hagen 71–2

Schulze, Herr 53

Schuschnigg, Kurt von 215, 255

Schwäbische Illustrierte xiii, 5

Schwägermann (adjutant to Goebbels) 319

Schwanenwerder 232–3, 234, 237–9, 240, 241, 248, 251, 260–62, 263–4, 266, 271–2, 274, 286, 314–16

SD 274

Second World War 4, 82, 94, 284–98, 299–301, 302, 311, 313–15

Seidel, Ina 11

Seine, River 85

Seligman, Max 195

Serbia 4

Sereny, Gitta 317, 320

Severin (Quandt farm) 131, 150–51

Sicily 278

Silberstein family 18

Silberstein, Hans 18

Silesia 253, 282, 303

Social Democrats 12, 29–30, 31, 32, 50, 75, 116, 122, 132, 144, 171f, 173, 214

Social Democratic Party 105
Socialist Workers Party (Palestine) 94, 194, 196
Sofia 197
Sombart, Werner 58
Soviet Union 287, 292, 294–5, 297–8, 299, 300, 307, 313, 318, 321
Sonnemann, Emmy 202, 218–19; see Göring, Emmy
Spain 243
Spanish Civil War 243, 248–9
Spartacists 32–3, 35
Speer, Albert 218, 249–50, 272, 278, 280–81, 284–5, 314, 315–17
SS 33, 126, 133, 157, 160, 175, 212, 214, 231, 254, 255, 274, 294, 296, 307: Einsatzgruppen (in Russia) 294–5
Stahl, Ilse 120
Stahl, Maria 215
Stalingrad 300
Stalin, Josef 292
sterilisation law (1936) 244
Sternau, Robert 22–3, 59
Strehl, Hela 210, 223
Steiner, George 111
Stern family 177
Stern, Fritz 212
stock exchange collapse 100
Stoeckel, Dr 165, 223, 246, 248, 251
Strasser, Georg 104, 157, 161, 212
Strauss, Richard 227
Stravinsky, Igor 85
Strength Through Joy movement 240
Stumpfegger, Dr 320
'Sturm-Lokale' soup kitchens 107
Sudetenland 270–71, 273, 278–9
'Support for the Fatherland' law (1916) 225
Switzerland 74, 91, 230, 310
Syria 56

Tannenberg, battle of 156
Tel Aviv 22, 55, 58, 78, 79–80, 193–5, 200
Tempelhof airport 317
Tennis Court Oath 10
Terboven, Josef 215

Thälmann, Ernst 157
theatre 229–30, 274–5
Thild 6
Third Reich 112, 143, 162, 168, 171, 173, 175, 179, 208, 216, 231, 250, 270, 283ff, 292, 296, 308–9, 311–12, 324
Thyssen, Fritz 154
Tucholsky, Kurt 101
Tikvat Zion (Hope of Zion) 23, 59, 187
Todt, Sergeant Karl 196
Tokyo 269
Trieste 54, 78, 183
Turkey 56, 196

Ufa Studios 237, 250
Ukraine 13, 57, 199
Ullstein publishing 69, 220–21
Umberto, Crown Prince of Italy 230, 234
unemployment 107, 115, 156
United States 10, 30, 88–90, 109, 163, 177, 296, 298, 313

Venice 238
Versailles, Treaty of 31, 36, 86, 116, 162, 219, 231, 254
Vienna 54, 86–7, 183, 214, 255–6, 257
Vilvoorde 6ff
Völkische Freiheit 70, 103
Völkische Freiheitspartei 104
Vorwärts 32, 161
Vossische Zeitung, 122, 155, 156, 171

Wagener, Otto 139–43, 145, 272
Wagner, Richard 172, 203, 281
  Die Walkure 172, 203
  Lohengrin 269
  Rheingold 214
  Tristan and Isolde 281
Wagnitz (Hitler Youth) 166
Wall Street crash 100
Walter, Bruno 175
Wannsee 209–10, 232
Warsaw 182, 188, 190, 286, 288, 294: ghettos 288, 294
Wegener, Paul 237

Wehrmacht 215, 219, 221, 231, 253, 255, 256, 288, 289, 292, 298
Weill, Kurt 101
Weimar 69, 101, 123, 124
Weimar Republic 59, 66, 100, 103, 107, 133, 167–8, 185, 213: Article 48 of constitution 133
Weiser, Moshe 194
Weiss, Bernhard 106
Weizman, Chaim 94, 181
Weltsch, Robert 185–7, 198
Werlin (director Mercedes factory) 202
Werner Siemens Realgymnasium (Berlin) 20, 24, 59
Wessel, Horst 112, 168
Wetekamp, Professor W. 26–7
W.H. Lennarts factory 63
Wilhelm II, Kaiser 10, 13, 17, 30–31, 51, 240

Wilna 294
Wilson, President T. Woodrow 30–31
Wirth, Chancellor Joseph 60, 70
Wittgenstein 101
Wolf, Friedrich 197
Wolff, Theodor 66–7, 69
Wolf's Lair (Hitler's HQ), 304

Yishuv 58, 74
Ypres 19

Zbasyn concentration camp 273
Zionism xi, 20–24, 27, 29, 36–8, 50, 54–9, 74–5, 77–8, 80–82, 93, 112, 135–6, 162, 181–2, 189–90, 192
Zionist Congress 22 (lst, Basle 1897), 181, 182, 188, 190
Zionist Workers' Party 190
Zlibanski, Jaakov 194